What the experts are saying about *Loosely Coupled*.

"Loosely Coupled is a visionary overview of web services at a time when the IT and business press is still groping to understand its significance amidst the usual vendor hype and noise. Doug Kaye's ability to weave nuanced, objective technology overviews together with practical, leading-edge advice make this an essential reference I can highly recommend to any web-services pioneer, from the software development lab to the executive suite."
  —**Scott Mace, IT journalist and radio/event producer**

"Loosely Coupled moves beyond the bits and bytes to examine the strategic issues organizations face when implementing web services. Whether you are a technologist or an IT manager, this book will give you the perspective you need to make sure that all of your web services bases are being covered."
  —**Tony Hong, Co-Founder, XMethods**

"Make sure you have this book within reach, because you'll want to refer to it again and again. It's an essential guide to the vital concepts and practical considerations that help you reap maximum business value from deploying the technology."
  —**Phil Wainewright, CEO, Procullux Ventures,**
    and founder of LooselyCoupled.com

"I wish all our customers would read *Loosely Coupled*. It would make my job a whole lot easier."
  —**Bob Hammond, CTO, Mirror-Image Internet**

"Loosely Coupled goes beyond simply echoing the hype surrounding web services, and offers invaluable guidance about the benefits to be gained and strategies for deploying web services initiatives that drive real business value."
  —**Mark Potts, CTO, Talking Blocks**

"This book gives a perspective of web services that just wasn't previously available. It will help you develop a strategic approach to bringing web services into your organization. Everyone who wants to make an informed decision in this area owes it to themselves to get this book."
  —**Tim McNearny, Navis**

Loosely Coupled

The Missing Pieces
of Web Services

Doug Kaye

RDS Press
Marin County, California

Editors: Alison Bing, Cessna Kaye
Cover photograph: Gary S. and Vivian Chapman/Getty Images

Printed on acid-free recylcled paper in the United States of America.

10 9 8 7 6 5 4 3 2 1

ISBN 1-881378-24-1

                    Publishers Cataloging-in-Publication Data
Kaye, Doug.
        Loosely coupled : the missing pieces of Web services / Doug Kaye. -- 1st ed.
        p. cm.
        Includes bibliographical references and index.
        ISBN 1-881378-24-1

        1. Web site development. 2. World Wide Web. I. Title.

        TK5105.888.K394 2003   005.2'76
                            QBI03-2002132

Library of Congress Control Number: 2003090298

To all my technical reviewers, but particularly the experts who so selflessly provided extraordinary feedback: John McDowall, Tim Mc-Nearny, Eric Newcomer, Mark Potts, and Phil Wainewright.

You are my true collaborators. Thanks for keeping me honest and on track.

Contents

Acknowledgements . . . . **xv**

Introduction **1**
   Who Should Read This Book 3
   What You Won't Learn Here 4
   Organization 4
   Stay in Touch 7

Part I: Perspectives **9**

   Chapter 1: Evolution **11**
      Vectors to the Holy Grail 12
      The ERP Backlash 14
      EAI and Business-Process Reengineering 15
      XML 17
      The Internet 18
      EDI and RosettaNet 19
      CORBA, DCE, RPC, DCOM, and RMI 20
      E-Commerce and the Dot-Com Bubble 21
      Y2K and the Economy 21
      CyberCash 22
      Microsoft v. Java Détente 23

Chapter 2: Web Services **25**
   The Elevator Pitch 27
   It's Not the Components—It's the Interfaces 28
   The Benefits 29
   Multiple Opportunities 31

Chapter 3: The Hype **37**
   The Gartner Hype Cycle 38
   A World Wide Web for Computers? 39
   A New Application Architecture? 40
   A Reason to Change Platforms? 40
   A Lingua Franca for Applications? 40
   A New Business Model? 41
   A Competitive Advantage? 42
   Automatic Linking to Unknown Partners? 42
   A Replacement for EDI? 44
   Well-Defined Standards? 44
   An Invention of… 44
   The Same As .NET? 45

Chapter 4: The Missing Pieces **47**
   Business Semantics 48
   Security 48
   Transactional Integrity 48
   Orchestration and Choreography 49
   Single Signon 49
   Reliable Asynchronous Message Handling 50
   Quality of Service (QoS) 50
   Contracts and Negotiations 50
   Standardization of New Business Models 51
   Billing and Accounting Services 51
   Intermediaries and Transformation Services 51
   Operational Infrastructure 52

Chapter 5: Critical Components **53**
   The 80/20 Rule of Strategies 53
   It's What You Don't Know 54
   The Web-Services Pyramid 55
   Milestones 57
   Simple or Complex? 58

Part II: Concepts **59**

Chapter 6: Application Integration **63**
Historical Solutions 64
Data Silos 64
Swivel-Chair Integration and SneakerNets 66
Screen Scraping 67
Enterprise Resource Planning (ERP) 67
The Shrinking Common-Technology Subset 70
The Intermediate Canonical Alternative 73
Enterprise Application Integration (EAI) 76
Reality Check 78
E-Commerce 79
Prepare to Be Externalized! 80

Chapter 7: Objects and Web Services **83**
History 84
Objects 84
Components and Containers 85
Distributed Objects 85
Object-Oriented Architectures 86
CORBA 87
Web Services 88

Chapter 8: Service-Oriented Architectures **91**
Why Services? 92
Traditional Application Architecture 93
Applications as Services 94
The Web-Services Model 95
Interfaces Versus Applications 97
Messages 98
Message Exchange Patterns (MEPs) 98
Intermediaries and Routing 101
Service Aggregation 102
Synchronous Services 105
Asynchronous Services 107
Documents or Remote Procedure Calls? 109

Chapter 9: Asynchronous Messaging **113**
Synchronous Interactions 113
Asynchronous Interactions 114

Procedural Design 116
Event-Driven Design 117
Context 118
Documents 119
Message Queuing 121
Reliability 123
Scalability 124
Still a Missing Piece 128

Chapter 10: Loose Coupling **131**
A Matter of Style 132
Asynchronous Messaging 134
Document-Style Messaging 136
Message Routing 138
Heterogeneity 139
Delayed Binding and Published Schemas 140
Transformations 142
Broad Applicability 143
Unintended Consequences 143

Part III: Technologies **145**

Chapter 11: Transactions **147**
Transaction Basics 148
ACID 149
Resource Locking 150
One-Phase Commit 151
Two-Phase Commit 152
The Web-Services Challenges 155
Loosely Coupled Transactions 158
Compensating Transactions 160

Chapter 12: Orchestration **163**
Business Processes 164
Process Representation in XML 166
Dynamic Processes 167
Complex Outcomes 168
Negotiated Commitments 168
Distributed State 169
State of the Art 169

Chapter 13: Security—The Challenges 171
Security Contexts 172
Space 173
Time 175
Security for Asynchronous Web Services 176
The Building Blocks 177
Integrity 178
Authentication 179
Authorization 185
Confidentiality 186
Non-Repudiation 192
Defensive Security 193

Chapter 14: Security—The Solutions 195
Network-Layer Security 197
Host-Based Security 201
Peripheral-Service Security 205
XML/Application Firewalls and Proxies 207
Web Services Networks 211
All of the Above 214

Chapter 15: Deployment Options 217
The Evolution of Solutions 217
Mixing Metaphors 219
Web Services Networks (WSNs) 220
Vertical Hubs 226
Distributed Web-Services Networks (DWSNs) 226
Specialty ISVs 228
Gateways, Proxies, and Appliances 228
Web-Services Delivery Networks (WSDNs) 231
Major Vendor Support 232
Web Services Providers (WSPs) 234

Part IV: Strategies 237

Chapter 16: Strategies and Projects 239
Adoption Strategies 240
Grass Roots 241
Complexity 241
QoS Asymmetry 242

Mapping Complexity to Strategy 243
Critical Components Revisited 244

Chapter 17: Simple Projects 245
A Stepping-Stone Template 246
Journey or Destination? 249

Chapter 18: The Timing of Complex Projects 251
Business Semantics 252
The 800-Pound Gorilla 252
Identifying the Critical Component 253
Strategic Timing 254
Launch Dates 255
Adoption Life Cycles 256
Timing is Everything 258
Adoption of the Critical Components 259
Positioning Your Industry 260
Your Adoption Profile 262
Finding Your Launch Date 262
Finding Your Start Date 263
The Decreasing Cost of Implementation 265
Lead Time 268
Postponing the Critical Component 271

Chapter 19: Service-Level Agreements 273
Communications 274
The Realities of Parity and Clout 275
Guarantees and Due Diligence 276
Performance SLAs 277
Reactive SLAs 279
Proactive SLAs 281
Beware of Weak SLAs 283
Service-Level Measurements 284
The Devil in the Details 285
SLAs for Aggregated Services 287
Penalties and Incentives 288
Nagging Little Penalties 291
Automated SLAs 293

Chaper 20: Providing External Services 295
A Service Mentality 296

Revenue Models and Payment Mechanisms. 297
Usage-Based Pricing 298
Aggregation and Settlements. 300
Contracts and Human-Process Overhead 300
Application and Infrastructure Robustness 303
Semantics 307

Appendix: A Strategic Checklist **309**
Inventory 309
Project Requirements 313
Planning 316
Evangelizing 319

Notes **321**

Index **325**

About the Author **333**

Acknowledgements

I'm deeply indebted to a superb team of technical reviewers. The following reviewed one or more chapters of the manuscript, which was extensively revised in response to their comments:

Jason Bloomberg, ZapThink LLC
Bob Hammond, Mirror Image Internet
Tony Hong, XMethods
Scott Loftesness, Glenbrook Partners
John McDowall, Grand Central Communications
Tim McNearny, Navis
Dennis Moser, Glenbrook Partners
Eric Newcomer, IONA
Mark Potts, Talking Blocks
Brent Sleeper, The Stencil Group
Phil Wainewright, Procullux Ventures
Phil Windley, former CIO, State of Utah
Dave Wright, Microsoft

In the process or researching this book, the following were kind enough to subject themselves to telephone or in-person interviews:

Ed Anuff, Epicentric
Leon Baranovsky, Reactivity
Derek Bildfell, IBM

Julian Bond, VoidStar
Sam Boonin, Blue Titan
Kris Carpenter, Grand Central Communications
Mike Clark, Lucin
Craig Donato, Grand Central Communications
Simon Fell, pocketsoap.com
Robert Ford, CyberSource
Fergus Griffin, Epicentric
Adam Gross, Grand Central
Bob Hammond, Mirror Image Internet
Kathleen Hayes, Epicentric
Pete Heisinger, Inovant
Tony Hong, XMethods
Ed Horst, AmberPoint
Russ Jones, Glenbrook Partners
Alan Kotok, Data Interchange Standards Association (DISA)
Carl Ledbetter, Novell
John Lilly, Reactivity
Scott Loftesness, Glenbrook Partners
Frank Martinez, Blue Titan
John McDowall, Grand Central Communications
Tim McNearny, Navis
Craig Mudge, Pacific Challenge
Eric Newcomer, Iona
Chris Overton, Keynote Systems
Carlos Perez, AdaptiveTrade
Mark Potts, Talking Blocks
Brent Sleeper, The Stencil Group
Dave Spicer, Flamenco Networks
Paul Tearnen, RosettaNet
Phil Wainewright, Procullux Ventures
Allen Weinberg, Glenbrook Partners
Phil Windley, former CIO, State of Utah
Ron Wolf, Keynote Systems
David Wright, Microsoft
Betty Zakheim, IONA

Introduction

We all know how the World Wide Web has changed our lives. It's how we buy books, make travel reservations, trade securities, track our favorite sports teams, and communicate with friends and family. The web also connects our businesses to one another, but not directly. My company can purchase goods from your company over the Internet, but only if someone at my end sits down in front of a computer and orders from your company's web site. The World Wide Web wasn't designed for direct business-to-business transactions. It's intended for use by people.

Web Services

Rather than place orders via your web site, I'd like my warehouse-management system to automatically re-stock items I buy from you whenever I start to run low, by communicating with your order-taking system over the Internet. That would be a true business-to-business conversation without the intervening human process, and that's what *web services* are all about. They're the second wave of e-commerce—a better way than we've ever had before of linking organizations.

Service-Oriented Architectures

Building the human-oriented World Wide Web was much easier than linking businesses over the Internet. Any company that wanted to open its doors for consumer e-commerce only had to develop interfaces between the internal systems already under its control and the new web standards: the *HyperText Transfer Protocol* (HTTP) and the *HyperText Markup Language* (HTML). But to deploy business-to-business web services, companies must link existing systems to an unpredictable variety of external ones—many based on decades-old technologies. Some of your partners' systems run Unix or Windows, while others are on older mainframe operating systems. Further differences in hardware and programming languages make linking these systems extremely difficult using their traditional *application-program interfaces* (APIs). Instead, you'll need to build systems that communicate using technology-independent *services*, and adopt *service-oriented architectures* (SOAs) designed expressly to meet the challenges of linking heterogeneous distributed systems.

Loose Coupling

Web services must also be more tolerant of failures, both in other systems and within the Internet's infrastructure. Web services can cope with unexpected changes in remote applications, allowing your company to build systems that can adapt and respond to unanticipated events. These are the benefits derived from *loose coupling*.

If this book has a mission, it's to spread the loose-coupling gospel. Loose coupling allows you to link to your partners, while at the same time protecting the integrity of your systems and insulating them from inevitable, unpredictable changes. Loose coupling delivers business agility—arguably the most in-demand commodity in all of IT.

But web services can be misused, and there's a huge risk that companies adopting this new technology will continue to use it in the same tightly coupled ways they've always known. In that case, they'll get the same old results, and web services will become just another empty promise in a long line of over-hyped disappointments. Developers, managers, and IT executives must learn to think in terms of loose coupling and service-oriented architectures. Only then will they be able to reap the true rewards of web services.

Missing Pieces

There are dozens of books that will introduce you to the basic technologies and protocols of web services: XML, SOAP, WSDL and so on. But few of them emphasize the importance and benefits of loose coupling. Perhaps it's because web services are new—so new, in fact, that the web-services puzzle is still missing a number of pieces, some of which are critically important if web services are to be used for anything other than simple tasks. Rather than re-hash the established protocols and standards of web services, *Loosely Coupled* focuses on how you can complete the web-services puzzle for your organization, and plan, build, and operate high-value and truly loosely coupled web services.

Who Should Read This Book

Developers: You can get a simple web service up and running in a few hours. But then what? You'll find that the technologies of simple web services aren't all that different from those you're used to, but the missing pieces of complex web services are unlike any problems you've encountered before. *Loosely Coupled* will be your guide to the worlds of service-oriented architectures and complex web services, filling in the details of technologies you may not yet be exposed to: transactions, security, asynchronous messaging, and the unique deployment options for web services.

Managers: Web-services projects shouldn't happen by accident. If you're responsible for creating and executing project plans, *Loosely Coupled* will help you identify the *critical components* on which your projects' success depends. It will also be your team's in-house textbook, covering the advanced concepts critical to complex web services that aren't addressed elsewhere.

IT executives: You've been inundated by press coverage of web services, and your developers are already experimenting with them. But when should your company make a *strategic* commitment to web services, and what should that commitment be? Does it make sense to begin with a *skunkworks* team and take the conservative stepping-stone approach? Or should you dive into complex projects that cost more but offer greater returns? *Loosely Coupled* will help you answer these questions and guide you through the process of developing a web-services strategy that's right for your organization.

What You Won't Learn Here

There are no source-code listings or even XML fragments in this book. And although you'll find something called the *web-services pyramid*, you won't find a protocol-stack diagram anywhere in these pages. If you're a developer or architect, and therefore need to understand the web-services protocols and standards, pick up one of the *Understanding...*, *Introduction to...*, or *Essentials of...* books. But when you're ready for more advanced topics such as transactions, security, reliable asynchronous messaging—the missing pieces of web services—this is the book for you.

Organization

With its focus on the advanced topics of web services, *Loosely Coupled* covers a lot of ground. The book is organized so that you can read it in sequence, but you may find that you'd rather jump straight to the topics that interest you most. The following will give you a sense of what's in store for you in each section.

Part I: Perspectives (for all readers)
1. Evolution
2. Web Services
3. The Hype
4. The Missing Pieces
5. Critical Components

If you're new to web services, these chapters will give you the background you need. Experienced pros will take away a deeper historical and technological perspective on web services. Chapter 5 explains why you need to identify the *critical components* in order to guarantee success as you develop and deploy your web services.

Part II: Concepts (for all readers)

6. A History of Integration
7. Objects and Web Services
8. Service-Oriented Architectures
9. Asynchronous Messaging
10. Loose Coupling

This section introduces the concepts that set web services apart from earlier technologies. Chapter 6 outlines the relationships between web services and ERP, EAI, and e-commerce, and Chapter 7 connects the dots between web services and object-oriented (OO) technologies. The last three chapters of Part II explore the more advanced topics that are probably new to most IT professionals: SOAs, asynchronous message and queuing, and the all-important yet elusive concept of loose coupling.

Part III: Technologies (for developers and managers)

11. Transactions
12. Orchestration
13. Security—The Challenges
14. Security—The Solutions
15. Deployment Options

Of all the missing pieces of web services, three are notably unique to web services and SOAs: transactions, security, and the deployment options. For example, even if you're familiar with the principles of ACID-style transactions, you'll discover why they're inappropriate for asynchronous web services.

The security issues surrounding web services are so significant that we've dedicated two chapters to the topic. Chapter 13 explores the challenges associated with this missing piece of web services, including requirements for integrity, authentication, authorization, confidentiality, and non-repudiation. Chapter 14 introduces the various means to address these security problems, such as SSL, VPNs, and XML firewalls.

Part III ends with a survey of infrastructure options for web services, including web-services networks (WSNs), gateways, proxies, web-services delivery networks (WSDNs), and web-services providers (WSPs). Chapter 15 also introduces the strategic concept of the *solution-evolution timeline*, which shows how technologies and standards evolve over time.

Part IV: Strategies (for managers and executives)

16. Strategies and Projects
17. Simple Projects
18. The Timing of Complex Projects
19. Service-Level Agreements
20. Providing External Services

Part IV of *Loosely Coupled* shows you how to differentiate simple and complex web projects, and address each type with the appropriate project-management methodology. For those starting with simple projects, Chapter 17 provides step-by-step guidelines that will allow you to increase complexity over time. Chapter 18, on the other hand, helps you determine whether you'd be better off diving into complex projects from the start, and when to time that entry.

SLAs for web services are still in uncharted territory, but Chapter 19 maps them out from both the provider and requestor perspectives. In Chapter 20, we'll look at the issues unique to those who are ready to take the plunge and provide web services to external business partners. We'll study revenue models, payment methods, contracts, and the robustness requirements for applications and infrastructure, to help you determine whether your systems, processes, and staff are ready for 24/7 operation and 100% uptime.

Appendix: A Strategic Checklist

Finally, to pull it all together, we've provided a checklist that highlights the significant issues presented throughout the book, complete with cross-references to the more detailed discussions.

Stay in Touch

Web services are among the most rapidly changing technolgies, and we urge you to take advantage of the online content that support this book in order to keep up-to-date on the latest developments.

Updates. You'll find as-needed updates to *Loosely Coupled* at *www.rds.com/webservices*. You can find the latest version of the web services pyramid (see Chapter 5) at *www.rds.com/webservices/pyramid*, and the strategic checklist (Chapter 21) at *www.rds.com/websercices/checklist*.

Free newsletter. RDS publishes the *IT Strategy Letter*, an email newsletter for IT professionals, which offers our most recent strategic thoughts on web services and other leading-edge IT issues. You can subscribe for free at *www.rds.com/newsletter*.

Errata. If you discover errors of any kind in this book, please report them to our editors at *errata@rds.com*.

Contact the author. I look forward to your feedback of all kinds. In particular, let me know what you think should be added to this book or revised.

I wish you the best of success with your adventures in web services. May they be loosely coupled.

Doug Kaye
doug@rds.com

Part I

Perspectives

Chapter 1

Evolution

On April 3, 1860, the Central Overland California and Pike's Peak Express Company (commonly known as the Pony Express) began operation. It revolutionized the movement of information by transporting letters from St. Joseph, Missouri, to Sacramento, California, (roughly 1,500 miles) in only ten days.

On October 21, 1861, Western Union spliced its eastern and western wires together, thus creating the first transcontinental telegraph network. Just three days later—after less than 19 months in service—the famed Pony Express went out of business. The widespread deployment of electronic data communications had begun.

This shift to new business communications technologies has been repeated many times during the past century and a half. In the early 1920s, Western Union's Morse-code keys and sounders were replaced by teletypewriters, which in turn gave birth to the worldwide Telex network. In the 1970s, "What's your Telex number?" was an often-heard question. But by the late 1980s, it had changed to, "What's your FAX number?" And by the late 1990s, it became commonplace—no, imperative—to have our email addresses on our business cards.

From the perspective of a 200-year calendar, these transitions and the introductions of new technologies seem nearly instantaneous acts of creation, but in reality each was the result of a sustained process of evolution, not revolution. For example, at the time the Pony Express was made obsolete by the telegraph, Western Union had been acquiring and linking local telegraph companies for ten years. The FAX machine struggled for decades and finally achieved critical mass when the technology was merged with inexpensive plain-paper laser printing. Even email has traveled a relatively long road. It was 1971 when Ray Tomlinson first sent messages to himself. It would take more than 25 years for email to exceed the ubiquity of FAX for business communications.

Vectors to the Holy Grail

Now at the start of the 21st century, web services are poised as the next technology to change the way we link businesses. It seems as though web services have appeared suddenly, just as the transcontinental telegraph appeared to have been instantly created at the moment its eastern and western wires were joined. But web services haven't burst onto the scene any more quickly than FAX or email. Like the telegraph, web services are the result of many decades of invention.

There's long been a search for the Holy Grail of data communications: that perfect technology for linking all systems, large and small, wired and wireless. Ask any CIO or CTO what he or she wants in this regard, and you'll probably hear something like this:

- to link to any organization, anywhere in the world, but with only a single connection to the network;
- to communicate with all business partners using just one universal set of protocols, documents, and business processes;
- to communicate securely, reliably, and without concern for scalability (i.e., the volume of usage);
- to use the same technology to communicate within the organization as is used externally;
- to *loosely couple* organizations so that they don't need to know the internals of one another's business processes or technologies;
- to be able to reuse data and processes in order to reduce costs;

- to be able to change components or swap out one for another without breaking anything; and
- to make money by providing data and services to others over the network.

It's a long list, but it isn't new. Look at the list again, but this time, consider how each objective applies to the FAX machine. Then read it once more with the telegraph in mind. You'll have to bend a few definitions here and there—they didn't use the term *business processes* in the days of the Pony Express—but the concepts haven't changed. The list has been fulfilled by every successful generation of data-communications technology. The list remains the same as the technologies continue to improve.

For example, there's always been a data communications network, even if it was based on a relay of riders on horseback. Likewise, it's always been important to have a single connection to the network, in whatever form it might be. Western Union made certain you could walk into one office and reach someone located near any other office. Today, with one FAX machine connected to one telephone line, you can reach any other FAX machine in the world.

What CIOs, CTOs, and those with other titles decades before them have tried to do hasn't changed. The objective remains the efficient linking of organizations. What's new is that web services are the first technology that promises to achieve this objective in the 21st century, by directly linking our computer systems via the public Internet.

Why was this objective so elusive? What were the missing pieces? Was the Internet the only catalyst we've needed to discover this Holy Grail of computer-to-computer communications? If so, then why haven't we been doing this since the mid 1990s when the Internet first got our attention? What have we been waiting for? If not the Internet, was it the invention of XML, the eXtensible Markup Language, that's been universally adopted as the basis for web services? Is that the missing piece? Why now? And why all the hype?

Like the splicing together of the eastern and western wires to instantly create the transcontinental telegraph, the arrival of web services was preordained by the convergence of a number of technological developments and economic and political events. We'd been trying to create the equivalent of web services for many years, but it wasn't until all the planets came into alignment that web services suddenly appeared—as if out of nowhere.

Twelve vectors—a collection of both successes and failures—have converged at this one point in time and space to bring life to web services as illustrated in Figure 1-1.

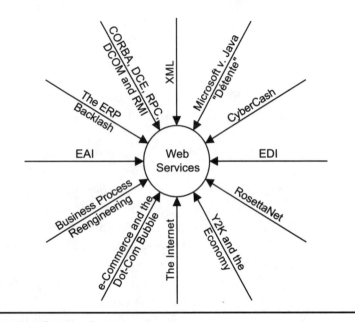

Figure 1-1: Web Services Convergence

Let's take a brief look at these converging vectors, one by one. We'll revisit many of them in greater detail later in this book.

The ERP Backlash

The 1990s saw an increase in the popularity of large monolithic systems such as Enterprise Resource Planning (ERP) that addressed multiple related applications such as integrating manufacturing and inventory management. ERP and other application packages, such as customer-resource management (CRM) and human resources (HR), do solve important problems, but they're extraordinarily inflexible and brittle. The applications are difficult to change, and if a change is introduced in one area, other areas tend to break easily. These packages also tend to be *silos*—isolated from other systems. This, in turn, means it's difficult to link them to other applications.

Then came the boom of the late 1990s. Suddenly, mergers and acquisitions were flying everywhere. Companies were being bought, sold, merged, and spun-out in feverish attempts to increase stock prices. Integrating two merged companies' ERP systems—even if they were based on the same package—was remarkably difficult because of the closed nature and brittleness of these application suites. Trying to combine ERP systems typically caused everything to break.

In the sober light of the post-boom dawn, senior executives and IT managers are now questioning those massive integrated application suites and looking for ways to develop systems that are friendlier to one another. We want applications that can interoperate as a matter of course and not require a yearlong integration project and dozens of expensive consultants.

There's a growing demand for applications built from smaller components that can be removed and replaced with others. This allows systems to grow incrementally—in small, inexpensive, and low-risk stages. No longer do we want to make $5 million or $500 million all-or-nothing decisions about integrated ERP systems as was common in the 1990s, when time-to-completion was often more important than cost or future-proofing. Today, we want to make $50,000 decisions, and we want to try things out and see if they work before taking the next step. We want to derive benefits at each stage.

Web services allow us to shift front-loaded expenditures and cliff-style deployments (as in, "jump off the cliff") to a more manageable strategy of smaller incremental investments with shorter-term returns. They provide us the opportunity to make tactical improvements over time, rather than having to get everything right, up front, and forever being stuck with our naïve decisions. Although ERP and other monolithic systems still play an important role—one not easily replaced—their cost and inflexibility make them yet another vector towards more component-based systems and web services.

EAI and Business-Process Reengineering

Enterprise Application Integration (EAI) packages were developed in the 1990s as a solution to the monolithic silos of ERP and other systems. In particular, many EAI systems allowed analysts to create *workflows* that scripted the movement of data from one application to another, usually mirroring or supporting existing human-based processes.

As valuable as EAI has become, most packages are only slightly more flexible than the applications they connect. The business processes supported by EAI tend to be *static*—difficult to change. Recently, businesses have searched for ways to create more agile *dynamic* workflows—those that can support rapidly changing business processes such as supply-chain or demand-chain integration. In particular, organizations want to extend their process integration to include the systems of their suppliers and distribution and sales channels—a task for which EAI systems were never intended.

In his book, *Out of the Box*, John Hagel wrote,

> "The business process reengineering movement that gripped the imagination of business executives around the world in the early 1990s promised radical improvements in performance, but all it really did was reengineer the same box. In part, this was not the fault of the methodology; it reflected the limitations of the existing IT systems. Yes, you could reengineer major business processes to make them more efficient, but you would need massive investments to implement the IT systems required. What you got at the end of the effort was typically another rigid set of platforms that were difficult to improve further. Given the effort required and the results achieved, this reengineering effort was not something executives (much less the rest of the company) wanted to undertake very often.
>
> "Proponents of business process reengineering would often talk about the importance of taking an end-to-end view of the business process. When they discussed examples, though, it became abundantly clear that their end-to-end view usually stopped at the edge of the enterprise. More enlightened proponents would occasionally include direct business partners of the enterprise. None expanded the notion of end-to-

end to include the entire value chain, extending from raw materials to the finished products and services used by consumers. The boundaries of the enterprise were simply too formidable for even the so-called revolutionaries to breach."[1] *[Reprinted by permission of Harvard Business School Press. From* Out of the Box *by John Hagel III. Boston, MA 2002, pp.4-5. Copyright ©2002 by John Hagel III. All rights reserved.]*

Business-process reengineering delivered not only processes that were limited to internal use only, but also mostly static business processes that weren't sufficiently agile to support modern real world collaborative business activities such as just-in-time manufacturing. From this we learned the need for technologies and systems that could support rapidly changing—even ad-hoc—business processes that extended beyond the limits of the enterprise.

XML

Rarely in the history of technology has one standard been as widely and rapidly accepted as XML. It's one of the simplest and most elegant of standards. For all practical purposes, XML is stable; it's not changing, and it has no competitors. There are debates about almost every other protocol in the web-services stack, but XML is nearly as widely accepted as the TCP/IP protocols on which the Internet itself is built.

XML solves one fundamental problem that has plagued programmers for years: It gives us a universal format for the representation and transmission of structured data. Everything from purchase orders and invoices to chemical formulas and music can be represented in XML, and in a manner that isn't tied to any particular hardware, software, programming or written language, character set, file system, or vendor.

XML provides the common *syntax* for web services. The secret of its success lies in its simplicity and the fact that its designers didn't endow it with features to support any particular class of application. XML, therefore, can be used to solve problems that weren't anticipated at the time it was created. This concept of preparing for *unantici-*

pated consequences has been applied to other web-services technologies and protocols, as we'll see throughout this book.

The Internet

One of the major challenges of linking businesses electronically has always been the physical connection—the wires and circuits. Before 1985, the state-of-the art solution involved deploying private networks based on dedicated point-to-point leased lines. But very few businesses could afford the extraordinary costs, and most found the trusty FAX machine or telex to be about as high-tech a solution as they could justify.

In the mid-1980s, EDI *value-added networks* (VANs) appeared as an interim solution to this problem. Rather than link separately to each business partner, a company can install a single link to a VAN's *hub*, where the VAN provides the routing and other services to move information among the companies. The VAN creates logical paths between all parties' physical connections.

VANs have two weaknesses, however. First, they're still expensive. Second, there isn't a single VAN used by everyone. You may need to connect to one VAN in order to reach your customers, to another VAN to reach your suppliers, and so on.

The Internet, on the other hand, is the first ubiquitous data network. Just as the telephone network allows us to speak to anyone, anywhere, anytime, the Internet provides a comparable service for data. You only need a single connection to the Internet to send email or to transact business electronically. Furthermore, the cost of that Internet connection has become so low, that it rarely enters into the equation for most web-services budgets.

In his white paper, *Web Services Infrastructure: The Global Utility for Real-Time Business,* Phil Wainewright points out,

> "The internet has ceased to be solely a content transmission network. It has become a computing execution network, processing commercial transactions and business applications."[2]

As its contribution to web services, the Internet has given us the universal data-communications infrastructure we never had before. But the Internet isn't a direct replacement for VANs, for it provides only the data-communications infrastructure. The equivalents of the high-level services offered by EDI VANs are, in the case of web services, supplied by the parties themselves or by third-party mediation or transformation services, which we'll explore in detail in Chapter 15.

EDI and RosettaNet

Just as XML is the vector that provides the syntax, EDI is historically responsible for web services' business-to-business *semantics*—standards for the expression of meaning. Born in the 1960s and widely adopted by large companies in the mid-1980s, the concept of EDI is that a consortium of companies (possibly competitors) within a particular vertical industry will come together and agree on standard formats for the exchange of data between *trading partners*.

Today, there are two EDI bodies, each developing its own standards. One is the United Nations Electronic Data Interchange for Administration, Commerce and Transport (UN/EDIFACT). The other is the Accredited Standards Committee (ASC) X12, chartered by the American National Standards Institute (ANSI). The Data Interchange Standards Association (DISA) serves as the secretariat for ASC X12.

The number of acronyms and the length of the organizations' titles are the first hint: EDI, in its current incarnation, is large, complex, and expensive. It's only for the big guys. For example, the X12 standards cover finance, government, materials management, transportation, and insurance. There are no X12 or UN/EDIFACT standards that address the needs of small and medium businesses.

But EDI has planted some important seeds for web services by answering questions like, what do those standards look like? How do you debug them? And just how do you get competitors to sit down and agree on standards? That's no small feat.

In 1998, 40 technology companies that wanted the best of three worlds—XML, EDI, and the Internet—formed RosettaNet, a consortium that now includes more than 400 electronic-component,

information-technology, and semiconductor-manufacturing companies worldwide. RosettaNet created XML-based standards for the
exchange of electronics-industry business-process data directly over
the Internet.

RosettaNet demonstrated the practicality of a federated (i.e., distributed) architecture in which the parties communicate directly, as
opposed to centralized architectures that were based on hubs such as
used in EDI. Both EDI and RosettaNet have made major contributions to web services.

CORBA, DCE, RPC, DCOM, and RMI

Over the past two decades, many technologies have been designed to
link the components of separate systems. The most notable are:

- the Common Object Request Broker Architecture (CORBA),
  first released in 1992;
- The Distributed Computing Environment (DCE) and its
  Remote Procedure Call (RPC) component, delivered by The
  Open Software Foundation (OSF, who later merged with The
  X/Open Company to form The Open Group) in 1993;[3]
- Microsoft's Component Object Model (COM) released in
  1993 as a way for applications running on the same computer
  to communicate with one another. This was followed in 1996
  by Distributed COM (DCOM) that supported communications between applications running on separate computers;
- Sun's Remote Method Invocation (RMI) technology as part
  of its Java™ 1.1 platform, also released in 1996.

All of these technologies had their problems, and subsequent versions of each of them improved, based in part on what they learned
and stole from one another. But none of them attempted to solve
some of the problems addressed by web services. DCOM and RMI
are specific to the Microsoft and Java environments, respectively, and
therefore aren't a universal solution. CORBA isn't appropriate for the
role played by web services, because CORBA couples systems tightly,
requiring participating systems to be acutely aware of the internals of
others.

Although these predecessors were intended to solve problems that are tangential to (i.e., close, but not the same as) those solved by web services, they have enough in common that the success of web services owes a great deal to these technologies that came before.

E-Commerce and the Dot-Com Bubble

On October 14, 1994, the World Wide Web went mainstream when Netscape released the first commercial version of the Mosaic web browser. Four short years later, the world started taking e-commerce seriously when Amazon.com's holiday sales put it over the $1 billion mark in annual revenues. But on May 18, 2000, highly visible Boo.com folded—the first major casualty of the dot-com era. The bubble had burst.

We learned that no one would get rich by selling pet food online at below-cost prices, but we also learned a great deal about how to build Internet-based commerce systems. Those lessons survived as well as the people who learned them and the technologies they developed. Web-based e-commerce was the catalyst for *application servers* and for the *three-tier architecture*, as examples—both technologies that play a major role in web services, the second wave of e-commerce

Y2K and the Economy

Fears of the Y2K threat induced a worldwide cross-industry IT buying frenzy. Coincident with the rush to capitalize on e-business, Y2K caused a technology over-expenditure of $130 billion spanning a two-year period.[4] Rather than following the usual hardware and software replacement cycles, everyone replaced everything all at once. The resulting imbalance between increasing demand and inadequate supply drove up prices of products and services, as well as the profits of hardware and software vendors and the consultancies that were called in to stitch it all together.

Obviously it wasn't sustainable. It was just good (or bad) timing. After the first quarter of 2000, when the Y2K-accelerated replacements had been completed, everyone stopped their IT spending all at once. It didn't help that the dot-com bubble burst at precisely the same time. On April 14, 2000, the top 100 NASDAQ-listed companies began a precipitous two-year 75 percent decline in market capitalization and a drought in the venture financing that had been keeping the dot-coms afloat.

Along with the recession came necessary IT budget cuts. In the post-boom reality, IT organizations were asked to do more with less, to deliver short-term ROI on every project, and to reuse existing solutions wherever possible. These demands for efficiency, reuse, and incremental improvements rather than large high-risk projects further helped set the stage for web services.

CyberCash

The first e-commerce web sites had no real-time connections to credit-card processors. Most merchants printed a hard copy of each transaction, which was then typed into a PC-based software package such as *ICVerify*, which in turn communicated with a *gateway* and from there to the processing company. From the end-user's perspective, the transaction appeared to occur in a matter of seconds, but in reality, it often wasn't completed until the following day.

Founded in 1994, CyberCash was one of the first companies to offer credit-card payment processing over the Internet. The company's *Merchant Cash Register* was an application that could be installed on an e-commerce web server. It would accept authorization requests directly from e-commerce applications such as storefronts, then forward the payment information in real time over the Internet to the centralized CyberCash gateway. In 1997, the company released a *thin-client* version of its product, which consisted of small libraries that could be called by any web application.

Although the protocols between the client and the gateway were proprietary, the CyberCash solution to credit-card payment processing was the first major *service* to support e-commerce applications over the Internet. Architecturally, the CyberCash model was the forerunner of many simple *remote procedure call* (RPC) web-service interfaces.

Microsoft v. Java Détente

On December 23, 2002, a US federal judge ordered Microsoft to include Sun's Java runtime environment with the Windows family of operating systems. Two years earlier, Microsoft settled a lawsuit brought by Sun Microsystems, and agreed to pay Sun $20 million. Sun may have won these battles in the courts, but the victories were largely symbolic because Microsoft managed to find an end-run solution around the attempt to make Java ubiquitous. Microsoft has bigger plans, and they're based on web services. Here's just one example:

Microsoft controls the desktops of the world, but it has far less clout in the market for small mobile devices such as PDAs and cell phones. However, rather than roll over and play dead—giving up the mobile market altogether—Microsoft has another opportunity to take the lion's share of mobile-device revenues.

As cell phones and PDAs become commodities, the value of device-resident software (such as operating systems, games, and other programs that run within the devices) will approach zero. Few people will pay more for a Java-based phone than for one that isn't. But the market for extra-cost and remotely hosted services for those devices will continue to increase. These services include mobile e-commerce (m-commerce), instant messaging (IM), location-based services (LBS) such as advertising-driven restaurant finders, and many others.

Java was supposed to be the "write once, run anywhere" technology. Its model is based on portable source and executable intermediate code. Web services, on the other hand, are the "write once, access from anywhere" solution. No porting is required. Services can be utilized from anywhere. There's little inherent value in a programming language, but there's tremendous value in a universally accessible service.

To win the lucrative remotely hosted service business, Microsoft (or anyone else) needed to find a way that its services could work with all mobile devices, not just those based on Java or some other platform. The key was to convince all handheld device manufacturers to use one technology. It could have been Java, in which case Sun would have been able to control the technology used to link the mobile devices to remote services. But that didn't happen. Java isn't ubiquitous.

The only way to convince all vendors to adopt a single interface technology was to truly give it away—not under some strict licensing program as Sun did with Java, but free and unencumbered. Web services is such a technology, and by convincing virtually every vendor to support it, Microsoft guaranteed it will be able to deploy services that can be reached by every device, even those based on Java. It's a brilliant strategy, and one that allowed Microsoft (and others) to leapfrog over Java. The competition is no longer about the language or even the platform. Instead, thanks to web services, vendors' offerings can interoperate at a higher level—above the operating system or programming language.

The agreement by competing vendors to work together to develop full web-services interoperability is a vector that's critical for the emergence and success of web services.

———————

There have been other converging vectors that set the stage for web services, but these twelve were the most influential. Web services are no accident. They didn't appear from out of the blue. They're the evolutionary result of 150 years of trying to get it right.

Chapter 2

Web Services

Unlike the telegraph, the FAX machine, and email, web services didn't result from any one person's invention. Had someone actually come up with the concept of web services in a Ph.D. thesis, that paper likely would have gathered dust for years. Anyone who actually read it would've probably dismissed the concept as science fiction, since it was unlikely that all the required pieces would fall into place at the same time.

But all the pieces *have* fallen into place. In less than a decade, we've managed to make EDI less expensive by replacing VANs with the Internet and stopped thinking in terms of client/server. Spurred on by recession, we slashed our budgets for monolithic applications and the expensive consultants that nurse them. After watching Microsoft and Sun battle over Java, we asked the major vendors: "Can't we all just get along?" They took our point, and began to change their ways.

These are the converging paths that led us to web services. But now that we're here, where are we exactly? We have a label for this beast called web services—but what is it, and how is it an improvement over what's come before? To get a handle on just what web services are, consider the story of the three blind men and the elephant. In case you haven't heard it, the story goes like this:

> Three blind men, walking together across the plains of Africa, stumble upon a grazing elephant.
> What is it?" asks the first.
> "It's a tree," says the second blind man, feeling a leg.
> "No, it's a snake," says the third, touching the elephant's trunk.
> The first blind man, holding the elephant's tail in his hands, says, "You're both wrong. It's a rope."

Defining web services can be just as tricky. Explanations in the press are often less than fully informed, and vendor-provided definitions tend to be self-serving, touting only the benefits of web services that emphasize that vendor's tools. But ultimately, a web service is nothing more than an application with which other applications can communicate via a network, most often using XML.

Note that in this definition, the use of a network is the only technical constraint. Many gurus and pundits will disagree with this, and insist that you've got to use XML and higher-level protocols such as SOAP and WSDL to build a true web service. Others will reject any definition that doesn't include references to business processes or the Internet. Some experts argue that web services are all about application integration, while an equal number claim that web services aren't about integration at all, but rather the basis for a new application-development paradigm.

There's no reason to exclude any of these definitions from the scope of web services. In the chapters that follow, we'll look at a broad spectrum of web-services applications and architectures. We'll consider web services that connect the business processes of separate organizations, those that work only behind the firewall, and even those that link software modules running within a single computer. We'll see how web services can be used to perform such relatively simple tasks as converting US dollars to Euros, and functions as complex as long-running multi-party business transactions.

The Elevator Pitch

Imagine you're riding the elevator down to the lobby of your office building. At an intermediate floor, the door opens and in steps the CEO of your company—someone you rarely see or speak with. You've been developing your web-service strategy, and unbeknownst to you, the CEO has heard of your work-in-progress. He or she says, "So what's this I keep hearing about web services? What are they, and why are they so important?"

You've got until the elevator stops at the lobby to deliver your pitch. You may never get another chance. What will you say? What's your executive summary, or *elevator pitch*? How about this:

> Web services allow computer systems of all types to communicate over networks, including our corporate intranet, our extranet or the public Internet. They're written to strict standards to work with other web services, and will enable systems in different organizations to communicate with one another. We can use web services to link to our business partners, or to connect many of our own systems. Web services can facilitate our electronic commerce with an increasing number of business partners, while reducing the time and cost of setting up each new relationship.

> Most importantly, web services are *loosely coupled*, which means they'll help us achieve interoperability among systems in a way that's easier to change and accommodate unanticipated applications.

> Web services are still a work in progress. Some of the standards are new and not fully tested, and many of the potential business benefits are only beginning to be realized. But thinking strategically, we should start planning for web services, and insist that our vendors support web services in their products.[5]

It's Not the Components—It's the Interfaces

To help your managers and others understand what makes web services unique, first you'll want to explain the difference between *components* and *interfaces,* as illustrated in Figure 2-1.

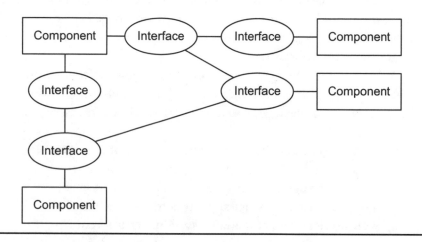

Figure 2-1: Components and Interfaces

Web services make use of highly standardized interfaces that are separate from the internal operation of the components. The interfaces do not change the individual functions of the components, but they do allow otherwise disparate components to provide services to one another.

The Stencil Group came up with this helpful explanation to describe the importance of interfaces apart from the components they connect:

A common-sense analogy can be drawn to a major milestone in the development of the home electronics industry. Before RCA's introduction of its device for connecting radio receivers with other devices, stereo systems were closed, monolithic cabinet systems. As more manufacturers began to adopt the RCA jack, stereo components could interoperate without regard to vendor. Consumers benefited from a wealth of choices. No longer locked into one company's solution, customers could construct a home stereo system on a *best of breed*, component-by-component basis. Enthusiasts could *scale* a home entertainment system with just the right mix of equipment, and replace individual elements as budget and needs dictated.[6]

In other words, it's the universality of the interfaces that allowed stereo systems to incorporate additional components and expand the stereo's function far beyond the original intentions of the designers. With this RCA-jack analogy in mind, let's take a closer look at some of the benefits made possible by web services.

The Benefits

The oncept of software components isn't a new one. Component-based technologies such as *object-oriented programming* (OOP) have existed for years, as have applications that communicate with one another through various *application-program interfaces* (APIs). But while web services have borrowed a great deal from these earlier technologies, through *service-oriented architectures* (SOAs, explained in depth in Chapter 8), web services solve a number of problems that haven't been solved satisfactorily by component-centric systems. Unique benefits of web services include the following:

Independence

Web services allow applications to communicate with one another, even if they're written in different programming languages or run on operating systems or hardware from different vendors. Since they're generic in this way, web services significantly reduce vendor lock-in.

Standardization

The widespread acceptance and adoption of web-services standards means that we finally have a universally accepted technology for application integration and communication. As with FAX and email, web-services collaboration with partners will become the rule rather than the exception.

Modularity and Granularity

The components in a stereo system interface with one another at the "box" level, making it easy to interconnect components from different manufacturers. You can even plug in all-new devices (such as DVD players) that weren't invented at the time the interfaces were designed.

As a point of comparison, consider the PCI bus. This is an important interface for linking the components within a PC, but it does little to enable the interconnection of one PC to another, or a PC to an Apple Macintosh.

Older software technologies such as Enterprise Java Beans (EJBs) and Microsoft's DCOM are based on rather *fine-grained* components, much like hardware components that use the PCI bus. On the other hand, web services are based on a smaller number of *coarser-grained* pieces, and therefore can be linked at a level that's more abstract and general purpose. With larger building blocks, fewer interconnections must be made, so the cost to build complete systems is lower.

Reusability

Modularity allows for the reuse of services for applications other than those for which they were originally designed. The ability to reuse existing services means a reduction in time-to-market for business applications. But as we'll see in Chapter 10, reusability in web services doesn't require reusable or portable software. It's the *service* that's reused, not the source or object code.

Lower Costs

The reusability and service-oriented architecture of web services mean a better return on investment. The high degree of standardization of web-services interfaces will make the integration of a new system and linkage to new business partners into more generic, easily repeatable processes than they are today. Ultimately, web services will allow us to replace unplanned, one-off integration projects with a predictable, one-to-many practice that is much less costly.

Loose Coupling

When linking two systems, programmers are tempted to take short-cuts that save time and therefore money up front. For example, if the two systems both store character strings using the same encoding, a programmer's first instinct might be to use that encoding when transmitting strings from one system to the other. That works fine, until a third system enters the picture using a different encoding scheme. Which systems should be converted to match which format? There's no obvious right answer—and that's when the nightmare begins.

Loose coupling is a philosophical and stylistic approach that allows disparate systems—those that use different technologies and processes—to be linked without the need for one party to have knowledge of the technologies used by the others. This avoids the problem described above, since loosely coupled systems can communicate using system-independent formats and techniques.

Reduced Brittleness

As the above example of character strings suggests, tightly coupled systems—even those based on components—are likely to break when pressed to work in ways beyond their original design objectives. Web services are built using loosely coupled SOAs, so the systems they create are less brittle, or less likely to break when the internals of one service are changed and new services are connected.

Scalability

Reuse and standardization of web services allow us to develop one-to-many rather than one-to-one solutions. Since much of the technology used to link to multiple business partners is the same as it is for a few, the incremental cost of adding an additional partner to an existing web-services system trends towards zero.

Multiple Opportunities

Like the elephant approached by the blind men, web services can take on many different forms depending on where you're coming from—

that is, what problem you're trying to solve. Indeed, one of the benefits of web services is that they can be applied to solve problems in a wide range of environments, as illustrated in Figure 2-2.

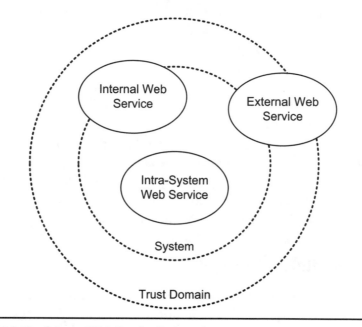

Figure 2-2: The Scope of Web-Service Environments

The dotted-line circles in Figure 2-2 indicate boundaries crossed by different categories of web services. For example, an internal web service crosses the boundaries that separate systems, while intra-system web services are contained within a single system. External web services cross the *trust domain* boundaries that separate departments, divisions, or companies, linking the systems controlled by these separate entities. .

As this diagram shows, web services can be used to link systems within a single trust domain, to connect trust domains with one another, or to connect components within systems. When you're developing a strategic plan, keep in mind that the cost and complexity of web services within these different environments can vary greatly. In particular, there's a major difference between external web services that cross the trust domain boundary and those that don't, mostly because there are additional control and security issues to consider.

If you control the systems on both ends of a web-services interface, your task in designing, building, testing, operating, and maintaining those systems will be far simpler than if you have to collaborate with and trust another party—even if it's just another division or department of your own company.

Internal Web Services

Internal web services are those that operate within a single trust domain. They're often used to solve *enterprise application integration* (EAI) problems, such as linking customer information in an accounting package with customer information in a help-desk system. Such a web service could allow help-desk personnel to see all of the available information about a given customer on a single screen, including purchase dates, customer warranties and service details. Internal web services are often described as *behind-the-firewall* web services, since they can't be accessed or used by outside trust domains, which could include business partners or other company divisions. Internal web-services requestors (clients) and providers are controlled by a single entity, such as a company or a department. The basic architecture for web services in this category is illustrated in Figure 2-3 and will be the focus of Chapter 6.

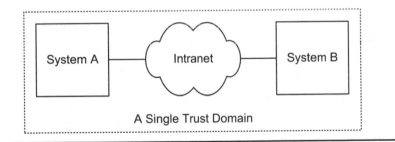

Figure 2-3: Internal Web Service Architecture

External Web Services

External web services connect two or more independent trust domains, and are sometimes referred to as *beyond-the-firewall* web services. In this model, the physical connection, business models, and processes are extended to include systems controlled by others. These web services are shared with specific business partners, or perhaps made available to the public. Some examples include:

- Linking to fraud-detection and credit-card processing services to automate real-time transactions.
- Linking a customer's ordering system and a vendor's invoicing system to automate the supply chain.
- Linking the databases of two merged banks so that their customers can access their accounts from ATMs operated by either bank. (Before and during a merger, the banks will certainly be separate trust domains.)

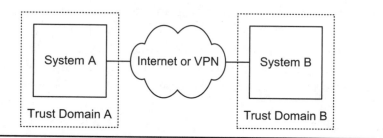

Figure 2-4: External Web Service Architecture

External web services are generally more difficult to design and implement than their internal counterparts because the expanded scope introduces an additional set of challenges. These include:

Security. If a web service can be accessed by a party outside your control, how can you guarantee that the web service will be accessible only to those who are authorized, and only for intended purposes?

Business agreements. Before you allow an external partner to make use of a web service, what contracts and other agreements must be in place?

Technology agreements. Even though web services give you the ability to exchange information with your business partners, you've still got to agree on the semantics or meaning of that data.

Support agreements. When something goes wrong, who's going to diagnose the problem, and who's going to fix it?

Intra-System Web Services

Intra-system web services are a special case, linking components or modules within a single system as shown in Figure 2-5. This system may be either a single computer (i.e., all of the modules operate within one box) or multiple computers that are tightly coupled.

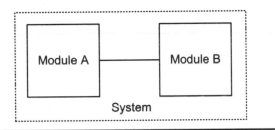

Figure 2-5: Intra-System Web Service Architecture

Some purists insist that intra-system web services aren't actually web services at all, because they're not intended to interoperate with remote systems based on different operating systems or programming languages. The best example of this model is found in the portion of Microsoft's .NET platform that deals with how Windows-specific components communicate with one another. In the versions of Windows prior to .NET, this mechanism was widely known as the Distributed Component Object Model (DCOM), which wasn't based on either the XML or SOAP protocols we associate with web services today. Now under the .NET umbrella, all of these linkages are based on a binary (non-XML) version of SOAP technology.

One elegant aspect of .NET is that—at the SOAP layer—it uses similar protocols to communicate on an intra-system basis as it does for both internal and external web services. This means that programmers working in the .NET world can use the same tools and skill sets whether they're developing applications that use Microsoft-specific services or web services that are based on universal standards and intended for use beyond the single-vendor environment. The

.NET platform includes a rich and complex array of features and technologies that go far beyond web services.

———————

In a sense, web services are like the elephant encountered by the three blind men, because they take on different forms depending on problem at hand. They can be applied to a wide variety of problems, including some integration issues we have only just begun to pinpoint. But though web services are superior to many previous approaches to application development and integration, they remain one of the most misunderstood and hyped technologies in recent memory, as described in the next chapter.

Chapter 3

The Hype

From all the press and vendor attention they've received, you might get the impression that web services will be as revolutionary as the Internet itself. But while web services may change business interactions as much as the World Wide Web changed business-to-consumer communications, they're just the logical next step in the evolution of distributed-system technology.

It's easy to get carried away with the enthusiasm, but we need to adopt a skeptical perspective if we're going to develop a strategic plan for web services. If the enthusiasm is infectious, we need to build up immunity by exposing ourselves to mild doses of the hype surrounding web services. This chapter will serve as an inoculation to trigger our anti-hype protective mechanisms.

First let's examine what's been said and written about web services, and separate the hype and misunderstanding from reality. Then, after we sort out what web services can and can't do, we'll identify the elements required to meet our more realistic expectations for web services.

The Gartner Hype Cycle

Gartner Research regularly publishes a graphical representation of the *hype cycles* for various industries and technologies, as shown in Figure 3-1.

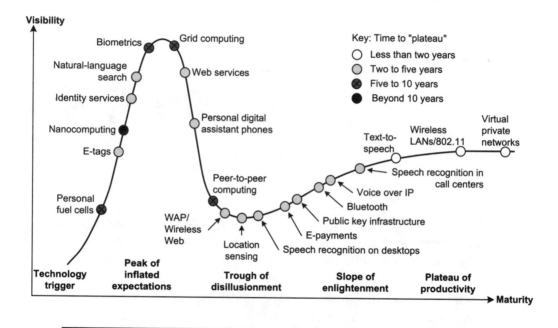

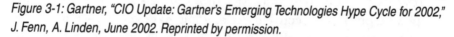

Figure 3-1: Gartner, "CIO Update: Gartner's Emerging Technologies Hype Cycle for 2002," J. Fenn, A. Linden, June 2002. Reprinted by permission.

Hype can be calculated as the ratio of *visibility* to *maturity*—in other words, the ratio of talk to actual adoption. As you can see, in 2002 web services were near the peak of the hype cycle and two to five years from maturity, which Gartner expects will be preceded by a period of disillusionment.

Similarly, John Hagel believes enterprises go through binge/purge cycles in which they obsessively embrace new technologies only to burn out and eventually reject them, claiming they were the wrong solutions to begin with. Hagel points out that we saw it with client/server and again with some of the object-oriented (OO) technologies.[7] Both of these once-heralded technology families have become whipping posts; the IT community loves to blame them for past disappointments. In reality, both OO and client/server are now deeply engrained as mainstream technologies. They may not be today's hottest fads, but they're still widely used.

When the hype dies down, and web services enter Gartner's Trough of Disillusionment, will they be purged like client/server and cast aside like last week's news? Hagel and most other futurists and analysts don't think so. They believe web services will be highly regarded for far longer than client/server. Like TCP/IP, web services will quietly fade into the background as they become universally adopted. But before we plunge into Gartner's Trough of Disillusionment, let's consider which of the many claims made about web services are legitimate, which are hype, and which are just plain wrong.

A World Wide Web for Computers?

The simplest answer to this question is: Not exactly. Remember, the web and the Internet aren't one and the same. The Internet existed long before the invention of the World Wide Web, and it was based entirely on computer-to-computer communications. The older (but still in use) protocols such as TCP/IP, SMTP, and DNS were intended for machines, not people.

While email (SMTP) and news (NNTP) were designed to carry human-readable information, they don't specify how that information should be presented. They're only used to carry the data from computer to computer. So it's a bit peculiar that we hear web services described as the World Wide Web for machines, since the Internet was created for those machines long before we humans had a web we could use. In this sense the World Wide Web is an aberration, because it's the only Internet application that's designed with a human-user interface in mind: the browser. It's unfortunate that we call them *web* services. *Internet* services would have been a more accurate name, avoiding an association with the World Wide Web, web sites, and web pages.

A New Application Architecture?

As an evolutionary technology, there's nothing fundamentally new about web services, but it's fair to say that web services represent a culmination of technologies that now allow us to "do it right." Microsoft's huge .NET umbrella strategy uses web services as a replacement for its older DCOM technology, allowing Microsoft to link its Microsoft Office products. IBM has a top-down initiative to enable its entire product line (including Lotus Notes and its DB2 database) using web services as the interface to its *grid-computing* architecture. In the Java universe, web services will replace RMI. Likewise, the messaging features of CORBA will be replaced by web services in many situations, particularly in distributed-application systems that cross trust-domain boundaries.

These older technologies were true innovations. But like any first-round inventions, these are refined into long-lasting solutions only later, through good engineering. Web services are one such evolutionary refinement.

A Reason to Change Platforms?

This is what the vendors would have you think—particularly those whose products you're not currently using. But the whole point of web services is that they're vendor-independent. The programming language, operating systems, and tools you use will be invisible to otehrs with whom you communicate. Since the choice of tools will have no effect on the ability of others to interoperate with your web services, the best tools are the ones that are most compatible with your existing systems, skills, and processes. If you're already a Microsoft shop, web services aren't a good reason to switch to Java or vice versa.

A Lingua Franca for Applications?

The term *lingua franca* describes a mode of communication between people who speak different languages, and it's often used when describing the benefits of web services. But Clay Shirky, a well-known consultant on Internet technologies, makes an important point: "Web services can't create a framework in which any two arbitrary applications can interact, because XML doesn't provide shared languages, merely shared alphabets. XML is not only not a *lingua franca*, it isn't even a *lingua*."[8]

Even when combined, the basic technologies of web services— HTTP, XML, SOAP, and WSDL—don't address *semantics*, or meaning. These protocols give us a shared *syntax*, or structure for a language along the lines of rules for sentence construction and punctuation. But since they lack a vocabulary, the protocols only tell us how documents should be structured and not what they *mean*.

Suppose you want to accept electronic purchase orders from your customers. Web services provide a mechanism for transmitting those orders, but the basic web-services protocols don't know anything about purchase orders. An *XML schema* can define the structure of a purchase order, for instance, but it still won't tell a system how to interpret the description of an item.

As we discussed earlier, these semantic issues have historically been within the domain of EDI, and RosettaNet broke new ground by defining the semantics for a specific industry. The same breakthrough will have to happen for other industries and value chains in order for web services to achieve their potential.

A New Business Model?

The rumor is that soon we'll all be able to create new revenue models and charge for the use of our web services. While this is true for some companies, there's nothing inherently valuable about the web-services delivery mechanism. If we learned anything from the dot-com debacle and from the failure of the generic *application service provider* (ASP) model, it's that you only make money when you provide value.

Think about your local plumber. He owns a truck, but that's not why you pay him. You pay him to fix your leaks. The value he provides is his ability to solve your plumbing problems. The truck is merely a mechanism for getting him to and from your house.

Likewise, web services are just a mechanism for moving information from one system to another. If you already have information or something else of value to offer, web services may be a good way to deliver that value to your customers. But don't be in awe of the delivery mechanism. Just because your information is offered as a web service doesn't make it more valuable.

A Competitive Advantage?

Do your FAX machines or email give you an advantage over your competition? Probably not, since your competitors likely have FAX and email, too. Perhaps web serviecs will offer a competitive edge for a brief period, as long as they're new to your industry. But once they're commonplace, web services won't be business differentiators any more than email or a FAX machine. Web services will be *required* in virtually every industry. Even local Mom and Pop storefronts will use web services to communicate with their suppliers and manage their inventories.

Today, you may be able to achieve some short-term advantage from web services if your competitors don't offer or use them—but at some point, the tides will turn. Once web services become common in your industry, you'll be at a disadvantage if you *don't* use them.

Another point to remember is that there's little advantage in being the first kid on your block to launch external web services. You might derive some short-term benefit from the attention you receive, since it's a good excuse to send out another press release. But just like the first company with a FAX machine, you may not find anyone out there to communicate with.

On the other hand, there are very real, immediate opportunities to gain a competitive advantage by using web services as an *integration technology*. You don't need to wait for the other kids; you can get a head start on them by using web services internally.

Automatic Linking to Unknown Partners?

The proponents of this concept would have you believe that your computer systems will be able to identify a new business partner through a directory of web services, and establish both the business relationship and communications interface to that partner without any human intervention.

Imagine a scenario in which a web-services shopping bot locates the online bookstore with the lowest price for a particular book identified by its ISBN number. The problem is, how does the bot know which vendor to *trust*? Is the lowest-cost vendor legitimate? Which vendor can actually meet its delivery commitment?

Compare this to the Yellow Pages in the phone book. Just because a company advertises there is no guarantee of its honesty, integrity, or quality. For trivial transactions such as book purchases, fully automated partner discovery might work—but it's hard to imagine turning an automated system loose on mission-critical business relationships.

This idea of automatically discovering and linking to new business partners is pure science fiction, hyped by futurists with no experience implementing commercial-grade systems. Their theory is that multiple competing vendors will offer technically identical web services and that your computer systems will be able to find these services, select one, and automatically link your application to the selected web service. The example used most often is credit-card processing. In this scenario, all credit-card processors list their services in a directory and your e-commerce system selects and links to the best one, all without human intervention.

In reality, most high-value web-service interactions will be conducted between known, trusted business partners, not anonymous parties. Once two parties have established a relationship of trust, the technologies for automated discovery can certainly be used to advertise, locate, and enable new services between them, plus link to new versions of existing services—but only after a relationship is established.

When it comes to the automated discovery of new business partners, Clay Shirky contends:

> "Web services are actually best at automating private, previously negotiated conversations. The idea of unknown but perfectly described capabilities existing out there in the cloud—at once unfamiliar enough to need to be discovered, tailored and reliable enough to build a business on, and not so critical that they need to be hosted locally—describes a small and fairly

trivial set of possible services. The ASP business ran aground on this issue, and there is no sign that the web services solution will work any better…Web services can't replace developers but may let them get through the gritty details faster, once they've worked out the high-level agreements."[9]

A Replacement for EDI?

Yes, thank goodness. This claim isn't hype. EDI was the best we could do with 1980s technology, but it's too complex, inefficient, and expensive for most companies. Once two or more organizations have a valid business reason to work with one another, web services can substantially reduce the effort and time it takes to develop the standards for integration and to implement those links.

Well-Defined Standards?

Not quite, but we're getting there. The old maxim still applies: "The greatest thing about standards is that there are so many of them." Although some of the fundamental standards are stable and widely accepted, others are not—particularly those required for mission-critical business applications.

Don't be misled by the apparent integrity of the web-services protocol stack as described by vendors and analysts. The stack is still evolving, and anyone trying to implement a heterogeneous system based on web services will tell you that dealing with those still-evolving protocols can be a nightmare. But standards become stronger the more they're used and problems get corrected, so the standards supporting web services are being tested and improved at a remarkable rate. The lack of standards shouldn't stop you altogether, but be realistic about the risks and costs of diving in too early. (We'll discuss the topic of timing in Chapter 18).

An Invention of…

Sun claims it invented XML,[10] which is true if you ignore the fact that XML was based on the Standard General Markup Language (SGML).

Microsoft and UserLand Software both claim to have invented SOAP, and they did. But who cares? What difference does that make to us, the consumers of the technology? After all, Xerox invented the mouse, the laser printer, and the modern *graphical user interface* (GUI). But that doesn't mean we necessarily turn to Xerox as the best source for products based on these inventions.

While we appreciate the contributions made by technology innovators, it's important to set who-invented-what considerations aside when it comes time to make strategic plans and purchasing decisions. Historical firsts are irrelevant when it comes to planning web services—on the contrary, it's the vendor independence of web services that's so important.

The Same As .NET?

Oh, how Microsoft hopes you'll think so. In fact, .NET is a huge umbrella of technologies and marketing efforts that includes much more than web services. All of the major vendors—not just Microsoft—hope you'll think of them first whenever you hear the words "web services."

———————

Now that we're aware of the hype surrounding web services, let's consider what we can realistically accomplish with them. This means tackling the most difficult task of this or any other planning process: coming to grips with what we don't know, and identifying the missing solutions that we may have to invent.

Chapter 4

The Missing Pieces

Fifteen years from now, web services will be about as exciting, dynamic, and newsworthy as TCP/IP is today. Web services won't be mentioned by the IT trade press, and the topic won't be tracked by analysts. Web services will become such an inherent part of distributed computing that even the name "web services" will disappear from our lexicon. (We won't miss it—it's not such a great name anyway.) Web services will continue to evolve slowly, as TCP/IP continues to do, but the web-services puzzle will essentially be complete. It will just be how we do what we do.

Today web services get a lot of attention, because the competition is on to become the first to complete the web services puzzle. In some areas there are multiple solutions competing for the same spot in the final puzzle. Although there are substantial benefits to be had by venturing into the world of web services before the requisite pieces of the puzzle are unambiguously in position, doing so has its risks and challenges. You'll have to come up with at least a temporary solution for each of the missing or unstable pieces, knowing that you'll probably have to replace it when a standardized and less expensive solution eventually appears.

Your greatest challenge is to determine which tools and solutions are available, and which you're going to have to invent. This is a classic buy-versus-build decision. Anything you've got to build or invent will cost more, take longer, and put your plan at greater risk than an off-the-shelf solution with a proven track record. Since this is a fundamental consideration in the strategic planning process, let's preview the missing web-services components we'll address in detail in the subsequent chapters.

Business Semantics

The existing standards of web services provide a grammar or syntax that allows applications and organizations to communicate, but far less work has been completed on the standards for semantics to convey intentions or meaning. The mechanisms exist to move purchase orders and confirmations around the globe at lightning speed, but we still can't reach a universal agreement on whether the buyer's name should consist of a single string of characters or must be broken into first, middle, and last names.

Security

Security is another missing piece. It's not that we don't know how to solve the security problems—we solved them for e-commerce and other environments before anyone ever heard of web services. But web services do add some new twists to old problems. In the past, the majority of authentication and authorization challenges have been contained within a single trust domain. External web services require that we develop trust mechanisms that span organizational boundaries and interoperate with disparate technologies. Some of the critical web-services standards for authentication, encryption, and non-repudiation (not being able to deny what you've done) have yet to be agreed upon.

Transactional Integrity

The lack of standards for the handling of complex transactions will delay the adoption of web services in many applications. Here's an example of the problem:

Suppose you need both an airline flight to New York City and a hotel room there. You don't want either unless you can get both. If you commit to the airline first but can't get a hotel room, you'll need to cancel the airline reservation. If you start with the hotel reservation and fail to get an airline reservation, you're stuck with a hotel booking you can't use.

This problem isn't unique to web services. We've solved this problem before with airline and hotel reservation systems that were closely coupled, or linked with a detailed knowledge of one another's internal workings. But we don't yet have agreement on a standardized way to manage complex transactions using web services when they involve multiple disparate systems.

Orchestration and Choreography

One of the promises of web services is that we'll be able to create ad hoc or agile multi-party business processes—possibly even disposable processes that are used once and then discarded. But before this can happen, we need to establish standards that can coordinate or *orchestrate* complex transactions and *choreograph* multi-party business processes.

Single Signon

Deployment of many web services has been delayed due to the unsolved *single-signon* problem. Here's an example that illustrates the need:

Suppose the airline system knows you as Bob, and the hotel system knows you as Robert. Let's say you also use a different password to logon to each system. In order to automate your reservation, one of the systems must have a way to share your identity with the other, with your permission, while protecting your privacy.

Although many single-signon solutions have been proposed, this problem has become a highly political and controversial topic. So far, a good single-signon solution that's acceptable to consumers, governments, and all vendors has proved elusive.

Reliable Asynchronous Message Handling

Systems that are both reliable and capable of handling high traffic loads require a robust *asynchronous messaging* system. The problem with unreliable systems is that messages are sometimes lost due to errors, bottlenecks, or outages. Here's an abstract example that illustrates the problem:

If application A needs a small piece of information from application B, A may be able to send a request to B and wait for the response. But what happens if it takes a while for B to find and deliver the answer? Should A keep waiting forever? Suppose the answer depends on application B in turn asking a question of yet another application?

The solution to this problem is a system that queues and saves messages until delivery is known to have occurred. Again, we know how to do this—we just haven't adopted a standard so that everyone does it the same way.

Quality of Service (QoS)

Many web-services transactions are time-sensitive and therefore require an up-front guarantee that they can be completed promptly. At present, there's no consensus on how to manage or measure this concept of Quality of Service.

Contracts and Negotiations

A successful web-services strategy must include plans for more than just the technology. Before business partners can be linked via web services, there has to be agreement as to the terms and conditions of their relationship. Once web services allow us to solve technical problems more quickly, we're going to find that our negotiation and contractual processes have become the new bottlenecks. We're going to have to streamline these non-technical steps of establishing new business relationships.

Standardization of New Business Models

Many people are excited by the potential of web services to enable new business models. But we have yet to determine exactly how these business models will operate, and which of them will ultimately succeed or fail. Will software be delivered as web services rather than downloaded or on CD-ROMs? Will we pay for web services by the month, by the user, or by the transaction? As with many of the dotcoms, a number of innovative companies may be born and die trying to provide the answers to these questions.

Billing and Accounting Services

We're going to need mechanisms for tracking the usage of some web services, based on a pay-per-use business model. The modularity of web services will eventually allow us to stitch together web services from multiple parties to create larger and more valuable *aggregated* web services, which means we're also going to need mechanisms for *settlements* allocating shares of revenues among multiple parties. Some usage charges will be fractions of a cent per transaction, but such *micropayments* are historically inefficient to collect and account for. These problems have been solved in other situations, such as broadcast-rights management and long-distance telephone network charges—but we still need similar solutions for web services.

Intermediaries and Transformation Services

Although web services are standardized, many variations are permitted, so we'll need a way to reconcile those variations or transform information from one variant to another. For example, the provider of a web service may offer it via the HTTP protocol, whereas a subscriber to the web service may want to access it using SMTP. Similarly, a buyer may want to obtain a price quote in Euros, whereas the seller may only offer the information in dollars. Packaged software and services vendors and any other intermediaries will have to support the conversion of these and other formats and protocols. At the moment, many of these transformational solutions are proprietary, implying that relying on a single vendor may produce lock-in. Eventually we'll need standards for transformation services, and the business opportunities for third-party intermediaries will have to stabilize.

Operational Infrastructure

We have little experience with the operational-infrastructure requirements for web services, just as we had minimal understanding of such requirements for the World Wide Web when it was new and few web sites experienced much traffic. Although web-based e-commerce has taught us a lot about outsourcing, web hosting, redundancy, backup and recovery, we have yet to transfer that experience to web services.

For example, many existing business applications are shut down daily or weekly for backup and maintenance. This won't be acceptable for many web services in the 24/7 world of the Internet. Web services intended for use by external business partners may have to be up and running at all times, but many of the legacy applications that provide the back-end functionality of those web services weren't designed for such levels of availability. IT departments will have to solve many physical plant and staffing issues in the web-services world.

One consistent theme emerges from the long list of what's missing from web services: Even though the IT community really does know how to solve most of these problems, we haven't yet reached agreements on which solutions should be adopted as standards. All of these issues will be resolved in time, and standards will be adopted and implemented. But for now, venturing into web services can mean taking many risks and having to invent—rather than purchase—solutions to many of these problems.

Managing the risks and unknowns is the most important part of a web-services strategy, and in the next chapter we'll see how to segregate the broad spectrum of web-services technologies. This will help us identify key unknowns and quantify the risks associated with them.

Chapter 5

Critical Components

In 1906, Vilfredo Pareto, an Italian economist, observed that twenty percent of the Italian people owned eighty percent of their country's accumulated wealth. One hundred years later, we're still using Pareto's Principle, also known as the 80/20 Rule.

There are 80/20 rules for just about everything, as you can learn by querying Google™ for "80/20 rules." Here are just a few out of "about 1,660,000" matches:

- 80 percent of a budget comes from 20 percent of the items.
- 80 percent of a manager's interruptions come from the same 20 percent of the people.
- 80 percent of your website traffic comes from 20 percent of your pages.
- 80 percent of the decisions made in meetings come from 20 percent of the meeting time.
- 80 percent of the outfits we wear come from 20 percent of the clothes in our closets and drawers.

The 80/20 Rule of Strategies

The key to developing any successful strategy is not to focus your analysis on the 80 percent of the problem you already understand or can easily find answers to, but to tackle the 20 percent that's difficult, risky, or potentially even impossible. You may spend 80 percent of your time and budget on that 20 percent regardless, but you can plan for it rather than discover it the hard way.

As you develop your own web-services implementation strategy, 80 percent of the issues you'll face will be ones you've encountered before. These are the easy ones. You'll know with some degree of accuracy how to plan for them, including how much the solutions will cost, how long they'll take, and what resources they'll require.

Think about the way you approach desktop software decisions. Is it difficult to choose between Windows and an alternative operating system? Probably not. How about word-processing and spreadsheet software? Do you lose sleep worrying about those decisions? Not likely. They're the no-brainers.

But what about software for security and spam filtering? These are two components that require more attention. They're part of the 20 percent of decisions that are difficult and will take up 80 percent of managers' time.

The same is true with web-services implementations. It's not the 80 percent of the technology that's standardized and well documented that will get you—the relatively established technologies such as SOAP, XML, or WSDL won't keep you awake at night. It's that nasty 20 percent for which the solutions aren't yet standardized and documented, such as transactional integrity and security. These aspects of web services are the focus of Part III, *Technologies*.

It's What You Don't Know

Eighty percent of the challenges you'll face in implementing a web service will come from the 20 percent that you've never done before or that *no one* has ever done before. Remember, unless the pages of this book are yellowed with age, web services are still in their infancy, much as TCP/IP was in 1985.

In Chapter 4 we pointed out that many pieces of the web-services puzzle are still missing. If you need one or more of those pieces for your web-services projects, you'll have to buy proprietary implementations from vendors, or build them from scratch. Whether you buy or build a solution to meet your needs, it will cost more and take longer than if the pieces were available as standardized solutions.

For example, if your project requires an element of security (authentication, encryption, non-repudiation, etc.) for which no off-the-shelf standardized solutions exist, you'll have to license proprietary software, outsource to a specialty service provider, or develop an ad hoc solution in house. Such a requirement could be the catalyst that pushes a project over the line that separates simple and complex web services, and therefore causes the project to require a more elaborate plan.

There are usually a few technologies or components in any project that present the greatest challenges, cause most of the delays, and can make or break the project. Because these pieces of the puzzle have such an effect on the project's schedule and cost, we'll refer to them as the *critical components*. Once you've identified these critical components and established how, at what cost, and on what schedule you can buy or build them, you'll know whether the cost and time needed to implement a web-services project is significant enough to require formal strategic planning.

The Web-Services Pyramid

The *web-services pyramid* in Figure 5-1 shows the possible domains of critical components in web services.

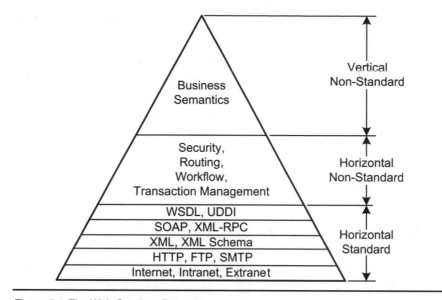

Figure 5-1: The Web-Services Pyramid

The web-services components in the bottom third of the pyramid are those that are more or less *standardized* and readily available. For instance, you can buy inexpensive SOAP toolkits from nearly any software-platform vendor. In many cases, SOAP services are already part of the underlying operating system or application server. These components are *horizontal*, because they make up the foundation of *all* web services regardless of the industry or type of application.

The middle tier of the pyramid contains the components of web services that are also horizontal (i.e., not specific to any industry or application), but are either not yet standardized or not readily available as off-the-shelf implementations. Over time, some of the components in this *horizontal non-standard* layer work their way down to the *horizontal standard* layer as they become standardized and more widely available. For instance, before they were standardized and readily available, SOAP, WSDL, and UDDI were in this middle tier. Today, they're readily available, so they've made their way to the lowest tier.

Finally, at the top of the pyramid are the business-semantic components. These are the industry-specific (i.e., *vertical*) document and message formats, transaction types, and specifications. This layer is the final frontier of standardization. Today, precious few standards exist in the rarified atmosphere at the top of the pyramid. Over time, many industry-specific business-semantics standards will be created—but if history is any lesson, it's going to take many years. While some particularly automated industries such as financial services, automotive, and electronics have made great strides in standardizing business semantics, this is not the case for many less sophisticated verticals. Among your own network of partners, the use of industry-specific standards might not be such a priority, so you may not be able to wait for your industry to reach a standard definition. But to keep your project as streamlined as possible, you should attempt to minimize the number of business-semantics interfaces your organization has to work with.

Milestones

As we delve deeper into strategic planning for web services in Part IV, *Strategies*, we'll identify the dates when web services have achieved (or will achieve) certain milestones. For instance, it may be important to know when it will be possible to hire contractors with previous experience with a particular technology. But since a web-services project includes a wide array of components that have different levels of complexity and standardization (as illustrated by the pyramid), we'll need to *determine those milestones for each individual critical component*.

For example, let's say we're estimating the date when the final standard will appear for a web service that will be available to multiple external business partners. In this case, the milestone date we're looking for is when the business semantics become standardized. Because the web-services project hinges on this critical component, the milestone for the critical component *is* the milestone for the overall web service.

Now assume we're dealing with a web service that will only be deployed internally or with one business partner at most. Here the important milestone is when the required middle-layer components are standardized, because they're the critical components for that web service. Once again, the critical component determines your project milestones—and hence your project schedule.

Simple or Complex?

In Part IV, *Strategies*, we'll segregate web-services projects according to their complexity. One of the criteria we'll use is whether a project requires linking to one or more external (i.e., beyond-the-firewall) trust domains, in which case the project falls into the *complex* category.

Because simple projects by definition never require linking to systems beyond your control—and hence avoid the political issues associated with semantics—their critical components always reside in the middle layer of the pyramid. You may determine that one or more of the critical components for an otherwise simple project will require a substantial investment of time or effort. In this case, consider treating the project as complex instead, or delaying the project until the critical component becomes simpler and less expensive due to standardization and the availability of lower-cost solutions.

The most important takeaway from these past two chapters is this: Don't treat all web-services technologies alike when it comes to planning a project. Some components are far more mature than others, and some don't exist at all. The success of your web-services projects will be determined by the degree to which you *focus on the least mature technologies*, or those highest in the web-services pyramid. This pyramid concept is a useful tool, and one we'll refer to throughout the remainder of this book.

Part II

Concepts

Concepts

Imagine the owner of a horse and carriage in 1910 seeing for the first time a Model T Ford parked by the side of the road. Walking around it and scratching his head, he might have wondered where to attach the horse harness. It would have taken this fellow a while to come to grips with the fundamental change that had taken place in transportation technology. Judging solely from his previous knowledge of buggies and a quick glance at the Model T, he might conclude that this new buggy wasn't all that different from his old one.

You can hitch a horse to a Model T, but then you'd be missing the point, wouldn't you? An automobile isn't just a carriage that happens to have an internal-combustion engine stuck between its two front wheels. It's an entirely different vehicle.

While the advanced concepts of web services aren't new, they're often as mysterious and unfamiliar to many programmers as the Model T was to some buggy owners for years after its introduction. And just as it's possible for a horse to pull an automobile, it's also possible to develop web services without ever understanding the more advanced concepts of service-oriented architectures (SOAs), asynchronous messaging, and loose coupling. But doing so would mean passing up some of the greatest benefits of web services.

In Part II of *Loosely Coupled*, we're going to explore the advanced concepts of web services. We'll begin in Chapter 6 by studying the history of application-integration technologies that preceded web services. In Chapter 7, we'll look at the relationship between object-oriented programming (OOP) and web services. In the subsequent three chapters, we'll explore the concepts of SOAs, asynchronous messaging, and loose coupling. By the end of Part II, you'll understand these concepts, and how they can help you take full advantage of the benefits of web services.

Chapter 6

Application Integration

Most CIOs consider linking computer systems within their organizations to be a necessary evil. It's necessary because without integration, information remains locked away in the databases of separate divisions and departments, which inhibits the automation of critical business functions. But integration can appear evil because it's become so extraordinarily expensive. Of course integration *should* be viewed as an exciting opportunity to increase IT's efficiency and capabilities, but it's rarely perceived that way.

Non-IT executives are as frustrated as CIOs by the cost of integration. After investing millions of dollars in applications to solve departmental problems, CEOs and CFOs ask why they should have to spend millions more to get newly purchased applications to work with the old ones. Given all the brilliant minds in their IT departments, they wonder how it could be so difficult and expensive to make systems communicate with one another.

Forrester Research estimates that as much as 35 percent of IT staff resources are used for gluing together heterogeneous applications (i.e., those based on different platforms and technologies).[11] Gartner Research estimates that the average programmer spends 65 percent of his or her time performing integration tasks. No matter whether you prefer Forrester's 35 percent or Gartner's 65 percent, the fact remains: Application integration represents the single largest expense of most IT budgets, and application integration has become a nasty thorn in the side of most CIOs.

In this chapter and the ones that follow, we'll see how internal web services communicate within the confines of corporate firewalls to substantially reduce the cost and pain of application integration, all while creating opportunities to increase the value and agility of information systems. Beginning with historical perspectives, we'll see how web services are the next step along the evolutionary path of enterprise resource planning (ERP) and enterprise application integration (EAI).

Historical Solutions

How did we get to the point where at least one-third of our IT costs come from integration, and how might web services become our salvation? To answer this question, let's follow the history of integration solutions summarized by the timeline in Figure 6-1.

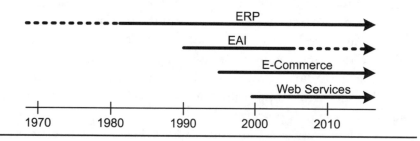

Figure 6-1: Integration History Timeline

Data Silos

Before the advent of ERP application suites, each departmental business function was typically supported by a separate software package: Finance departments had accounting packages, HR and manufacturing had isolated systems tailored to their unique needs, and so on. In most cases these applications replaced purely manual (i.e., paper-based) systems, so in that sense anything was an improvement.

Over time, these single-department applications grew without regard for their peer applications in other departments. Indeed, not all departments were automated, and there was little thought given to automating entire companies. It was done one departmental business function at a time.

As the applications improved, they increasingly supported functions at the periphery, where data flowed into and out of their departments. But because they varied so greatly in terms of technology and structure (i.e., they were heterogeneous), it was extraordinarily difficult to link one department's system to others'.

The department-specific applications and their associated databases became *data silos* or *stovepipes,* as illustrated in Figure 6-2 along with some typical data integration paths. The silo and stovepipe metaphors indicate the vertical (departmental) dedication of systems and their inability to be used directly by other departments.

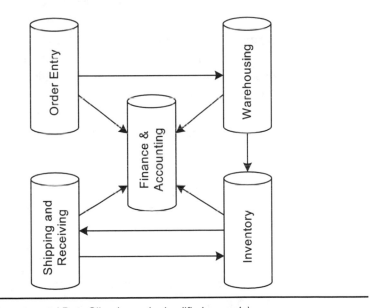

Figure 6-2: Departmental Data Silos (a much-simplified example)

Swivel-Chair Integration and SneakerNets

As computer-generated paperwork flowed out of one department, it was manually re-entered into the computer system of the next. An order-entry system might print out a hard copy of an order, only for it to be re-keyed into the warehousing system and again into the billing system, the accounting system, and so on. This *swivel-chair integration* became the norm for companies that invested in departmentally specific systems.

Some companies were able to coerce one department's application to read data files written by another's. These lucky organizations often resorted to *sneakernets*—transferring data on magnetic tape or floppy disks—to avoid the re-keying process. With the advent of LANs and WANs, electronic file transfers replaced most sneakernets.

But no matter whether the task was performed by swivel-chair integration, sneakernet, or file transfer, the process was always one-way. Data moved forward from one system to the next, but rarely in the opposite direction. This created a lack of synchronization among multiple versions of similar items. If an order was modified after it left the order-entry system, the change wasn't typically reflected in the original system. It was common for there to be two or more versions of an order, and no one knew for certain which one was correct.

Trying to resolve conflicts was a manual process requiring lots of phone calls between people who had become experts in one environment or another. Highly automated systems remained dependent upon individuals who could solve the inevitable problems that occurred. ("Call Sally down in Billing; she'll know how to straighten this out.")

As absurd as swivel-chair integration may sound, it remains in widespread use to this day. Why? Because it's a highly pragmatic solution. No matter how technologically incompatible two applications may be, and no matter how complex or obscure their internal technologies may be, it's always possible to take the output from one program and re-enter it into the other. Swivel-chair integration is the ultimate fallback: It takes almost no time to implement, requires virtually no IT investment, and can be adopted at any level within a company—without even asking the CIO. And yes, that's also one of its weaknesses. But the two main problems with swivel-chair integration are (1) it's very labor intensive, and (2) it's highly prone to errors—both of which are due to the fact that it's a manual process.

Screen Scraping

The first attempts to link applications programmatically weren't much more elegant than sneakernets. Early software packages had no application program interfaces (APIs) whatsoever. It was impossible to import or export data from these silos, even though the need to do so became overwhelming given the demands of real-world business processes. Out of desperation, programmers found they had no option but to write software that emulated the screens and keyboards of terminals attached to ERP systems.

The concept borders on the ridiculous, but early ERP systems were so inflexible and unable to link to external systems that programs were written that actually pretended to be people. The result was nothing more than automated swivel-chair integration. To retrieve customer data, for example, these *screen scraper* applications first simulated the keystrokes that an operator would use to find the customer record, then captured the data returned from the host system as destined for the display screen or printer. The screen-scraping program would then simulate the data-entry process on the receiving system.

Screen scraping is extremely brittle because if one application's screen changes, the interfaces to all others that depend on that screen will have to be updated. But it's also very easy to understand. Since it can be developed and maintained by relatively low-skill, low-cost programmers, screen scraping is still widely used even today.

Enterprise Resource Planning (ERP)

Instead of requiring separate systems in each department, ERP promises to build a single integrated system based on separate modules for each department or function, as illustrated in Figure 6-3. This way, you can license the overall package, start with the finance and manufacturing modules, then add HR at a later date. Using ERP, each department gets a customized application that provides its own window into the corporate system.

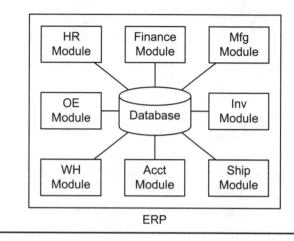

ERP

Figure 6-3: The ERP Solution

First conceived in the early 1960s, ERP software took off during 1980s and 1990s, when a generally strong economy both created the need for ERP and made funding available for its implementation. Companies were expanding at increasing rates, and many considered automating their business processes as a way to build competitive advantage. In addition, executives were willing to pay a premium to gain increased visibility into the inner workings of their organizations. ERP was thus a welcome solution.

But ERP was (and still is) tremendously expensive to implement and maintain. Meta Group analyzed the total cost of ownership (TCO) of ERP, including hardware, software, professional services, and internal staffing. Their evaluation estimated the time it takes for ERP to be adopted and absorbed into most companies at two years following installation. Among the 63 companies surveyed—including small, medium, and large companies in a range of industries—the average TCO was $15 million, the vast majority of which was spent not on software licenses but on systems integration and customization. The highest TCO was $300 million and lowest was $400,000. Meta Group also determined the cost on a per-user basis over that period was a staggering $53,320. [2]

Still, most companies that implemented ERP in the 1980s and 1990s were glad they did. Although the costs were high, the systems supported at least some level of enterprise-wide integration that had been nearly impossible to achieve before.

But then some companies that were initially glad to have ERP began to experience its limitations. The ERP paradigm is based on the idea that the centralized database is authoritative for all data and transactions, across all business units and departments. This presumes that any external system not part of the ERP system itself will be entirely dependent upon the ERP database and transaction system. The system assumes it's the master, and that any other applications are its slaves.

ERP packages include various utilities for extracting and reporting data, and they have real-time query (read-only) capabilities as well. Reading can usually be done in real time, as it's the one operation that doesn't alter the database. But it's virtually impossible for an ERP package to co-exist in an environment where—heaven forbid—there might be another application that could create or update objects such as orders, employees, or inventory items.

Naturally, ERP packages couldn't solve one hundred percent of all business automation needs. Soon there were other systems, such as those for CRM and e-commerce, and some of these had valid reasons to create or modify data as well as read it. Once again, CIOs found themselves faced with the data-silo problem, only this time on a much grander scale with substantially larger and even more isolated silos, as shown in Figure 6-4.

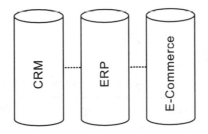

Figure 6-4: The New Data Silos

This closed architecture of ERP packages may become their ultimate demise. The inflexibility of ERP software has forced programmers to go to some extraordinary lengths to work around these limitations, and has also created opportunities for new categories of vendors and products focused not on creating new applications, but on integrating those already in place.

The Shrinking Common-Technology Subset

Whether intended for internal or external use, all integration solutions must address the problem of disparate technologies. Just exactly how does one select the technologies to link disparate systems? One approach is to focus on the technologies common among all of the systems. Another approach is offered by web services, which is to bank on technologies that are independent of any of the systems.

The traditional approach to integrating systems is *subtractive* in that it seeks to find the *common subset* of technologies between the systems, starting with a physical connection between the systems. That subset is the basis for the integration, and additional layers of technology are built on top of it.

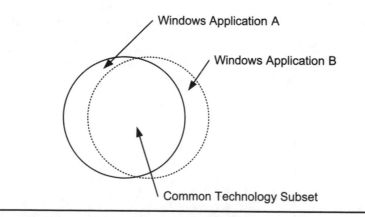

Figure 6-5: The Common Subset of Similar Applications

Figure 6-5 illustrates this subtractive effect with two Windows-based applications that are very similar. Because both systems run on Windows operating systems and may have been written using the same programming language, data exchanges between them require few transformations. The subset of technologies in common between these two applications is large, and there are many opportunities to use identical technologies and even common data representations to link the two systems.

Let's take a simple example of how this works in practice. Suppose you're trying to integrate systems for an industrial-products company, and your first goal is to allow the order entry (OE) system to retrieve customer records from the customer resource management (CRM) system. The OE system will supply a customer ID number, and the CRM system will return a complete customer record, as illustrated in Figure 6-6.

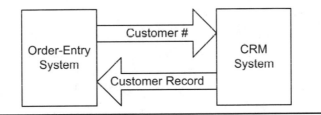

Figure 6-6: A Simple Query

Using traditional techniques and philosophies, you'd first determine what technologies the two systems had in common that might be used as the basis for the integration interface. For instance, if both systems were running on Microsoft Windows platforms, you'd likely use system-to-system DCOM calls to pass data back and forth. Not too difficult a task.

But what if the OE system is running on a J2EE (Java) platform, written using Enterprise Java Beans (EJBs)? Now the applications have far less in common, as illustrated in Figure 6-7.

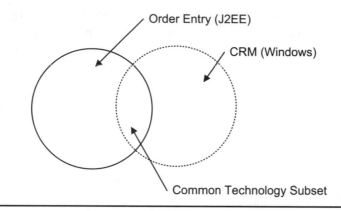

Order Entry (J2EE)

CRM (Windows)

Common Technology Subset

Figure 6-7: The Common Subset of Two Dissimilar Applications

Using a subtractive method for selecting integration technologies is somewhat more difficult here than with two systems that are both Windows-based. Programs in the J2EE environment can't communicate using DCOM, nor can Windows apps communicate using RMI, the preferred Java-only protocol. The integration task has become more challenging, because the two endpoints have less in common. And it's not just a matter of finding a compatible communications protocol—even if you solve that problem and find a way to transmit customer records from the CRM system to the OE system, the receiving system won't be able to *interpret* the data. That's because the data will be structured according to the data-representation standards of the particular programming language on the Microsoft (sending) platform. Each programming language and environment has its own proprietary rules for how numbers, character strings, and compound data structures are stored and transmitted. You've got to come up with a representation of the customer record that both sides can understand.

Since the customer record is inherently part of the CRM system, your first tendency might be to adopt that format as your de facto standard, and therefore write code on the OE system that can handle data transformations in each direction. In other words, you might make the OE system a slave, capable of communicating using the native protocols of the master CRM system. But if you go that route, what will happen if at some time in the future you add a third system into the mix, or a fourth? Every time you add a system that's not based on the same technology platform as the CRM system, you'll have to repeat the entire process. The ever-shrinking common-technology subset is illustrated in Figure 6-8.

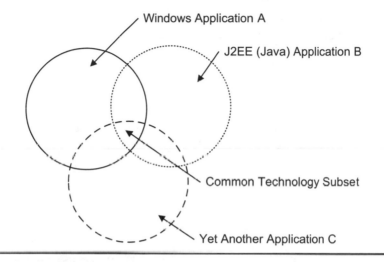

Figure 6-8: The Shrinking Common Subset

To make matters even worse, the process will be repeated not only for each additional system and application that needs access to customer information, but for other query types as well—even from the same applications. In other words, just because you solved the compatibility problem for the customer-record query doesn't mean you've solved it for other queries as well. You'll probably have to write new code on each system for each query. The total number of custom integration tasks will be the product of the number of applications and the number of interactions between each pair of systems. You're stuck with that old n^2 (parabolic) problem once again, and it's a losing battle.

The Intermediate Canonical Alternative

Rather than commit suicide by geometric progression, suppose you simply walked away from the n^2 confrontation. Change the rules. Instead of attempting to find that ever-shrinking common-technology subset, what would happen if you adopted an integration standard that was independent of *all* platforms?

At the time you begin the first integration project, it's important to think big. Think in terms of the CRM system providing a *service* to an entire community of other systems. The membership in that community may eventually include a wide range of disparate systems, some of which may ultimately even reside outside the company. So you'll want to make the data available in a way that's independent of the vagaries of any one system, and at the same time easy to translate into and out of any system.

Suppose that rather than looking for a common subset of technologies between two applications, you began by adding a standardized interface (or *adapter*) to each of them, as illustrated in Figure 6-9.

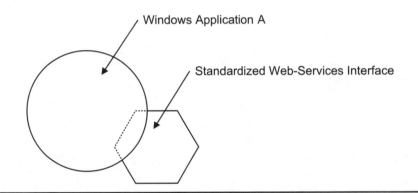

Figure 6-9: Adding a Web-Services Interface

Yes, your initial task might be more substantial, since you're adding to applications rather than taking the shortcut of exploiting non-universal compatibilities. But it's a reasonable investment, so long as the web-services interface is truly universal. There's additional expense associated with adding such an interface to each application, but it's a cost that scales *linearly* with the number of applications, not with the *square* of the number of applications. That is, it's something you do once per application, not once for every pair of applications that might want to communicate.

Figure 6-10 shows what happens to the subset of common technologies when a universally independent architecture is adopted.

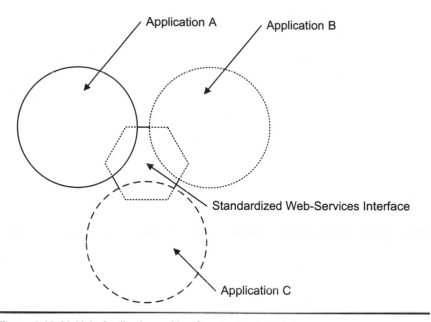

Figure 6-10: Multiple Applications with a Standardized Interface

Now there is only one common technology between the applications, but it's one designed for the sole purpose of application-to-application communications. You can add as many applications to this mix as you like, and you'll never again be worried about the shrinking common-technology subset.

This is a fundamental aspect of *loose coupling:* No longer are we concerned with the subset of common technologies. In fact, not only do the circles representing the applications in Figure 6-10 not overlap—they don't even touch. There's no assumption that any application has anything in common with any other application, other than the standardized interface. It would be a violation of loose-coupling principles to base the interface on any common-subset assumption. (We'll explore loose coupling in greater depth in Chapter 10.) This concept of a universal integration technology supported by adapters for each application isn't unique to web services; it's also used in most *enterprise application integration* (EAI) products as well.

Enterprise Application Integration (EAI)

By the early 1990s, many CIOs realized that although ERP had killed one monster, it had created another. ERP eliminated many of the individual data silos such as HR, finance, and manufacturing, but it replaced them with a new ERP super-silo of its own. Nothing external to ERP could be linked to these core systems that ran companies.

CIOs began to see how flawed the concept of one centralized ERP system was, and how dependent they had become on (a) a single software package, (b) the ERP vendors, and (c) the massive customization by expensive consultants required to make the inflexible packages do what was needed in the real world. Just as departmental data silos created the opportunity for ERP in the 1980s, the failings of ERP created yet another opportunity in the 1990s. The result was EAI.

EAI packages act as software data translators that take information from ERP and convert it into formats that other applications, such as CRM packages, can understand—and vice versa. Unlike the applications it links, however, EAI doesn't actually provide any business functionality itself. Instead, it supplies the glue that allows a company's multiple business systems to exchange data with one another. You can think of EAI as a communications and translation platform, rather than one on which applications are built.

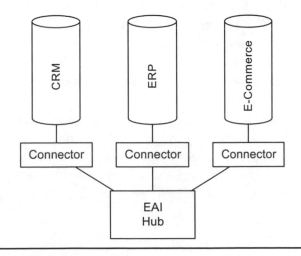

Figure 6-11: An EAI Hub and Connectors

EAI software typically runs on dedicated servers, often called *hubs* or *brokers,* as illustrated in Figure 6-11. EAI packages also include adapters or *connectors* to popular ERP and CRM application suites. For other applications not supported by adapters or connectors, the EAI vendors offer *developer toolkits*, which allow programmers to create their own customized links.

Integrating systems via EAI is a two-step process. First, you install the appropriate connector for each of the systems you want to link. This involves identifying the tables used in each system's database—in other words, you explain to the EAI hub how each application's data are organized.

Second, you create a *mapping* of each application's data into and out of a common (canonical) format. This is typically done using a graphical tool that displays the data structures of an application on one side of the screen, and the canonical data structures on the other. You simply draw lines connecting objects or fields from one side to the other. Let's say you want to link orders from the ERP package to the CRM package: First you define the canonical representation of an order, then create mappings for each of the ERP package's fields to the canonical form, and finally do the same for the CRM application's data.

Once you define the data structure for your ERP package, you can use that same information when linking to HR, CRM, and other applications, because they all convert into and out of the canonical form. This means the installation of the connectors and the mapping of the translations from each application to the common format need not be repeated for each pair of applications.

One problem with EAI, however, is that some applications can't be cleanly linked as is. For example, suppose the *address* field in one application is 40 characters long. What happens when it's mapped to another application's address field that can hold only 30 characters? There's no way around it: No matter what the canonical format may be, some data will be lost when moved from the first to the second application. Likewise, suppose the first application stores a *name* in a single field, whereas the second requires *firstname, middlename,* and *lastname*. It's possible to parse long names into three pieces, but this is an error-prone process. And the address and the name problems are two of the most trivial examples of application incompatibility.

But the greatest problem with EAI is its very high cost. (Do you see a recurring theme here?) The typical *basic* license fees for an EAI package are between $500,000 and $750,000, and that's just the tip of the iceberg. In most cases, you can count on additional professional-services expenses—either from the EAI vendor or a third-party systems integrator—of at least five times that amount. Gartner Research estimates that the total cost for EAI deployment ranges from 6x to 20x the cost of the software licenses,[13] or $3 million to $15 million.

Reality Check

During the late 1990s, when top-line (revenue) growth was the primary mission for many companies, few of them looked carefully at the returns on their ERP and EAI investments. As we said at the start of this chapter, integration was a necessary evil—a required expense.

But as the 21st century began, we had the opportunity to catch our collective breath and reconsider those ERP and EAI investments in light of an economic downturn and quests for profits. Today, many companies simply can't afford those same packages we bought in the 1990s. In those heady days there was more money than time, and it often made sense to throw money and consultants at problems in order to keep up with rapidly changing environments. Ah, how times have changed.

During the 1990s, it was also typical to rip out existing applications and to replace them with equal or more substantial suites. But due to the realities of sagging profits and less-than-unlimited lines of credit, no one wants to do that today. New applications must interoperate with those that already exist. No longer is there an opportunity to start fresh; everything must work within the status quo. Furthermore, organizations want to be able to make smaller, more incremental changes. Even when an ERP component must be replaced, companies want to do so at the component level, not by replacing entire suites of applications.

E-Commerce

Although EAI turned out to be a rather simplistic and inflexible solution, many CIOs were glad to have its tools and the help of the hordes of EAI consultants. But when e-commerce surfaced in the late 1990s as the latest application requiring integration into existing infrastructures, both ERP and EAI confronted new challenges they couldn't handle. Neither ERP nor EAI vendors were prepared for the onslaught of e-commerce. At the time, it was possible to obtain e-commerce add-ons to ERP packages, but they were developed and released slowly, and they never contained the features that state-of-the-art e-commerce systems required. And as we all remember, having those rapidly evolving e-commerce features was considered critical.

The only solution available was to license e-commerce modules from e-commerce vendors and integrate them into the ERP systems, in some cases via EAI hubs. The process required even more consultants, at a time when demand far outstripped supply. In other words, already high integration costs went through the roof.

Even after throwing money at the problem, we found many EAI packages weren't up to the e-commerce challenge. Most legacy applications operate in batch mode, meaning that data gets transferred from silo to silo on a scheduled basis, perhaps hourly or every few minutes. Many EAI systems converted these batch legacy applications into real time—but the results often weren't fast enough for e-commerce, where milliseconds matter. Furthermore, neither EAI nor ERP functioned well when asked to link to the world outside the organization.

To understand the scope of the problem, let's say you need to compute sales tax for online orders. The inflexible ERP sales tax modules aren't appropriate. They don't interface well with the website shopping cart software, which is a component you don't often get as part of your ERP system. Besides, your web and application servers are probably located at a hosting service far from the ERP system running in-house, behind your corporate firewalls. Furthermore, e-commerce has to be running 24/7, whereas it's common to shut down ERP systems for occasional maintenance. The systems mix about as well as oil and water.

An e-commerce system without access to web services performs its own sales-tax computations, which means it's nearly impossible to interface the e-commerce system to an ERP package that assumes it's the ultimate authority and will, therefore, compute the sales tax on each order. Convincing the ERP package that this computation has already been done outside of the ERP package is no easy chore.

E-commerce isn't the only rapidly evolving trend that ERP has proven unable to handle. Supply-chain management—the process of linking to one's vendors, their vendors, and so on—has become another glaring example. Designed as intra-company systems, ERP packages and even EAI add-ons were never intended to link to customers and vendors in value or supply chains—certainly not if those business partners used different software.

Given this still-evolving story, what will the next solutions to the challenges of application integration (i.e., web services) look like? They should:

- Put an end, forever, to the data silo problem;
- Not require the centralized hub of an EAI solution, and replace EAI adapters with standardized APIs;
- Not require that single-source adapters be installed on all participating applications;
- Not require hordes of expensive consultants to implement and maintain systems;
- Support integration of business processes, not merely the get/put exchange of data;
- Permit modular (incremental) development and replacement of applications and their components; and
- Allow real-time integration, not just batch updates of data.

Web services may not be the final chapter in the story of application integration, but they do offer many of the above qualities—a significant contribution to the state of integration technology.

Prepare to Be Externalized!

Before we end our exploration into the history of integration, consider what the next steps might be—because thus far, we've only scratched the surface of the possibilities. As you look at your legacy applications today, you probably see isolated silos of code and data. Does the thought of a new application evoke visions of pulling data out of one of these applications and transferring it to another? If so, you're still thinking of integration in a deconstructive sense. You're still focused on breaking down the barriers to get at the code and data.

Once you've exposed your applications as web services, you'll have a very different view of them. No longer will you see a collection of isolated silos or islands, but instead a homogeneous pool of services that can be stitched together to build *new* applications. This is the constructive view.

By all means, go for the low-hanging fruit gained from exposing applications as web services, but don't stop there. Think of that step as the means to an end: being able to build all-new applications by aggregating web services, whether those services are backed by your legacy applications or not.

When you expose an application as a web service, you're making it available within an environment in which access to such a function may have never been possible before. Doing so substantially enhances the value of that application to your organization. Ultimately, the greatest benefit from linking existing systems—and the eventual requirement for doing so—will probably be to deliver their functionality to external business partners. Companies that don't begin to expose their legacy applications for internal purposes now may not be able to deliver external web services to their partners when the time comes. As you develop plans to link your existing applications, keep in mind that the long-term benefit may be much greater than what you can perceive today.

Chapter 7

Objects and Web Services

The relationship between object-oriented (OO) technologies and web services is the subject of much confusion. Contrary to a common misconception, web services won't replace OO technologies. In fact, the two are very different beasts. Although the SOAP protocol commonly used in web services was originally known as the Simple *Object* Access Protocol, that's a misleading definition and has essentially been dropped. SOAP is more appropriately used to transport data in the form of *messages* than to access objects.

In this chapter we'll explore the history of OO technologies, their relationships to web services, and some of the misconceptions about those relationships. While programmers will continue to use OO technologies to develop and deploy applications, there are many other ways to develop web services—so that the underlying technologies of web services remain hidden and irrelevant. Finally, we'll examine a common shortcut strategy of *wrapping* objects in web-services interfaces, and see why that approach may not result in well-designed, loosely coupled web services.

History

Software methodologies have repeatedly evolved over the half-century of computing history in order to keep pace with advances in hardware and networking technologies. Figure 7-1 offers a timeline of the software technologies relevant to our current discussion.

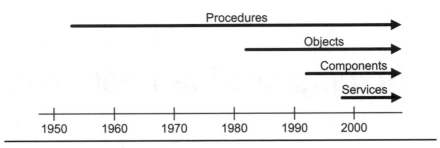

Figure 7-1: Software Technology Timeline

In 1952, FORTRAN was introduced as the first high-level programming language. It allowed programs to be organized *procedurally*, broken into functions and subroutines. Other procedural languages followed FORTRAN, most notably COBOL for business applications and C for scientific and systems programming. The few computers that existed in those early days were entirely autonomous. There were no networks and no needs for software that could link one system with another.

Objects

By the early 1980s hardware architectures had become more complex, and large application programs consisted of hundreds of thousands of lines of source code. It was increasingly difficult to maintain order, consistency, and reliability in such large projects.

Smalltalk, the first object-oriented programming (OOP) language, was created to increase the reusability of software. It included the concepts of objects, classes, messages, and methods that are now the foundations of most modern OOP languages, such as C++ (created in 1983), Visual Basic® (1991), Java (1995), and C# (a few years later).

During the 1980s, it also became increasingly common for computer systems to include multiple CPUs and for multiple systems to be linked in the form of *clusters*. With the development of local area networks (LANs), distributed computing architectures began to appear and focus attention on the incompatibility of disparate systems. Previously, it was only inconvenient that two computers had different standards for character-string encoding, bit- and byte-ordering, and so on. But when these heterogeneous systems were asked to communicate in real time over a LAN, their differences became major obstacles to that task. To meet the integration needs of these environments, *object brokers* were invented so that applications could locate and communicate with objects on local and remote systems, even if those objects were built using different programming languages and ran on systems acquired from different vendors.

Components and Containers

Objects are relatively *granular:* small units of data combined with their associated processes or *methods.* While an important aspect of OOP is to build increasingly complex objects out of simpler ones, in practice it can become unwieldy. In the late 1980s, this led to the introduction of *components*, most notably those of Enterprise Java Beans (EJBs). Components provided an additional layer of abstraction and packaging over the objects they contained, and were somewhat larger, or less granular.

Component *containers* allowed applications to be changed via *configurations* at run time, rather than at the time the applications were built. Containers' support for late-stage configuration is similar to the *delayed binding* of web services, which we'll discuss further in Chapter 10.

Distributed Objects

Objects and components can be accessed remotely as well as locally. A program on one system can reference objects on other systems and create, modify, or delete those objects by remotely invoking the associated methods. Consider a warehousing system that's linked to an order-management system. Rather than create its own local copies of the orders, and run the risk that the copies become out of sync with the originals, the warehousing system can locate, read, and modify the order objects within the order-management system.

The two systems for warehousing and order-management could be running within a single computer, or executing on separate systems. If the systems are separated, *distributed object architectures* allow objects on one system to locate and communicate with objects on the other.

Object-Oriented Architectures

Over the past decade, a number of technologies have been devised as platforms for the development and operation of OO applications. Their history is illustrated in the timeline in Figure 7-2.

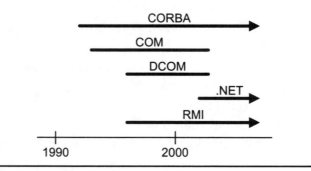

Figure 7-2: Object Technologies Timeline

The Common Object Request Broker Architecture (CORBA) was released in 1992 by a consortium of hardware and software vendors known as the Object Management Group (OMG). The fundamental CORBA concept is that of the Object Request Broker (ORB), a software agent that enables objects to locate and communicate with one another in a distributed system. CORBA is a fairly complex and expensive system, and after more than ten years it has still only caught on in some high-end IT shops. It's critical to those that have already built systems around it, but it hasn't captured the minds or the checkbooks of the majority of CIOs, programmers, and system architects—particularly those not responsible for large systems.

A year after CORBA was announced, Microsoft introduced its Component Object Model (COM). Unlike CORBA, which allows objects on different systems to communicate with one another, COM only linked objects within a single computer. Furthermore, while CORBA was a vendor-independent technology, COM was proprietary to Microsoft.

In fact, CORBA and COM solved very different problems. CORBA linked objects on distributed systems, perhaps manufactured by multiple vendors, whereas Microsoft's COM was simply the technique by which the various components within the Windows operating system and Windows-based applications communicated. In 1996, Microsoft released its Distributed COM (DCOM) to support communications between applications running on separate computers—but it was still a Microsoft-only technology.

In the same year Microsoft delivered DCOM, Sun Microsystems released the Remote Method Invocation (RMI) technology as part of its Java 1.1 platform. As its name implies, RMI allows objects on one system to invoke methods (that is, request operations) on another, possibly remote, system. Just as DCOM is proprietary to Microsoft, RMI only runs on systems written in Java.

CORBA

CORBA is an object-oriented, pre-web services answer to integrating disparate systems. It has proven to be effective within closely controlled application-development and deployment environments, where there's a high degree of cooperation between the participants. But CORBA's complexity, lack of extensibility, and relatively high cost have kept it from being adopted as a ubiquitous technology like web services.

Programmers will continue to use basic OO technologies when developing applications, and they'll use CORBA for many integration tasks involving potentially heterogeneous OO systems. However, they're switching from object-only services to more generalized web services as a way of making those applications available to a broader range of systems—particularly those outside of their organizations, and beyond their control.

Web Services

Although web services can be developed using object-oriented technologies, the two concepts are orthogonal in a number of ways:

Basic OO technologies are for proprietary-platform application development.

OOP is used by itself (that is, without the high-level language-independent features of CORBA) within a family of tightly coupled applications that can be distributed among multiple computers, as long as they're similar. DCOM and RMI are two such technologies that aren't intended to link disparate systems, and can't communicate with one another.

CORBA and web services are interface technologies, but...

Both technologies are capable of linking heterogeneous systems. But CORBA requires that the underlying applications be object oriented, because only OO environments can be CORBA compatible. Web services don't make that requirement. They can be developed using OOP or with procedural or simple scripting languages (such as Perl or PHP), and can communicate with other web services endpoints whether they're object oriented or not.

One can simply *wrap* existing objects and components in web-services interfaces, and thereby make them available to *any* remote application that's also capable of communicating using this architecturally neutral technology. Using such wrappers, web services allow formerly isolated systems based on the OO technologies (DCOM, CORBA, and RMI) to interoperate, as well as those coded in procedural languages. However, because such web services will retain the fine grain of the underlying objects, they'll remain as tightly coupled and inflexible as the objects themselves.

CORBA, DCOM, and RMI are tightly coupled.

With these technologies, the programs at each endpoint must have substantial knowledge of one another. When using DCOM, for instance, a programmer specifies the name of the remote program and the name of a specific method or function within that program that he or she wants to invoke. If the remote program is then replaced by another program with a different name, the invoking program must be modified accordingly. This is one example of tight coupling: The programs at each endpoint must have substantial knowledge of one another. Loosely coupled web services, on the other hand, don't depend on intimate knowledge of the endpoints. (We'll discuss loose coupling in detail in Chapter 10.)

Web services should be coarse-grained.

As mentioned above, another aspect of tight versus loose coupling is granularity, or the level of detail at which an interface is designed. Objects are small and granular, and components built from objects are somewhat larger and therefore less granular. But both tend to be too fine-grained as the basis for web services.

Service-oriented architectures (SOAs) are the foundations of web services, and can be based on objects, components, *messages*, or non-OO *parameters*. As we'll see in Chapters 9 and 10, web services based on coarse-grained messages deliver the loosest coupling between the service endpoints.

———————

Object-oriented technologies play an important role in the development of web services, but they're not inherently any more important than non-OO languages, tools, and runtime environments. If you choose to use OO technologies as the basis for web services, be careful that you don't just pour old wine into new bottles. Don't just throw SOAP wrappers around your fine-grained objects and call them web services. Simply mapping objects or components into XML representations isn't enough.

Instead, design your web services interfaces to be as coarse-grained as possible—preferably using asynchronous messaging where appropriate. You'll find you've created loosely coupled web services with broader applicability to support unanticipated future applications.

Chapter 8

Service-Oriented Architectures

Looking beyond the world of computer software at the greater scheme of things, we can see that *services* are the fundamental concepts of outsourcing. Services imply one party performing work for another. Most of us no longer install our own television antennas; instead, we subscribe to cable-TV or satellite services. Instead of walking to the corner store to buy our morning newspapers, we use delivery services. In business, we outsource our human-resources tasks to payroll services, our gardening to landscaping services, and our office maintenance to janitorial services.

Services are rapidly gaining ground in the IT world as well. Not only are functions previously bound into our applications now delivered over-the-wire by service providers, but services are also changing the fundamental model of software development. Services are a new way of building distributed applications. As web services mature, we'll increasingly create applications by combining services at runtime rather than by linking modules during development. The components of our applications will interact in a very different manner than in the past.

We have five decades of experience with traditional applications, but just a few years with those built from services. As a result of these recent experiences, however, a number of models or *architectures* have evolved. These *service-oriented architectures* (SOAs) are abstract descriptions of how the pieces of systems interact to achieve the desired results. In computer science, architectures tend to be more like philosophies than explicit specifications, so pinning down definitions can be challenging—but that's what we'll do in this chapter.

Why Services?

Let's begin with an example that's common to most interactive applications (those on the World Wide Web) as well as to web-services-based retail e-commerce applications: the calculation of sales tax or VAT. The traditional approach to integrating sales-tax calculations into an application is to license a software package, and subscribe to updates to an associated database or tax-rate table. A number of tax-calculation software vendors offer easy-to-integrate modules for a variety of programming languages, and they distribute updates to their sales-tax databases via CD-ROM or make them available for download over the Internet.

Sales taxes have a nasty habit of changing, which means you may need multiple versions of the database (and, perhaps, the code) running at the moment such changes take effect. And given the number of countries, provinces, states, counties, cities, and special districts with the authority to levy such taxes, these changes occur frequently. Consider what happens when not just the rates, but also the calculation algorithms change—then it's not just the data that must be updated, but the software as well.

Dealing with sales tax is most likely not one of your company's core business activities. You'd love to solve the problem just once, and let someone else worry about keeping that solution up to date. You'd probably like to receive sales-tax calculation as a service, just as you'd rather pay someone else to clean your office bathrooms.

Traditional Application Architecture

Figure 8-1 illustrates the architectural implications of an e-commerce application that uses a traditional solution for sales-tax calculation combined with a similar one for calculating shipping costs.

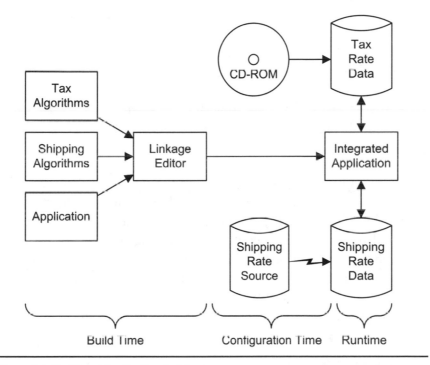

Figure 8-1: Traditional Application Architecture

In this example, the vendors of tax- and shipping-rate information provide both algorithms (code libraries) and data. The tax data is delivered on CD-ROM, while the shipping-rate data is downloaded periodically over the Internet.

Consider this application architecture in terms of its life cycle. There are three distinct phases, separated by time:

Build time. A developer builds the application by using a *linker* or *linkage editor* to combine the application module and the library routines that support tax- and shipping-rate calculations. The result is an integrated application, with the tax- and shipping-rate logic built in, but not the data. (With some programming languages, modules are combined at runtime using *class loaders*—but since the relationships are still determined at build time, the effect is the same for the purposes of this discussion.)

Configuration time. On a regular or as-needed basis, the tax- and shipping-rate vendors deliver updates to their respective data. These updates are then copied into local databases by operations personnel. Updates might occur weekly or monthly—certainly more frequently than re-builds of the application.

Runtime. At runtime, the application calls the linked-in rate-calculation algorithms, which in turn query the local databases and return their results.

We could have merged the data with the application at build time, but that would require that that we re-build the entire application every time a simple tax- or shipping-rate change occurs. By delaying the data-update process to the configuration phase, we've made the application less *brittle*, or better able to cope with change. This concept of postponing the reference to volatile data—or at least merging it as late as possible in the application life cycle—is an example of the concept of *delayed binding*, which we'll discuss in detail in Chapter 10.

Applications as Services

In the example shown in Figure 8-1, the shipping-rate information is obtained via electronic transfer in batch mode, perhaps using FTP. Suppose, instead, that the tax- and shipping-rate data were available over the Internet in real time. And suppose that through the use of web services, the algorithms that computed the tax and shipping rates ran at the sites of their respective vendors rather than at the application's site. The results would then look like Figure 8-2.

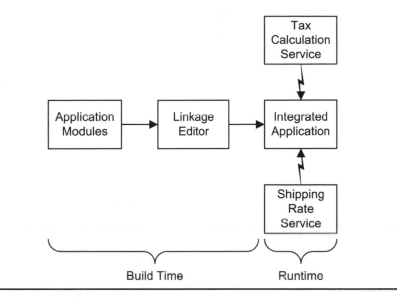

Figure 8-2: Service-Based Application Architecture

As compared to the traditional architecture, one based on services has two distinct characteristics. First, the algorithms and data are no longer parts of the application's local infrastructure, but are located off-site instead. The second and more subtle distinction is that integration of changes to the tax- and shipping-rate portion of the application have been deferred until run time—the last possible stage. In fact, this e-commerce application is now immune to—even ignorant of—any changes in the rate algorithms or data. There will never be any new code modules or database updates to worry about. The service-oriented architecture has *future-proofed* the application.

The Web-Services Model

At the highest level, virtually all web services are based on the model illustrated in Figure 8-3, which you'll find in nearly every introduction to web services and SOAs.

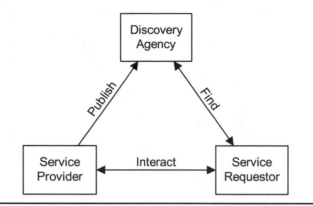

Figure 8-3: The Web-Services Interaction Model

This model includes three roles typically played by three different systems, and three actions among the parties. The roles are described below.

- **Service provider**. The system offering the service.
- **Discovery agency**. (Historically referred to as the *service broker*.) A secondary service that is well-known, or easy for the other parties to find, and acts as a repository for information about other services.
- **Service requestor.** The system that wants to discover and use the service offered by the provider.

The connecting arrows represent actions performed, which are as follows:

- **Publish.** The provider sends information describing the service to the discovery agency.
- **Find.** When a requestor wants to locate the service, it queries the discovery agent and receives in response the description of the service, where to find it, and how to communicate with it.
- **Interact.** The requestor then contacts the provider, they exchange credentials and negotiate options as required, and then they proceed to communicate as intended.

The diagram shown in Figure 8-3 is helpful up to the point of interaction, but it doesn't tell the whole story. What's missing is what happens next: how the requestor and provider actually interact and exchange information.

Interfaces Versus Applications

To understand how the endpoints communicate, let's begin by exploring a web service with a very simple architecture—one that accepts a value in dollars and returns the equivalent value in Euros, as illustrated in Figure 8-4.

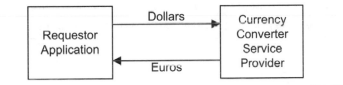

Figure 8-4: A Simple Web Service

Not only is this a simple web service, but the real-time currency converter application behind it is fairly straightforward too. If the currency-converter program already exists, it doesn't take much to add the web-services interface, enabling the application to be accessed by other systems.

The simplistic view of the currency converter in Figure 8-4 is more generally and accurately illustrated in Figure 8-5, where you can see that the web services and the applications are not one and the same. The web services are merely the *interfaces* to the applications.

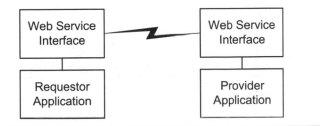

Figure 8-5: Applications Linked via Web-Services Interfaces

The complexity of the application isn't necessarily passed on to the web-service interface. Many web services are built on top of existing applications requiring relatively little additional planning or modification, so differences in the applications often aren't good indicators of the complexity of the web services they support. It's not unusual for a very complex application to be delivered through a simple web-services interface.

Messages

At the most fundamental level, web services are built upon the exchange of *messages* between *senders* and *receivers* as illustrated canonically in Figure 6.

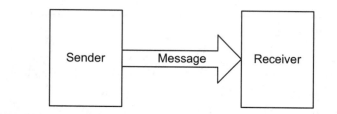

Figure 6: Basic Messaging

It's important to note that the roles of sender and receiver are independent, and function at a lower level than the roles of service provider and service requestor. As we'll see shortly, requests, responses, and other concepts are built on top of the sender/receiver messaging model. Requestors, providers, publishers, and subscribers all play the role of both sender and receiver at various times.

Message Exchange Patterns (MEPs)

Web services are built by combining messages in a wide variety of ways, but over time a number of recurring usage patterns have surfaced. These are known as *message exchange patterns* (MEPs), and can be categorized according to two criteria: synchronization and correlation.

Synchronization. When two endpoints exchange messages, they do so in one of three ways:

- **Synchronous.** After sending a message, an endpoint expects a response and waits for it.
- **Asynchronous.** After sending a message, an endpoint expects a response, but doesn't wait for it. Instead, the application is prepared to accept the response at any time.
- **Fire-and-forget.** The sender doesn't expect a response.

Correlation. When two endpoints exchange multiple messages regarding a single transaction using a synchronous or asynchronous model, there are three ways pairs or groups of messages are associated with one another:

- **Uncorrelated.** There is no need to associate one message with another; each is self-contained.
- **Transport-layer correlation.** The underlying transport-layer protocol is used to correlate associated messages, such as using HTTP's built-in support for request/response.
- **Message-based correlation.** Messages or message headers can contain the information necessary to associate two or more messages, in order to maintain a meaningful conversation when MEPs are complex or the transport can't provide correlation.

Using the above criteria to explain their differences, let's examine the most common MEPs: request/response, publish-and-subscribe, and broadcast/multicast.

Request/Response

One of the simplest MEPs is the request/response model of interaction. It can be implemented either synchronously or asynchronously, although the former—where the requestor waits for the response—is far more common.

Since there are only two messages, request/response has a very simple *correlation context*—which is why so many synchronous request/

response services use HTTP to tie responses to requests. Figure 8-7 illustrates the canonical request/response model.

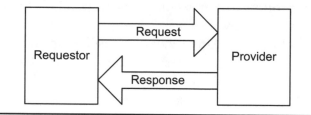

Figure 8-7: The Request/Response MEP

Publish/Subscribe

A somewhat more complex message exchange pattern is referred to as publish/subscribe, or pub/sub for short (see Figure 8-8).

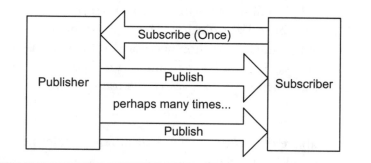

Figure 8-8: The Publish/Subscribe MEP

In the pub/sub MEP, a *subscriber* sends one message requesting to be notified of certain events. The *publisher* then sends a message to the subscriber each time such an event occurs. An example of the pub/sub MEP might be notification of the change in the status of an airline flight, or a stock's new trading price.

Broadcast and Multicast

In yet another variation, a provider can send a single message that is then received by all devices on a particular network. This is the broadcast MEP, as illustrated in Figure 8-9.

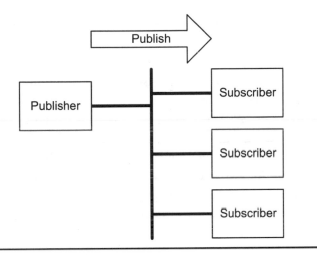

Figure 8-9: The Broadcast MEP

Because it doesn't transmit a unique message to each subscriber, the broadcast model can be particularly effective when there are a large number of subscribers, or when it's important that all subscribers receive messages at approximately the same time. Broadcast messages depend on a broadcast-capable network or data-link layer, such as IP or Ethernet, respectively. *Multicast* is similar to broadcast, but a single message is directed to a group, rather than to every device on the network.

Intermediaries and Routing

An option that can be used in combination with any MEP is to send messages through one or more *intermediaries:* services that can perform a variety of transformations or other tasks as illustrated in Figure 8-10.

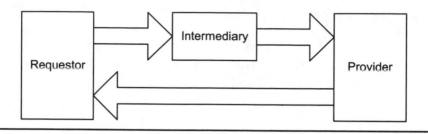

Figure 8-10: An Intermediary

Intermediaries can provide such services as auditing or translations of language or currencies. They can even strip off source identification, and thereby *anonymize* messages. Intermediaries can also convert the protocols and standards used by one endpoint into those of the other, all while maintaining the integrity of the message. Using the *routing* capabilities of web-services protocols, a sender can specify that a message is to follow a specific path on the way to its ultimate destination through particular intermediaries.

Service Aggregation

Moving up a notch on the complexity scale, let's consider an example of a travel-reservation service that can book airline flights and hotel rooms. This web service makes use of other web services, so we refer to it as an *aggregated* or *composite* web service. This type of request/response SOA model is illustrated in Figure 8-11.

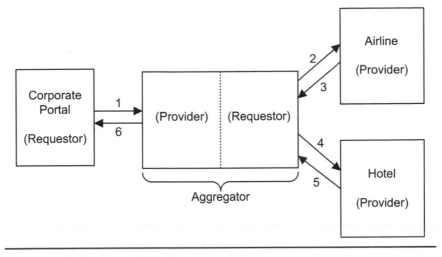

Figure 8-11: An Aggregated SOA Example

The requestor might be a corporate intranet web site or portal that supports business-travel reservations for the company's employees. In Figure 8-11 the requests and responses are shown as parallel arrows, but in this example there are three such pairs. Let's walk through these interactions, referring to the messages as numbered below and in the figure.

1. The requestor system sends a web-service request to the aggregator, a system that offers a web service for complex travel reservations. The aggregator, playing the role of web-service provider in this exchange, receives the initial request.
2. The aggregator breaks down the request into two parts: one for the airline, the other for the hotel. Then it switches roles to become a web-service requestor, and issues a new request to the airline's web service for the air-travel portion of the trip.
3. The airline's system, a web-services provider, checks availability and returns a response to the aggregator.
4. Still acting as a web-services requestor, the aggregator issues another request (for the hotel reservation) to the hotel's web service.
5. The hotel's system also returns a response to the aggregator.

6. The aggregator switches back to the role of provider, and transmits the ultimate response to the waiting corporate portal.

At least two other scenarios are possible. First, the aggregator could send its requests to the airline and hotel services in parallel, rather than one after another. Alternatively, the exchanges between the aggregator and the airline and hotel systems could be *asynchronous*, to be discussed later in this chapter and in greater detail in the next chapter.

Note also that the relationship between the corporate portal and the aggregator can be synchronous even if one or both of the other two relationships are asynchronous. In fact, any combinations of synchronous and asynchronous interaction models are possible in this example.

Because web services can invoke other web services, ad infinitum, it's not hard to see that aggregated services can quickly become far more complex than basic web services—although not necessarily from the perspective of the ultimate requestor. After all, the purpose of aggregation is to hide complexity and deliver a simplified service to the customer.

But aggregated web services introduce an entirely new class of potential problems. For example:

*   What happens if the hotel reservation fails (e.g., no rooms are available) after the airline reservation has already been booked?
*   Suppose the hotel reservation system goes offline and doesn't respond at all—what then?
*   How can the aggregator guarantee the quality of service (i.e., how long this complex transaction will take) when the aggregator depends on third parties over whom it has no control?

We'll look at solutions to these problems below, and in more depth in Part III: *Technologies*.

Synchronous Services

In most of our examples so far, the applications that issued requests assumed the responses they received would contain the desired data and would be returned promptly. This is similar to what happens when you use a web browser to access a web site. You click on a link or button, and your application (the browser) waits or *pends* for a few seconds until the web site returns the contents of the next web page.

We refer to web services that use this model as *synchronous* web services. The most basic form of this interaction style is illustrated in Figure 8-12.

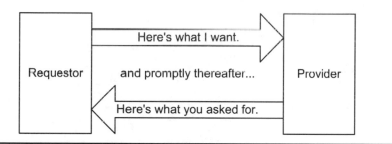

Figure 8-12: Synchronous Request/Response

The synchronous architecture has three important characteristics:
- The calling application (requestor) expects to receive the desired results in the response message. There's no facility to accommodate a response such as, "Thanks for the request. I'll call you back later with the answer."
- The requestor's application may pend or stop performing other tasks while it awaits the response.
- Because it's pended, the calling application needs to receive a response quickly—otherwise, it will *time out* (give up) within a short period of time, typically no more than a few seconds.

These characteristics will become important when we consider the limitations of synchronous architecture in a moment. The flowchart in Figure 8-13 illustrates the synchronization of the requestor and provider in this model.

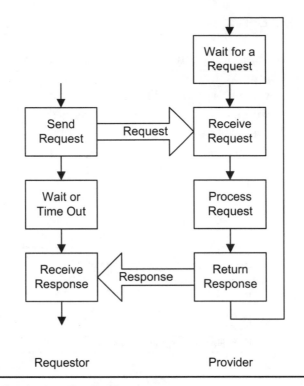

Figure 8-13: Synchronous Service Flowchart

After sending a request, the requestor waits until the provider has received the request, processed it, and sent the reply, and until the reply has been received. This is the essence of the synchronous interaction style: a requestor that pends between the times it issues a request, and the time it either receives the response or gives up.

Requestors that pend are simple to develop, test, and maintain. By not performing any other task while waiting, these programs have no trouble keeping track of their *state* or correlating requests with responses. They're only working on one task at a time, and hence don't need to save information about what they're doing for later retrieval.

Many web services can be built using a synchronous interaction style, which works for simple queries and updates such as package tracking, stock quotes, and weather reports. But there are many web services for which a synchronous design just won't work. For those, we need asynchronous web services.

Asynchronous Services

An asynchronous architecture differs from one that's synchronous in two ways:

- Rather than perform its task immediately, an endpoint may just acknowledge a request, perform the required task at a later time, and eventually return the results. An asynchronous service may not even issue any real-time acknowledgements at all.

- Because endpoints may not perform their tasks immediately, requestors and providers aren't expected to pend or wait for responses. They can send messages, and then go on to perform other tasks. In order to do so, however, they must keep track of the status of partially completed interactions and re-call that information at a later time. In other words, they must *correlate* related messages.

To illustrate the operation of the asynchronous interaction style, let's step away from web services and use a web-site transaction as an example. Consider what happens when you purchase a book from an online bookstore, as illustrated in Figure 8-14. This is a familiar transaction for which a synchronous architecture (whether for a web service or web site) would be inadequate.

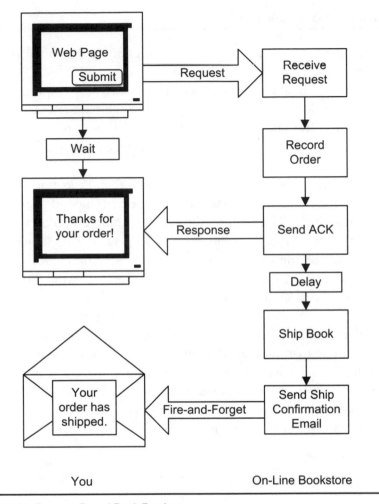

Figure 8-14: Browser-Based Book Purchase

After selecting your book and working your way through the on-line checkout procedure, you click on the final *submit* button. What you'd like to see is a web page with the package-tracking number and the expected delivery date. But the bookstore can't send you that information until the book ships, perhaps hours or days later.

Instead, the bookstore returns a web page containing an *acknowledgement* (ACK). Rather than complete the transaction, this page is a placeholder. It says, in effect, "Thanks for your order. The next event in this transaction will occur when we ship your book, and send you an email message." If the bookstore's web site didn't return the acknowledgement web page, and instead required your system to pend, you might be sitting in front of your computer screen watching the browser's little spinning logo until the book shipped days later. The acknowledgement page completes a subset of the overall transaction and allows you to get on with the rest of your life. But the transaction isn't complete; it's merely suspended. Eventually, the bookstore will ship your book and send you an email message telling you so.

We could consider each of the steps (ordering, shipping, confirmation) as separate transactions, but in fact they're all part of a single multi-step *business process:* the ordering and shipping of books. A system based on an integrated view of a multi-step process is far more valuable to the bookseller and its customers than one composed of discrete and unrelated steps. For instance, the ability to relate orders to shipments allows the company to generate a report of unfilled orders, which have been placed but not shipped. An order isn't complete until it's been shipped and received, and as a customer, your desire to purchase the book isn't fulfilled until the book arrives at your door. Likewise, the bookstore's goal of fulfilling your desires isn't achieved until you've got the book in your hands.

If we were only to deal with the individual steps rather than consider the business process as a whole, we would lose the benefit of this overall context. Orders and shipments wouldn't be linked (correlated) with one another.

As the customer, imagine what this process would be like if the steps weren't correlated. A book would arrive at your door, but you probably wouldn't know why—you wouldn't be able to relate the delivery to the order you placed a few days earlier. You may find yourself thinking, "I wonder what happened to that book I ordered," because you'd receive no shipping notification connected with your order. A business-process perspective allows you to see the big picture, and relate the individual steps to one another.

Documents or Remote Procedure Calls?

When version 1.1 of the SOAP protocol was published in May of 2000, it included (and still includes) two styles of messages: *document style* and *remote procedure call* (RPC) *style*. To this day, there remains a great deal of confusion regarding these variants and how they relate to the other attributes of web services. The differences between these styles also cause substantial incompatibility between the SOAP-based implementations from various software vendors. As of early 2003, Microsoft's tools default to the document style, whereas many Java-based packages default to RPCs. A quick look at the XMethods web site (a directory of web services located at www.xmethods.com) shows an almost perfect segregation by platform. Virtually all document-style services are implemented on Microsoft's .NET platform, and those on other platforms mostly use the RPC style. Unfortunately, an RPC-style sender can't communicate with a document-style receiver, and vice versa.

RPC Style

Much of the early interest surrounding uses of web services was in XML-based (platform- and language-independent) mechanisms for calling remote procedures. The idea was to create strong standards to represent the basic data types of numbers and strings, as well as compound data structures built from these basic types. The goal was to make it easy for developers to map existing language-specific data types, structures, and objects into XML, so that the procedures or methods on one system could be called or invoked from another system, no matter how different. The RPC-style interface therefore has the following characteristics:

Request/response. Virtually all RPC-style web services use a simple request/response model to emulate the call and return of a procedure or method. This isn't strictly required, however, since there's nothing to prohibit sending a request without expecting a response.

Synchronous. Although it's not strictly required, most RPC-style web services do operate synchronously. The RPC/document and synchronous/asynchronous distinctions are orthogonal, but they tend to be lumped together in many articles and books.

HTTP(S). The RPC specification allows for the use of any transport, but by far most RPC-style web services are implemented over

HTTP or its secure counterpart, HTTPS. These request/response transport protocols are a good fit for most RPCs, offering a combination of support for encryption (SSL) as well as built-in correlation of requests and responses.

Methods, parameters, and return values. An RPC-style request explicitly names the method or procedure it wants to invoke on the remote system, and contains XML-formatted parameters that match those of the remote procedure. The response messages contain the remote procedure's output.

Encoding. The SOAP protocol includes a default XML encoding scheme, which is used by most RPC-style web services. The scheme supports strings, numbers, dates, enumeration types, and so on, as well as *compound values* such as structure and arrays. Again, the objectives are language independence and ease of mapping to those languages.

The RPC style is ideal for simple request/response web services, but it has three drawbacks. First, being limited to the request/response MEP, it can't easily accommodate more complex conversations, such as those that support long-running business processes. Second, the RPC interface is based on rather fine-grained concepts: methods, parameters, and return values. This degree of granularity isn't appropriate for communicating in business-level terms, such as via purchase orders and invoices. Finally, because RPC-style services are so easily mapped to an application's existing model of procedures or objects, they create strong tendencies on the part of programmers to take shortcuts and design web services that are tightly coupled to those existing entities.

Document Style

Document-style web services differ from those using the RPC style in the following ways:

Documents. Unlike the RPC style, which deals with smaller units of data, the document style transmits complete XML documents from sender to receiver. These documents are typically self-contained, including all of the contextual information associated with the message. For example, a purchase-order document contains all of the information regarding an order, even though not all that information may be required by every web service that receives it.

One-way messaging. Because document-style web services communicate through self-contained documents, fewer messages are required to accomplish complex tasks than are required using RPCs. Frequently an entire process can be initiated by the one-way transmission of a single message, possibly routed through multiple services.

Asynchronous conversations. Document-style web services can be implemented synchronously or asynchronously. But because documents are self-contained, or have the ability to maintain their own state, the asynchronous style of interaction is more suited to complex interactions that involve multiple events.

Loosely coupled. The ultimate benefit of document-style interaction is the reduction of interdependencies between senders and receivers. The design of such web services emphasizes the documents and the business processes rather than the functionality of the endpoints.

———————

Service-oriented architectures are more of a big deal than they might have appeared at first. What began as a way to call remote procedures in a language- and platform-independent manner has rapidly evolved into an approach to implementing cross-organizational, long-running business processes. Along the way, web services have become not merely a technology to integrate existing applications, but a new model for building all-new applications based on services. The key to this evolution is the trend towards document-style asynchronous messaging, which can support complex, long-running business processes and improve the reliability and scalability of web services. We'll explore asynchronous messaging in greater detail in the next chapter.

Chapter 9

Asynchronous Messaging

As mentioned in the previous chapter, asynchronous web services can be used to automate complex processes that take more than a few seconds or minutes to complete. But by itself, the asynchronous model isn't sufficient. In this chapter, we'll explore three additional concepts that must also be applied to fully realize the benefits of asynchronous interaction: *event-driven design, documents,* and *message queuing*.

These concepts aren't new—in fact, all three were used in complex applications well before the invention of web services or even the World Wide Web. But many application programmers and even some architects have never been exposed to these concepts that are now so critical to the design of complex web services.

Synchronous Interactions

To again illustrate the differences between the synchronous and asynchronous styles of interaction, let's use the analogy of holiday gift shopping. Here's the situation: You have a list of three people for whom you want to purchase gifts, and you've got two choices. You can head for the shopping mall, or you can shop online. For the sake of the analogy, think of yourself (the buyer) and the clerk or online store (the merchant) as a pair of distributed systems.

Figure 9-1 illustrates the interaction of these systems when you shop at the mall.

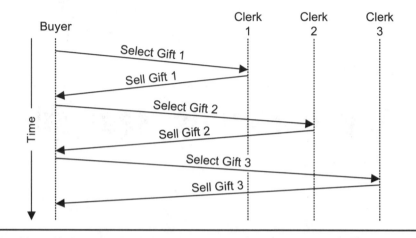

Figure 9-1: Synchronous Shopping At the Mall

The shopping-mall model is *synchronous* because it's composed of a series of predictable steps that cannot be re-ordered. Specifically, you and the sales clerks alternate roles: You select a gift, a clerk sells it to you, and you repeat the process for the remaining gifts. Your actions are synchronized with those of the clerks, and you won't move on to the next clerk before completing the exchange with the current one.

Asynchronous Interactions

Next, let's examine the interaction between the two systems when you shop online, as illustrated in Figure 9-2.

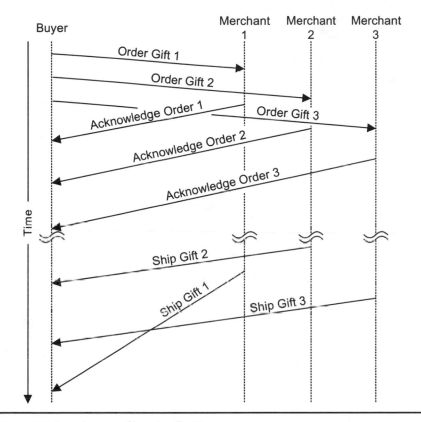

Figure 9-2: Asynchronous Shopping On Line

This is an example of the asynchronous interaction model, which differs from the synchronous model in two ways. First, the three ordering actions are predictable, but the three shipping actions are not. The shipments are initiated at seemingly random times and out of sequence, take different lengths of time, and arrive in yet another unpredictable sequence. Second, in the asynchronous model you can place all three orders, one immediately after another. The merchants send email acknowledgements in response to your orders, but you don't need to wait for one order to be acknowledged before placing the next. In other words, the buyer and merchant are no longer synchronized.

Procedural Design

How would a programmer implement each of these synchronous and asynchronous shopping systems as web services?

The synchronous shopping-mall scenario could be implemented *procedurally:* as a sequence of program steps that mimic human interactions. The results might appear similar to the flowchart in Figure 9-3.

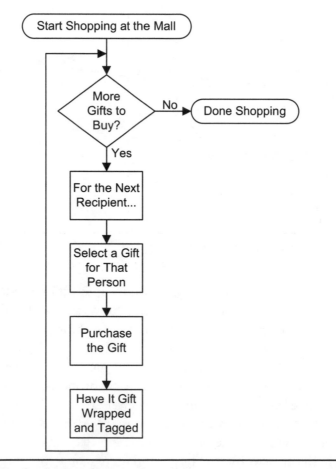

Figure 9-3: The Synchronous Shopping Procedure

This is the most obvious scheme, and one many programmers might well use—particularly those who have never been exposed to the concept of asynchronous services.

But designing web services for the online shopping scenario presents quite a challenge to anyone who is familiar with only the procedural approach. How can a step-by-step programming model in which there's a single logical flow deal with an unpredictable sequence of events?

Event-Driven Design

The key to designing asynchronous web services is to switch from a procedural programming model to one that's *event driven* as shown in Figure 9-4.

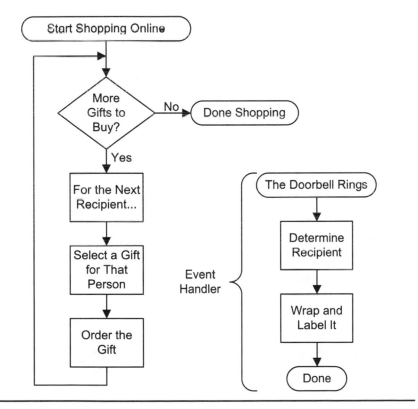

Figure 9-4: Event-Driven Asynchronous Shopping

In this event-driven model, there are two parts to the process. As shown on the left side of Figure 9-4, the first part is the actual shop-

ping procedure. The only difference between this shopping procedure and the one in the shopping-mall example is that here, you don't
actually complete the gift-buying process; you only go so far as placing orders.

Later, at a rather unpredictable time (and certainly in an unpredictable sequence), an *event* occurs: The doorbell rings, and you're handed
one of the gifts. You then have to go back to your shopping list,
identify the recipient of that gift, and finally wrap and tag the present.
Only then will you have completed the long, drawn-out gift-buying
process for that recipient.

Years ago, very few programmers had experience with event-
driven programming—but thanks to the World Wide Web, this
situation has improved. When a web server receives a request from a
web browser, that's an event. If it's a request for a simple, static web
page, the web server itself usually handles it. But if the request is for
a dynamically generated page, the web server dispatches the request
to a *handler* such as a Common Gateway Interface (CGI) script or a
Java *servlet*. These are similar to the event handler in Figure 9-4, in
that they receive control in response to events, process the events,
and then terminate.

Context

The problem of associating a just-delivered gift with its intended
recipient is one of *context*. At the moment the doorbell rings, you're
no longer in the process or context of ordering that gift. You've long
since gone on to other tasks. Upon receiving such an out-of-context
delivery, you must reconcile or correlate the shipment with an order
you placed earlier by locating your shopping list, and finding the gift
and the associated name.

You'll be in trouble if that list is lost or destroyed. If you only
ordered a few gifts, it won't be too bad—you'll probably remember
what you ordered for each person on your list. But if you happen to
be a large business that orders thousands of items, having to figure
out which gift is for which recipient can be a significant problem. The
solution to this context problem is to combine orders and their contexts into *self-contained documents*.

Documents

Have you ever received an email message that contained merely, "Yes" or "No," and didn't contain a copy of whatever question you originally asked? As with the online shopping example, this is a message that arrives without a context. The context must be inferred, making the message more difficult to process and prone to misunderstanding.

A well-written email message doesn't depend on implicit or external information to establish that context; the context is included within the message itself, usually with a quote from an earlier message. The same is true for web services, where self-contained documents can be used as alternatives to passing minimal data in *remote-procedure calls* (RPCs). RPCs include *parameters*, and typically depend on the context being understood by implication or conventions hard-coded into the sending and receiving applications. RPCs are appropriate for simple request/response exchanges, but not for web services that implement more complex processes requiring multiple exchanges—possibly even over extended periods of time.

Think back to the online shopping example. You'll recall that upon receiving each delivery, you had to refer to your shopping list to identify the gift recipient. Suppose instead that the online ordering process captured the name of the intended recipient, and that this bit of information was printed on the associated packing slip. This additional information is irrelevant to the ordering process, since the merchant doesn't care how you intend to use the items you order. But by sending what at first appears to be a verbose document, you'll be able to decouple the ordering procedure from the delivery-event handler, and you'll eliminate customer dependence on the shopping list to reconcile deliveries.

To further illustrate context and self-contained documents, consider the following example of a typical phone or instant-messaging conversation between two friends, Andy and Cliff:

Andy: Do you want to have lunch today?
Cliff: Sure, what time?
Andy: How about noon?
Cliff: 12:30 is better for me. Where?
Andy: Let's say the Italian restaurant on the corner, OK?

Cliff: That's good. Meet you there.
Andy: Great.

This is the way most people talk. It contains little wasted or redundant information, and makes for a natural and reasonably efficient conversation. But in order to grasp the gist of the conversation, you must have heard most of it from the beginning. If you join the conversation somewhere in the middle, you may not hear enough to know where and when the lunch rendezvous will take place. This is because the individual sentences can only be understood within the context of the sentences that have preceded them. They don't contain their own context. It's this lack of *self-contained context* that makes it impossible for latecomers to grasp the meaning of the conversation.

Now look at the same conversation, but with the accumulated context added to each sentence:

Andy: Do you want to have lunch today?
Cliff: Sure, I'm up for lunch. What time?
Andy: Is lunch today at noon okay?
Cliff: Lunch today at noon isn't good, but 12:30 will work. Where?
Andy: Let's have lunch today at 12:30 at the Italian restaurant on the corner.
Cliff: Lunch today at 12:30 at the Italian restaurant on the corner sounds good.
Andy: Great, I'll meet you for lunch today at 12:30 at the Italian restaurant on the corner.

Because each sentence includes all of the information previously exchanged, a third person can join the conversation at any point and instantly be up-to-date on all that has transpired. There's never a need to reconstruct the conversation.

The same principle can be applied to the design of web services. Rather than depend on implicit histories, documents can contain or reference everything necessary to understand them fully and in context.

Message Queuing

The difference between the synchronous and asynchronous models is like the difference between the user experience (not the underlying protocols) of instant messaging and email. If a friend sends you an instant message but your computer is turned off, the message will fail to reach you. The sender will have to try to contact you again later manually, or by other means. Using email, however, the sender doesn't care if you're at your desk, or if your computer or your company's email server are currently reachable. The sender knows that the *messaging infrastructure* will retry the transmission until it eventually succeeds.

Synchronous protocols operate in real time, which is to say that the endpoint services must be online and able to communicate with one another at the moment a request or response is sent. The communications infrastructure must also be available, including the Internet, intranet, or VPN. Using the synchronous model, failures of the network infrastructure or unavailability of a remote service must be handled by the applications.

Asynchronous protocols have built-in support for reliable messaging, such as retry mechanisms to work around short- and medium-term outages. By decoupling requests from responses, they decrease sensitivity to real-time constraints. Asynchronous messaging is based on a *store-and-forward* model, which means that intermediate servers retain copies of messages. This way, if there's a problem with the infrastructure or if an intended recipient service is busy or temporarily unavailable, transmission can be attempted at a later time (i.e., retried).

Figure 9-5 illustrates the flow of data between two services using asynchronous messaging. Note that each service is connected to a *messaging server* that contains a *message queue* for the temporary storage of messages.

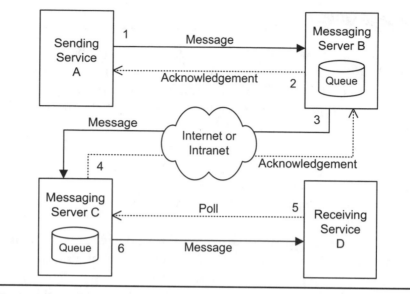

Figure 9-5: Asynchronous Messaging

It may be helpful to think of email as you read the following step-by-step description of what happens when a single message is sent from service A to service D. Although the Simple Mail Transfer Protocol (SMTP) is rarely used for web services due to its unreliability and lack of standardized security, an SMTP-based email system works in essentially the same way as the web-services example in Figure 9-5. Here's the basic procedure:

1. Service A transmits the message to its messaging server B, where a copy is stored in the local message queue until it can be forwarded.

2. Messaging server B immediately acknowledges receipt of the message from service A, which can then continue with other tasks. The acknowledgement implies that B will do everything possible to get the message through.

3. Messaging server B then attempts to transmit the message to the recipient's messaging server C through the Internet or intranet infrastructure. If it's unsuccessful, it will retry.

4. Once the recipient's messaging server C receives the message, it sends an acknowledgement to the sender's server B, which is then able to cease its transmission attempts and delete its

local copy of the message. The message is now safely stored in message-server C's queue.

5. With whatever frequency it deems appropriate, the receiving service D *polls* its local messaging server C to see if any new messages have arrived. Note that this is a *pull* procedure unlike the *push* of the earlier steps—in fact, this is the only pull operation in the process. Alternatively, the local messaging server C can push messages to the receiving service D, but then it must wait for an acknowledgement before pushing the next message so that it doesn't exceed D's capacity to receive messages.

6. The recipient's messaging server C removes the message from its queue and transmits it to the service D.

The above illustrates three important distinctions of the asynchronous model. First, services never communicate directly with one another, but rather through their respective messaging servers.

Second, because the receiving service may not immediately process the message, the only real-time response from the receiver's messaging system C is an *acknowledgement* that contains no application-layer data. Therefore, a complete semantic exchange between two web-services endpoints using the asynchronous model requires *two* messages, one sent in each direction. The second message (not shown in Figure 9-5) confirms *end-to-end* receipt of the first message. It can also contain an interim or final response from service D to service A. Hours or days may pass between the request message and the response message.

Third, a sender doesn't know whether a message it sends gets all the way through to the intended recipient. It only knows that it made it as far as its own message server. This is another reason that a separate end-to-end response message is typically required.

Reliability

A synchronous web service is sensitive to the latency and reliability of the underlying communications infrastructure. Even if a network is up and running, transport-layer protocols will time out if replies aren't received within a few seconds, whether those delays are due to the service or the network.

Compare this to the asynchronous model. When one messaging server has trouble reaching another it begins to retry, and will do so for hours or even days. Neither the sending service nor the recipient will necessarily be aware that this retry mechanism has kicked in. The underlying messaging protocols provide a *reliable transport*, which means they'll retry over an extended period of time.

Scalability

In addition to its reliability benefits, message queuing also delivers substantial improvement in the scalability of any transaction-processing application—-not just those that support web services. Message queuing improves scalability by allowing system architects to plan for *average loads,* as opposed to having to keep up with higher *peak loads* or even *burst loads.*

Imagine configuring the hardware and software for a web service that expects to process 25 transactions per second (25tps), when averaged over the course of an entire day. That's 25tps * 60 seconds * 60 minutes * 24 hours, which comes out to 2.16 million transactions per day. If our chosen application server can handle 25tps, a single application server should meet our needs.

However, we know transaction volumes will vary substantially over the course of each day, particularly for a service that's primarily used during business hours only and/or within a single country or time zone. When counting transactions over 30-minute periods, our transaction volume might look similar to that shown in Figure 9-6. Note that the number of transactions per second fluctuates by a 5:1 ratio depending on the time of day, and that this pattern repeats every day of the week.

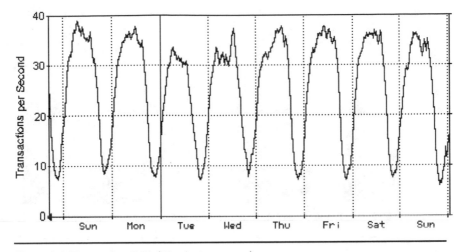

Figure 9-6: Transaction Rate (30-minute average)

Peak Loads

Figure 9-6 illustrates a key problem: Although the *average load* is only 25tps, during midday periods it occasionally reaches a *peak load* of 38tps. Our single application server that can only handle 25tps would be overwhelmed during peak hours, possibly when our most important business partners were trying to use our service. At that time, an average of 13tps would fail—roughly one-third of those submitted. Clearly, we should increase our capacity to a total of 50tps by adding a second 25tps server so that we can handle the peak load.

Burst Loads

Still, have we really solved the problem? We've been looking at the volume of transactions as averaged over 30 minutes—but just as the volume varies over the course of a day, it's also going to vary *within* those 30-minute periods. Take a look at Figure 9-7, which shows the traffic averaged over *one-second* intervals. Although the 30-minute average may be only 38tps, here we can see that our service is subjected to requests at much higher *burst rates* during each of those 30-minute intervals.

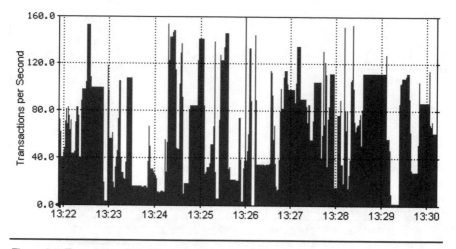

Figure 9-7: Transaction Rate (One-second average. Times shown are hours:minutes.)

Figure 9-7 shows the transaction rate between 1:22pm and 1:30pm on a typical day. When viewed on a second-by-second basis, we can see that this web service actually receives bursts as high as 150tps, not the 38tps we saw when we averaged the traffic over 30-minute periods.

So what should we do? We could plan for six (150/25) application servers in order to meet the burst demand—but that seems wasteful, since in the middle of the night our configuration capable of handling 150tps would handle only 10tps on 30-minute average.

What we need is some sort of a buffer that can smooth out the bursts and peaks to reduce the transaction load to a level closer to the daily average of 25tps. And that's exactly what message queuing does, as illustrated in Figure 9-8.

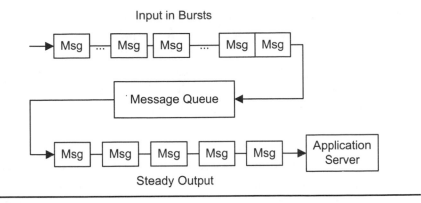

Figure 9-8: Message-Queue Buffering

Using a queuing mechanism, messages may *arrive* at high burst rates, but they can be *consumed* by the web service's application server at whatever rate it can process them. The only requirements are that over *some* period of time (many hours or even days), the web service can handle the *average* traffic load, and that the queue has the capacity to store a sufficient number of transaction messages.

Figure 9-9 illustrates the results obtained from inserting a message queue between the arriving requests and the application servers.

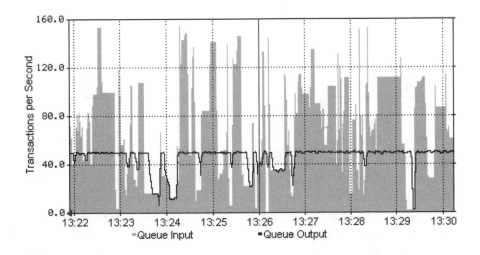

Figure 9-9: Message-Queue Input versus Output (One-second average. Times shown are hours:minutes.)

The gray area here shows the average burst demand per second—that is, the rate at which web-service requests are added to the message queue. The black line represents the rate at which the web-services application server polls for messages, removes them from the queue, and processes them. Note that while as many as 150 messages are received each second, our service—which is only designed for 50tps—can handle all of them. Although the application servers top out at 50tps, they keep on working even when messages arrive faster than the application servers can process them. The queue accumulates messages during these busy moments, and once the arriving-message rate falls below 50 per second the application servers begin to catch up. Eventually, the message queue empties, and the output rate falls below the maximum of 50tps because there is less for the application servers to do.

In this example, no message waits for more than 30 seconds or so before being processed. In fact, if we're willing to accept longer delays, we could even deploy a system based on just a single 25tps application server. During peak times, some messages might wait in the queue for many minutes, or even hours. But so long as the queue is large enough and there are no more than 2.16 million messages to process in any given day, all the messages will be handled. A message-queue based configuration designed to handle only 25tps would likely cost far less than one that could handle the burst load of 150tps without message queuing.

Still a Missing Piece

You rarely get something for nothing, and the increased cost of asynchronous document-style web services stems from their additional complexity. The good news is that all of the complexity is in the messaging infrastructure, thereby simplifying the applications. Once you've got the infrastructure in place and have implemented your first few web services, the incremental cost of deploying additional asynchronous services on top of that same infrastructure is substantially less. Furthermore (as we'll see in Chapter 18), tools for asynchronous messaging and solutions to the other missing pieces will become less expensive over time.

In addition to the initial cost of a message-queuing system, the other problem is that the standards and protocols for reliable messaging infrastructures are not mature. This issue is critical to the success of your complex asynchronous web-services projects, and it's another topic we'll address in greater detail in Chapter 18.

In the meantime, if cost or lack of standardization are keeping you from implementing the infrastructure of asynchronous messaging, consider outsourcing your message-queuing infrastructure to a web-services network (WSN) as we'll discuss in Chapter 15.

The asynchronous style of interaction based on event handlers, messaging, and message queuing is a cornerstone of loosely coupled SOAs. Many of the benefits of web services can't be realized until asynchronous interaction becomes well understood and widely practiced, and some high-value applications can't be deployed properly or at all without it.

We'll look more closely at the concepts of documents and messaging in the next chapter, as we wrap up our exploration of web services and SOAs with the critical concept of loose coupling.

Chapter 10

Loose Coupling

"I shall not today attempt further to define pornography...but I know it when I see it."

—Justice Potter Stewart, U.S. Supreme Court
Jacobellis v. Ohio, 1964

Talking about loose coupling is like talking about pornography: Many people use the phrase "loosely coupled," but few can tell you precisely what it means. This is because loose coupling is a methodology or style, rather than a set of established rules and specifications.

Loose coupling is an approach to the design of distributed applications that emphasizes agility—the ability to adapt to changes. Loose coupling intentionally sacrifices interface optimization to achieve flexible interoperability among systems that are disparate in technology, location, performance, and availability. A loosely coupled application is isolated from internal changes in others by using abstraction, indirection, and delayed binding in the interfaces between the applications. As compared to traditional, tightly coupled applications, loosely coupled applications aim to be more reusable and adaptable to the unexpected.

A Matter of Style

Unfortunately, the practice of loose coupling doesn't come naturally. At times, it even goes against the grain of much that the IT community previously tried to accomplish. The tendencies of many programmers and system architects are to tightly couple applications in order to achieve short-term, more easily measurable benefits, most notably in performance. But even when tight coupling results in better performance, it usually does so at the expense of agility, reliability, and scalability.

Loose coupling is a difficult concept to grasp, much as older software-engineering concepts such as structured programming, modular programming, and object-oriented programming are sometimes awkward for newcomers. Once you "get it," you can clearly see the benefits of each of these approaches—but they're confusing until you do.

Perhaps the best example of coming to grips with a new software-development methodology is a programmer's introduction to a new programming language. In the early 1980s, C++ became the first widespread language based on object-oriented programming (OOP), an all-new concept to many programmers at the time. C++ soon became the rage. But in fact, if you examined the source code of many early C++ programs, they looked just like C because their authors hadn't yet been exposed to (or didn't understand) the benefits of OOP. These programs were *degenerate cases* of the new programming paradigm—merely old C wine poured into new C++ bottles. Although they were syntactically correct C++, these programs failed to take advantage of any of the concepts that differentiated C++ from C. (Anyone who has ever recruited programmers, and asked applicants to provide sample programs, can tell you how much more you can learn about attitudes and skills from source code than from résumés.)

Just as OOP languages eventually delivered significant benefits over their procedural-language predecessors, so too will web services and their accompanying paradigms of loose coupling and *service-oriented architectures* (SOAs) prove to be advancements over tightly coupled *application program interfaces* (APIs) and traditional application architectures. But if history repeats itself, it will be some time before the concepts and strategies of loose coupling and SOAs sink into the minds of programmers and system architects. We'll try to move that process forward here by exploring the differences between tightly and loosely coupled systems, as summarized in Figure 10-1.

	Tightly Coupled	Loosely Coupled
Interaction	Synchronous	Asynchronous
Messaging Style	RPC	Document
Message Paths	Hard Coded	Routed
Technology Mix	Homogeneous	Heterogeneous
Data Types	Dependent	Independent
Syntactic Definition	By Convention	Published Schema
Bindings	Fixed and Early	Delayed
Semantic Adaptation	By Re-coding	Via Transformation
Software Objective	Re-use, Efficiency	Broad Applicability
Consequences	Anticipated	Unexpected

Figure 10-1: Tight Versus Loose Coupling

We've already covered the first two rows of this table in Chapter 8, so we'll mention them here only briefly, with an emphasis on exactly what it is about asynchronous document-style messaging that creates loose coupling. Then we'll explore each of the remaining rows of Figure 10-1 in detail, in some cases combining them for the sake of clarity.

To illustrate the differences between tight and loose coupling, we'll occasionally refer to a simple purchase-order application example. In this example there are four discrete applications, each running on a separate system:

- an inventory-management application that can tell us what's in stock;
- a customer-information application that can provide shipping and billing addresses and related data;
- an order-processing application to which we can submit orders; and

- our own application, which creates orders by using the services of the other three.

For the sake of later comparisons, Figure 10-2 illustrates how these four systems might interact using a tightly coupled model based on synchronous, RPC-style messages.

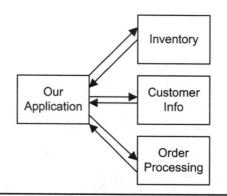

Figure 10-2: A Synchronous, RPC-Style Approach

There's no question that one can successfully build this distributed application using RPC-style synchronous messaging, but as we'll see, it can be substantially improved using document-style messages and asynchronous interactions.

Asynchronous Messaging

The system shown above might be a *long-running process* (as introduced in Chapter 8), since it could take hours or even days between the time our application first sends the purchasing document to the inventory system and the time the document is returned by the order-processing system. If we added an approval step to the process, many days might elapse between the time the operation commenced (e.g., when a purchase requisition is issued) and the final stage of the operation (acknowledgement of delivery).

Synchronous requests will time out and signal errors to their applications if they don't receive responses within seconds or minutes, so they can't be used as-is in this environment. Asynchronous web services more closely resemble real-world business processes that involve humans, who can't always complete their tasks promptly. Messages can wait in underlying queues until the next application is able to deal with them. In this way, asynchronous messaging decouples applications in time.

Without message queues, a message receiver must be available at the same time the sender is online and must have the capacity to accept and process the request. Message queues serve as buffers, allowing recipients to get behind on processing requests and even be taken offline altogether. Since the sender can operate independently of the presence and availability of the receiver, the application becomes more loosely coupled.

Resilience and Error Handling

The Internet and other infrastructure components aren't 100 percent reliable, so all web services must have ways to handle error in the network and failures of remote services. Synchronous web services are responsible for handling errors above the transport layer (or above TCP/IP in the protocol stack), whereas asynchronous messaging protocols include their own retry mechanisms that can deal with failures that last minutes, hours, or even days.

Let's consider what our purchase-order application should do when it doesn't receive a response from, say, the order-processing system. Should it re-issue the request? Or suppose the request has gone through, but our application never received the response. Might the order-processing system book the order twice? Implementing the error handling that answers these questions could become the most complex part of an otherwise simple application. Our application must understand the behavior of each of the three remote services in case they report errors. For example, how will all of the applications together recover from a partially completed transaction? The effect of such coordinated problem-solving is that all four applications will become increasingly intertwined—in other words, they'll be tightly coupled.

The use of asynchronous interaction allows the system to be far more tolerant of errors. Messages still may become lost or stuck in queues, but the frequency of such problems—and the need to address them robustly within the application—can be substantially reduced by using asynchronous messaging.

Document-Style Messaging

In addition to the improvements attributable to asynchronous interaction, there are two others that can be achieved by switching from RPC-style to document-style messaging, as introduced in Chapter 8.

Business-Logic Locus

Our sample application for creating and submitting purchase orders contains many logical steps and involves many rules. Collectively, these are the *business logic* of our application. For example, if there isn't sufficient inventory, the overall system must somehow decide whether to cancel the order or take some other action. What should happen if there's sufficient stock of one item but not another? The business logic determines whether a partial shipment should be sent.

When a business process involves multiple applications, as in our example, the question arises: Where does the business logic reside? Where is it manifested? Traditionally it would be hard-coded into our application, just as it would be in a non-distributed environment (i.e., one based on a single application running on a single server.) But there's a tempting alternative: Distribute the business logic to the various applications or services.

For example, it's possible to design the inventory-management system to make the partial-shipment decision, and either forward the order to the next service or reject it and send it back to our application. But if the business logic is distributed in this way among multiple applications or services, they become very difficult to maintain. A single change in the business logic could cause a cascade of changes in multiple programs on many different servers. Such interdependence among applications is a symptom of tight coupling.

Distributing the business logic also requires that applications deal with concepts that are otherwise outside of their domains. According to the principles of modularity, for example, an inventory application should process only inventory-related requests. It should keep track of what's in the warehouse and what needs to be re-ordered, but the inventory application should have no notion of what a purchase order is. The inventory application certainly shouldn't be expected to manage a partial-shipment policy, nor should it have to distinguish among items removed for customer orders, for promotional activities, and for a factory recall. To an inventory system, these distinctions are irrelevant.

From this example, you might infer that the best solution is to keep the business logic within our application and control everything centrally, as suggested in Figure 10-2. But there's a better way to manage the business logic: Express it within the purchase-order document itself, or in a document or file that's separate but accessible to all applications.

Consider how the inventory system functions when the business logic is contained within the messages it receives. The inventory system only needs to look up the inventory information for items listed in the document, execute the business logic specified within the document, and follow the routing instructions. The inventory system isn't sensitive to the type of document it receives, which could be a purchase order or any other document that specifies fundamental inventory operations such as add, remove, and report. The system must know how to locate the inventory-related portion of the document, but it doesn't need to know how to read or understand the rest of the document. In fact, it should understand how to locate the inventory business rules in *any* document, not just a purchase order. That way, new document types can make use of the inventory application without that application needing to be modified.

The inventory application in this new model includes a highly generalized business-logic engine, which allows it to execute any business logic associated with any document so long as the rules are related to inventory. To forward the purchase order (or any other document) to the next application along the route when the time comes, the inventory application doesn't need to know the function to be performed by the next application—only its address. Creating a new application then becomes a process of codifying the business logic and specifying the routing of the associated document.

Performance

While more processing and communications resources are required to generate and parse a large, document-style message than a small, RPC-style one, the ratio isn't linear. When RPC-style interactions are used, the *payloads* represent a small percentage of the total data exchanged. The XML and transport-layer *overhead* is high. Document-style interactions are more efficient than RPCs because they require the transmission of fewer messages. Although it takes more time to process each message, the total overhead required to affect a transaction is actually less than when RPCs are used.

Message Routing

Another way in which asynchronous messaging loosely couples applications is through the *routing* of messages. To see why, let's compare how the four systems might interact using asynchronous, message-based web services (as illustrated in Figure 10-3) as opposed to the earlier synchronous style (in Figure 10-2).

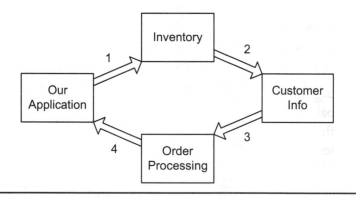

Figure 10-3: Message Routing

Unlike a synchronous service that expects an immediate response, an asynchronous web service moves information (the purchase-order document in our case) in one direction only. Our application first creates the purchase order, and (1) sends a message containing the document to the inventory system. If stock is sufficient, the inventory system then updates the order document and (2) forwards it to the customer-information system, which adds the shipping and billing information, and (3) routes the document to the order-processing system. Finally, the order is processed, the document is updated once again to reflect this, and (4) it's returned to our application.

Web services using routed messages are more loosely coupled because they're easier to change. Modifying message routing is usually simpler than modifying an application that created it, and it's even possible for downstream applications to modify the routing as necessary. Each application can accomplish what it needs without informing other applications, thereby decreasing the coupling between them.

While message routing can, in theory, be used with synchronous as well as asynchronous messaging, this is rarely done. One reason is that the asynchronous model is often supported by message queues (as we saw in Chapter 9), and queues can introduce delays that are unacceptably long to some of the transport protocols used to support synchronous services.

Heterogeneity

System architects used to think standards were the answer to interoperability. We hoped our vendors would eventually agree to do things one way, such as providing Java on every platform, even on Windows. Of course, we never achieved such a homogeneous state of technology. The IT world consists of heterogeneous programming languages, operating systems, and development environments, and it probably always will.

Given this reality, the key to loosely coupling heterogeneous technologies is to standardize the *interfaces* and not the source code. Once parties agree to the interfaces, they're free to implement the underlying services using whatever technologies they desire. Since our sample purchase-order application is based on loosely coupled web services, it's indifferent to the technologies used on the remote systems with which it interacts. Prior to web services, all of the systems would have had to agree on many internal details and were thus more tightly coupled.

Delayed Binding and Published Schemas

Once two parties have agreed to communicate via the exchange of
XML-formatted data to solve low-level data-type compatibility issues,
they still have a problem: How should they create a shared understanding of the syntax of those exchanges? Even when both parties'
applications are based on the same vendor's platform and developed
using the same programming language, the respective developers still
need to agree on the structure of the data.

Using customary methods, one programmer drafts a specification, which, after some discussion and negotiation, is accepted by the
other. The two parties thereby create a shared understanding through
agreement or *convention*. This shared understanding is established not
at runtime, but well in advance of any exchange of documents. The
programmers' objective is to standardize the specification as *early* as
possible in the process, and the early completion and approval of a
detailed specification is often heralded as a significant achievement.
But contrary to programmers' instincts, the earlier in the process such
issues are resolved, the more tightly coupled the parties will be to the
specification and to one another. To deploy a change to such a tightly
coupled system, the programmers must first agree to a modification
of the specification and then simultaneously implement that change
within their respective systems.

Using loosely coupled web services, the need for further conversations and coordination between programmers is substantially
reduced. In loosely coupled systems, the syntax of information
exchange can be entirely decoupled from how that information is
stored in a database or manipulated in an application. This means
the party offering the service can publishes a *schema* and a *description*
in standardized XML files specifying all of the data structures, documents, and methods supported by the service. The requesting applications can query the description and schema, and discover up-to-
date details at runtime. This information source also allows new applications to be developed without knowing certain details in advance
and without lengthy consultations between programmers.

Interface designs that are expressed indirectly through published
specifications can be extended more easily, without breaking the applications that depend on them. For example, XML schemas allow
a provider to add elements or attributes without affecting existing

requestors. This is a major advance over previous technologies, and another example of the *delayed binding* and *discovery* concepts we introduced in Chapter 8. Delayed binding is critical to loose coupling and should be applied wherever possible. The goal of delayed binding is to avoid any fixed or hard-coded bindings to data typing, structure, location, or network connection. Delayed binding also helps ensure that new versions of a web service are both backwards-compatible and future-proofed, allows for incremental development and change, and even encourages experimentation.

A delayed binding is one that can be changed at runtime, rather than when an application is designed or compiled. Here's an example of delayed binding with which we're all familiar: Every host or server on the Internet has an IP address such as 207.44.140.97, but we don't typically reach those systems by typing in their numerical IP addresses. The *domain name service* (DNS) binds a symbolic *hostname* (such as www.rds.com) to an IP address, which allows us to refer to the host via its name rather than by its address. In this way, a server can be transparently relocated to another IP address, and all applications and individuals will continue to find it regardless of the change. The extra steps of using DNS to convert hostnames to IP addresses introduce slight (20ms to 100ms) delays in the process of communicating with remote systems, yet we find those delays acceptable because we get flexibility in return.

The DNS example and the general concept of delayed binding show how optimizing for performance tends to tighten the coupling between systems. An application that uses the hard-coded IP addresses of remote systems can contact those systems a bit more quickly than can another application that uses hostnames, which must first be resolved to IP addresses using DNS. But if the remote system is moved to a new IP address, the application that used hard coding would instantly break. Even if the IP addresses were stored in a local "hosts" file to eliminate the need to query DNS, someone would have to update that file at the same moment as the remote system changes its IP address. Clearly, this tightly couples the two applications.

Transformations

Although web services define vendor- and technology-independent syntax and data types, they don't offer the same degree of standardization for the meaning or semantics of information. Frequently, two parties will discover that although their services are standardized and syntactically compatible, they still don't align on certain semantic issues. A simple example is of one web service that assumes currency is expressed in US dollars, while another expects it to be communicated in Euros.

The tightly coupled solution to this incompatibility is for one party or the other to write additional code, so that it can communicate and conduct business in the currency used by the other. Not only is this a non-trivial task, but it also requires that the adapting party develop and maintain expertise in exchange rates—possibly through licensing third-party databases that are frequently updated.

A loosely coupled solution allows the parties to agree to disagree. Service-oriented architectures support third-party *transformation services* (intermediaries) that can mediate or transform syntax or semantics from those used by one party to those used by the other, as shown in Figure 10-4.

Figure 10-4: Transformation as a Service

Although many web services won't require mediation or transformation, good design allows for the potential use of transformations in the future. If a new requestor comes along later who is unable or unwilling to use an existing service in its current form, the newcomer can employ the services of an intermediary to solve any incompatibilities that might exist. What's more, the intermediary can be inserted into the flow of documents and messages without any change whatsoever to—or even awareness of—the original web service. In loosely coupled web services, the capability to utilize such intermediaries is the rule rather than the exception.

As we'll see in Chapter 15, it's not only content and format that can be transformed. Loosely coupled web services also make it possible to mediate different transport protocols and security models, including authentication and authorization schemes.

Broad Applicability

Over the half-century history of software development, there's been a constant push for *reusable code*. On the face of it, the merits of reusable code seem obvious. Software development is expensive, and if a company's investment can be reused, the company should receive a better return on that investment. Reuse implies that code or class libraries will be shared by the software components within a system. But this is a tightly coupled practice and assumes (at the very least) that subsequent applications will be developed using the same programming languages or operating environments.

While reusable code has proven to be an important concept in software engineering, in the loosely coupled world of web services there's less of a need to port source code or utilize libraries when creating new applications. Instead, the code can be left to execute where it is, and its functionality offered as a web service to other applications and web services. In such a world, it makes sense to design web services for *broad applicability*—to be as useful as possible to the broadest set of applications—rather than to be reusable in the traditional sense. The code need not be portable, but its interface must be universal.

Delayed binding allows applications to be reused at runtime, when they're no longer language-dependent, rather than at build time. This means loosely coupled web services are available to more applications and hence applicable to a broader range of problems.

Unintended Consequences

"Innovation will come from APIs that support 'unintended consequences'."

—Tim O'Reilly[14]

Tim O'Reilly's comment captures perfectly the concept of *broad applicability*, which suggests that the eventual uses of any given service can't be predicted at the time the service is created. As with the older reusable-code paradigm, the service you develop today may become part of applications you can't yet imagine. You should assume that systems you currently know nothing about and are controlled by organizations you've never even heard of will someday want access to the same interfaces. In other words: Design and implement your web-service interfaces to handle anything that might be thrown at them.

"Easy for you to say!" you're thinking. And before the advent of web services, your reaction would have been justified. It was one thing to preach universality and interoperability, but another to pull it off. Now it's quite practical, and not considering your web services as being part of a grander scheme will substantially diminish their long-term value.

Unlike reusable code that's typically confined to operating within an organization, web-services applications may be running on systems controlled by business partners in faraway places. Keep this in mind as you expose your legacy functions and applications as web services. It's very possible they'll develop lives of their own, far beyond your original intentions.

As you evaluate opportunities and plan your own web-services projects, keep the objectives of loose coupling in mind. As choices appear, take the more loosely coupled alternative—or at least understand the tradeoffs you're making by taking the more tightly coupled path. Avoid the same impulses that might lead someone else to hard-code an IP address, a filename, or a URL in order to gain some efficiency and supposed simplicity. Instead, consider the benefits of loose coupling: insulation from change, and broad and unanticipated applicability. Remember, the applications you design and develop today will someday be legacy applications—*your* legacy applications.

Part III

Technologies

Chapter 11

Transactions

Most non-programmers think of transactions as associated with buying and selling, credit-card authorizations, and the like. But in the jargon of computer science, the word *transaction* has a very specific meaning: *the interaction and managed outcome of a well-defined set of tasks.* If that definition still sounds rather vague or abstract, it's because the scope of what's considered a transaction has expanded over the past two decades, and the older simpler definitions are no longer adequate. Computer systems have been connected via networks, and applications are more distributed in nature. The theories and practices of transactions have been repeatedly stretched to their limits, re-evaluated, and extended. Now, because of web services, we're once again expanding that definition to include *long-lived loosely coupled asynchronous transactions.*

In this chapter we'll look at transactions from the web-services perspective, beginning with a review of the history of transaction technology. Entire books and many Ph.D. theses have been written about transactions, so don't expect this chapter to be the definitive work on the subject. (For a thorough treatment of transactions, see *Principles of Transaction Processing*, by Philip Bernstein and Eric Newcomer.[15]) Instead, we'll focus on the pragmatic questions: What problems do transactions solve? How have they been solved prior to the invention of web services? What's unique about transactions in the web-services environment? What solutions have been devised to date? And finally, what pieces are still missing?

We'll cover the theory of transactions, but with an eye towards the real-world challenges when software and hardware break, communications links fail, and external parties behave in unpredictable and sometimes malicious ways. For anyone not familiar with the theory of transactions, the first part of this chapter will serve as an introduction to the topic. For others, it should be a helpful review. By the end of the chapter, you'll have a solid understanding of what transactions are in a variety of applications and environments, as well as the issues surrounding transactions in the context of web services.

Transaction Basics

Most database operations are simple, and thus don't qualify as transactions per se. For example, when a customer-service application wants to look up a customer's phone number, the application sends a *query* message to the database. It's a read-only operation that involves only one record in a single database. But most importantly, it's a one-step *(atomic)* operation that doesn't interact or conflict with other applications that may be interacting with the same record or even the same database.

More complex database operations require multiple steps that must all be completed for the operation to succeed. We refer to these operations as *transactions*. The traditional definition of a transaction is a single *unit of work* composed of two or more *tasks*. If any of these component tasks cannot be completed, the entire transaction fails, leaving the data in the state it was in before the transaction was initiated. In other words, a transaction is a collection of tasks that either all succeed, or all fail. Achieving this *consistent termination* of a unit of work is the goal of a traditional *transaction-processing monitor* (TP monitor) which is software that manages lower-level database operations.

An example of a simple transaction is a transfer of funds from one account to another within the same bank. The transaction's unit of work consists of two tasks: the debiting from one account, and the crediting to another. Ideally, both tasks will execute properly *(commit)*, but even more important is that if one task can't be accomplished, *neither* will be executed (i.e., they'll both *abort)*. It's okay if the matching credit and debit both fail—the application initiating the transaction can always try again. But it's a serious problem if the credit is executed without the associated debit, or vice versa.

ACID

As the results of their theoretical studies of transactions, Theo Häerder and Andreas Reuter published a 1983 paper, "Principles of Transaction-Orientated Database Recovery,"[16] in which they presented the requirements for systems that could process multiple-task units of work (transactions), and would not be corrupted by hardware, database, or operating system failures. The paper is most famous for its specification of the principles of Atomicity, Consistency, Isolation, and Durability (ACID). A system that conforms to these so-called ACID properties guarantees the reliability of its transactions. We'll review the ACID properties here, since they'll help us understand the requirements of transactions in a web-services environment, and why the traditional ACID properties are therefore insufficient.

Atomicity

Atomicity is another name for the all-or-nothing aspect of a transaction. Much as an atom can't be broken down further without destroying its defining characteristics, an atomic transaction must be completed in its entirety. If one component is committed, then all must be committed. If any one component cannot be committed, no components shall be committed. In our bank-account transfer example, atomicity guarantees that either both the credit and debit tasks will succeed, or neither will take effect.

Consistency

Whether a transaction succeeds or not, all data must end up in a consistent state. Using our bank-account transfer example, there should be no residual effect on data on either system if the transaction fails due to a problem with the database, the operating system, the hardware, communications links, and so on. No matter whether the transaction succeeds or fails, the accounts must end up without inconsistencies.

Isolation

The effects of a transaction should be invisible to and isolated from other transactions until it has been committed. Again, using our bank-account transfer example, this means that the credit/debit operations performed on behalf of our transactions should not interfere with any other transactions affecting the same data *(resources)*. If money is being withdrawn from or deposited to one of the accounts at roughly the same time as the account transfer is taking place, the two transactions must not interfere with one another.

The principal of isolation also states that if transactions overlap in time (i.e., they occur in parallel), the results must be identical to those they'd get if they were instead to occur sequentially (in series). The most common technique for assuring isolation is to *lock* database records between the time a transaction is initiated and the time it's completed.

Durability

Once a transaction has been completed successfully (i.e., it's been committed), the resulting changes must not be lost even if the hardware or software fails. For our sample application, this means that before the account transfer can be committed, the database must have logged the respective changes to reliable backup media or otherwise assured that they won't be lost.

Resource Locking

Consider a situation in which two people—let's say a married couple with a joint account—separately attempt to withdraw the last bit of funds from the same account at the same instant, but at two different branches. Of course, the bank must ensure this can't occur. Let's assume for the sake of our example that both branches are connected to the same computer and database, and that the teller-terminal application executes two tasks: First, it verifies that there are sufficient funds, and then it debits the account.

If the withdrawals occur serially, there's no problem. The husband goes to the first branch, and asks to withdraw all the remaining funds. The teller queries the account, sees that there's a balance of, let's say, $252.43, then debits the account that amount, and hands the money to the husband. When the wife makes the same request at the second branch, her teller reports that the balance is zero. The wife may not be happy about it, but the bank won't lose any money.

Now imagine a scenario in which both withdrawals occur at roughly the same time. The husband's transaction proceeds as described above, but if the teller at the wife's branch checks the balance any time before the teller at the husband's branch debits the account, the wife's teller will also see a balance of $252.43. If the wife's teller hands her the cash, the bank will be out that amount. The problem arises because the two transactions were allowed to occur in parallel, with different results than would be obtained had they been executed serially.

To *serialize* the transactions, the withdrawal application brackets the balance-verification task and the debit task as a single transaction, during which the application locks the database record for the account balance. During the brief time between when the teller at the husband's bank queries the account balance and the moment when his teller debits the account, all other teller terminals are forbidden to read or write the database record that contains the account balance. For a few seconds, the teller at the wife's branch will be unable to see the balance. The period could be so brief as to go unnoticed, but the effect is critical: By the time the wife's teller gains access to the account-balance record, it will read zero. Through locking, the transactions are serialized and hence isolated in conformance with the ACID requirements.

One-Phase Commit

In our earlier example, funds from one account were transferred to another within the same bank. The debit of one account and the crediting of the other must be bracketed as related tasks to ensure the atomicity of the transaction. This is managed by the database *transaction manager* (TM), which has the ability to reverse database operations. In this instance, the TM tracks the progress of the two tasks (debit and credit) to make sure they are both successful. If only one change succeeds for any reason, the TM reverses that operation such that both records are left in their pre-transaction state. The database management system then reports an *abort* (failure) of the transaction to the requesting application. Only when it's certain that both changes to the database have been permanently applied and thus satisfy the ACID requirement for durability does the TM return an indication of *commit* (success) to the application. When all of the resources are under the control of a single TM as in this example, this simple *one-phase commit* process is sufficient to guarantee the atomicity of the transaction.

Two-Phase Commit

When all of the data involved in a transaction resides on a single database, only one TM is required to maintain atomicity. But applications and databases are increasingly distributed, such as those linked by web services. The challenge for web services is to maintain atomicity by guaranteeing the mutual success and durability of all of the elements of such a *distributed transaction*, so named because it involves a *distributed unit of work*. In other words, multiple steps are required that involve two or more databases.

The traditional model for distributed transactions utilizes a single *transaction coordinator* and one or more *resource managers*, each responsible for its own data as illustrated in Figure 11-1.

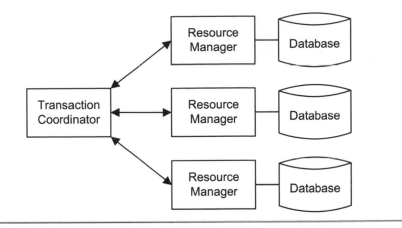

Figure 11-1: Distributed Transaction Management

The traditional method for handling distributed transactions is known as the *two-phase commit*, which, as its name implies, breaks transactions into two cooperating phases. The two-phase commit protocol is illustrated in Figure 11-2, and described in the following sections using the travel-reservation example introduced in Chapter 8.

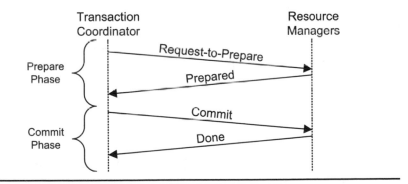

Figure 11-2: The Two-Phase Commit Protocol

Prepare (Phase 1)

The transaction coordinator is a process running on one system that sends a *request-to-prepare* message containing the details of the transaction to all of the resource managers, which are processes running on each of the database systems. Upon receipt of a request-to-prepare message, each resource manager responsible for data to be changed by the transaction writes the post-transaction state of that data to durable media.

The request-to-prepare message is really a question that asks, "Have you logged the updated state of all resources to reliable and stable media, so that if there's a failure, the effect of this transaction will persist?" Each participating system then responds to the coordinator with a *vote:* either a *prepared*-vote message, acknowledging that the resource manager is prepared to commit the transaction; or a *no*-vote message as illustrated in Figure 11-3, if for some reason it can't prepare for the transaction by durably recording the update.

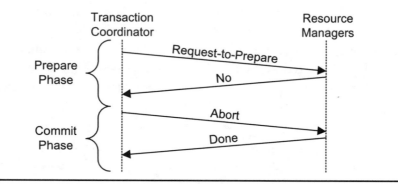

Figure 11-3: The Two-Phase Commit Protocol Abort

Commit (Phase 2)

If the coordinator receives prepared votes from all of the participants, it then sends out a *commit* message, instructing the participants to apply the transaction. If it receives a *no* vote from any of the participants, it sends an *abort* message to all participants, who in turn then relinquish their commitments, and cancel the local effects of the transaction. In either case, the resource managers respond by sending final *done* messages to the controller.

The two-phase commit process assures the atomicity of the distributed transaction. It's clean and simple—except when things go wrong. Due to hardware, software, or communications failures, it's possible that one or more messages may be lost, resulting in an uncertain state for one or more of the resource managers. As it turns out, however, only the loss of a commit message can cause a serious problem. Losses of other message types are less critical. If a resource manager fails to get the *request-to-prepare* message, it will simply fail to respond. The controller will give up waiting for the resource manager's response and send out an *abort* message. The other resource managers will not have committed any of their changes. The same occurs if one or more of the response messages is lost. And if a *done* message is lost, no action need be taken, since all of the resource coordinators will have committed the transaction.

The most serious problem occurs when a resource manager prepares for the transaction but never receives either a *commit* or an *abort* message from the transaction coordinator. Once a resource manager has sent its *prepared* response, it's in limbo. It can't commit the transaction, and it can't release any resources locked on behalf of the transaction. (Resource locks are under the control of the individual resource managers, not the transaction controller.)

In fact, there's no simple solution to this problem. As Bernstein and Newcomer point out,[17] no two-phase commit protocol can protect against all failures. The possibility will always exist that a communications failure can cause a resource manager to become *blocked*, or unable to commit or abort. (Bernstein and Newcomer describe in detail the mechanisms for handling such failures.) Still, even with its limitations, the two-phase commit protocol remains the mainstay of distributed transactions.

The Web-Services Challenges

The ACID model has been the focus of transaction technologies for twenty years. It's widely used for both local and—via the two-phase commit protocol—distributed transaction systems. But as valuable as the ACID model has proven to be for tightly coupled distributed systems, it falls short for long-lived, loosely coupled asynchronous transactions.

Long-Lived Transactions

As technology author Jon Udell wrote, "Web services tackle business processes that are widely distributed in both time and space."[18] They're far more complex in terms of time and space than the transactions for which the ACID concepts were developed. Whereas ACID-based transactions may span many seconds or even a few minutes, loosely coupled web-services transactions may extend over hours or even days. As described in the purchasing-application example in Chapter 10, considerable time can elapse between the preparation and commit phases. Using ACID-style transactions in such long-running business processes would mean that participating resources could be locked and unavailable for extended periods of time—which is unacceptable to many local applications that use the same databases and pend until the resources they require are released.

Reliability

ACID-style transactions are designed to cope with failures in hardware, software, and communications, but only in otherwise reliable environments where such failures occur relatively infrequently. Most ACID-style distributed transactions systems are based on synchronous, connection-oriented protocols, which maintain communications paths between transaction coordinators and the participating resource managers for at least the duration of the transaction. These synchronous protocols assist in handling such errors by signaling the transaction-coordinator or resource-manager software when a communication failure occurs, so that the coordinator or resource manager knows it can no longer communicate with the service at the other end of the connection. When a communications link fails, all synchronous transactions that depend on that link are promptly aborted.

Short-term communications failures are therefore fatal errors for tightly coupled synchronous transactions, but they must be routinely handled by the systems that support long-lived, loosely coupled asynchronous transactions. As we saw in Chapter 9, the latter are based on a *reliable-messaging* infrastructure that delivers messages with a high degree of assuredness, even in cases where the recipient and the intervening infrastructure may be down for extended periods of time.

Trust

Because the resource locks typically used with ACID-style transactions may block applications, it's critical that they be held for as short a time as possible. If an application dies after locking a resource, that resource could be orphaned forever. If the resource in question represents the availability of an airline seat, that seat might never be filled. A resource manager therefore manages its resources like a mother hen, making sure that locked resources are never abandoned. If a local application requests a lock and then terminates, the resource manager must clean up the mess by unlocking the resource. Before a resource manager allows transactions to be initiated by remote transaction coordinators, a great deal of trust must exist among the resource manager, the remote coordinators, and other resource managers participating in the transactions.

Suppose it's not the link that fails, but rather the remote transaction coordinator. Although the messaging software won't signal a communications error (the communications link is still operational), the local resource manager has the ultimate fallback: It can rely on timeouts to protect its resources. Unfortunately, timeouts can't be used for long-lived transactions, because by definition they execute over extended periods. Again, the techniques that support ACID-style transactions won't work with those that are long-lived, loosely coupled, and asynchronous.

Cancellation Risks and Abuses

External web services introduce a number of risks just by exposing internal systems to access by others. Allowing externally initiated transactions increases what's known as *cancellation risk*. For example, consider airline seats purchased at full price a few months before the flight. If they're cancelled at the last minute, the airline may be unable to sell them.

The problem becomes more acute when business processes are automated by web services, because accidental or even intentional abuse can so easily go undetected. For example, imagine how an unethical travel aggregator might exploit an airline-reservation web service. Months in advance, the aggregator reserves every available seat on a particular flight—but at the last minute, cancels them. In a panic to sell the seats, the airline puts them on sale at a deep discount. The unscrupulous travel aggregator then repurchases the same seats at this much lower price.

Accepting a reservation carries an inherent risk of such a last-minute cancellation. This problem exists even without web services, but there are systems in place to detect and prevent most abuses. Airlines manage this risk through overbooking. Concert and theater ticket agencies protect themselves using no-refund policies. But many other businesses—particularly those in wholesale trade—have no formal methods for managing cancellation risks. The risks and abuses of cancellations will probably increase and spread to other industries as external web services are deployed. Web services will ultimately need to express and negotiate the policies under which such transactions are made.

Loosely Coupled Transactions

Clearly, the web-services requirements for transactions far exceed what can be accomplished using traditional technologies. The more loosely we couple systems—separating them in time, space, and control—the more difficult it becomes to manage transactions distributed among them. Loosely coupled transactions, it would seem, come at a cost of increased complexity. That's true, but only so long as we keep trying to apply, refine, and improve traditional approaches based on ACID-style concepts. Instead, let's consider how we can build an all-new transactional system based on the loosely coupled web-services technologies explored in earlier chapters: asynchronous communications, reliable messaging, and document-style interaction. Let's use an example of a tightly coupled transaction, then see how it can be improved.

You're in your car, listening to the radio, when you hear an announcement that your favorite musician will be performing in your town. You grab your cell phone and dial the ticket-sales agency. A friendly salesperson answers the phone, and you launch into your request—only to be interrupted by the salesperson telling you, "I'm sorry, but our computers are down right now, and we don't know when they'll be back up. You'll have to call again later."

You've just stumbled into one of the drawbacks of synchronous transactions: In this case, there's nothing you can do but abort the transaction. You (the requestor) and the reservation system (the provider) must be available simultaneously. There's no point leaving your information with a salesperson who's just an intermediary, with no store-and-forward capability. Even if the salesperson were willing to take down your information, would you trust that person to complete your order? The responsibility for recovering from the system failure and restarting the transaction falls entirely on you, the requestor.

Half an hour later, you call back (retry), and learn that the system is now available. Of course the context of your transaction has been lost, so you've got to start from the very beginning. As luck would have it, the agent submits your request only to report, "Sorry, but all of the orchestra seats are now sold out. The best I can do is row J, seats 103 and 104 in the upper mezzanine." For a period of a few minutes, the reservation system locks the database records that represent those two seats while you make up your mind. If other customers are placing orders through different agents, they won't be offered those same seats. (This is now a synchronous transaction.)

You tell the agent you'll take the tickets, but your cell phone goes dead just as you're about to jot down your confirmation number. Now what? Did the transaction complete? Do you really have two tickets for the concert, or do you need to call back and place another order? If you do, will you end up with four tickets instead of two? Unfortunately, there's no way to know. Such are the problems of tightly coupled transactions without a reliable asynchronous messaging infrastructure.

Wouldn't it be great if you could just leave a voice-mail message (a self-contained document) including not only the obvious details, but instructions (the business logic) for what to do in case your first-choice seats aren't available? Your voice-mail message would then enter a message queue along with those of other customers, and be processed in sequence. As a result of your request, the ticket agency would call you back or send you an email message confirming your purchase. The acknowledgement would complete this long-lived, loosely coupled asynchronous transaction.

Long-lived Transactions

By communicating asynchronously, you've eliminated the real-time constraint of the transaction. You can make your request in the middle of the night. Even if a human agent must review your order, that person need not be available at the time you submit it. Although the vendor's voice-mail system must be able to accept calls at a reasonable rate, the actual transaction system that processes the request benefits from the scalability discussed in Chapter 9. Even if the transaction system goes offline, all orders will get processed in due time as long as customers can submit voice-mail orders. You can see how a reliable asynchronous messaging system is key to long-lived, loosely coupled asynchronous transactions.

Isolation Without Locking

You've also eliminated the need for record locking. So long as all requests are submitted through a single queue, the ticket agency can process its requests serially. And provided only one ticket request is being processed at a time, the application doesn't need to simulate serialization by locking resources.

Compensating Transactions

Once a transaction has been committed, it can no longer be aborted. Yet in the real world, there are often times when the effects of a transaction must be undone. The problem is that some transactions can't be reversed because their effects are permanent, and/or conditions have so changed over time that restoring the previous state would be inappropriate. As an example, consider a transaction that triggers the manufacturing of an item. Materials are consumed, and money is spent. It's impossible to simply wipe out the transaction. You can't un-manufacture the item. Instead, other actions must be taken, such as charging the customer a cancellation fee and offering the item for sale to other parties. In the earlier example of an unscrupulous travel aggregator who cancelled airline tickets at the last minute, we saw how the airline chose to put those seats on sale at a discount in order to make sure they'd be sold and the airplane would be full.

These are examples of *compensating transactions* that can be applied after an original transaction has been committed in order to undo its effects, without necessarily returning resources to their original states. Many transaction managers support compensating transactions—and as we'll see in the case of long-lived, loosely coupled asynchronous web services, compensating transactions can actually be used instead of resource locking.

Optimism

ACID-style transactions are *optimistic*, and assume a high likelihood of success. You can imagine a human coordinator of a simple two-phase commit transaction commanding the participants. Phase One: "Okay, here's what you need to do. [Coordinator enumerates the requirements.] Has everyone prepared for the transaction by safely storing the results? Good." Phase Two, after receiving affirmative votes from all participants: "Now everyone...GO!" There's no need for the coordinator to ask whether anyone was unsuccessful, since all of the participants promised in Phase One that they could do as requested. The key to the success (and integrity) of the transaction is the locking of the resources between these two phases.

On the other hand, a loosely coupled transaction coordinator must take a *pessimistic* view of a transaction's outcome. Even with a reliable messaging protocol, many other errors can occur due to the long-term nature of the transaction. Rather than reserve their resources in advance, loosely coupled participants prepare compensating transactions that will undo the local effects in case the first phase is unsuccessful. If the transaction is later aborted, all participants execute their compensating transactions.

When using compensating transactions, our human coordinator might say in Phase One, "Okay, here's what you need to do. Don't do it yet, but in case this doesn't work, I want each of you to figure out ahead of time how to recover. Now everyone...GO!" Then, in Phase Two: "Great...did that work for everyone, or do we all need to run our back-out scenarios?"

Compensating transactions are one of the technologies that decouple systems from one another, and are a first step towards filling in the missing pieces of complex web services.

———————

In this chapter we've covered not only the foundational technologies of transaction processing, but also the challenges and some of the solutions for transactions that support complex web services. Much of what we've explored is already available in one form or another, although not necessarily as adopted and universally accepted standards. In the next chapter, we'll look at the future of long-term, loosely coupled asynchronous transactions in the context of inter-company workflow and business-process automation.

Chapter 12

Orchestration

If there's a singular bold vision for the future of web services, it's to automate workflows and the complex business processes between organizations. Not surprisingly, this is also the vision of the web-services puzzle with the greatest number of missing pieces. The vision suggests a fundamental shift in the way we'll build future applications, based on long-lived loosely coupled asynchronous transactions.

The terms *business process* and *workflow automation* aren't in the everyday vocabularies of many programmers who build only simple applications. Even developers who are familiar with ACID-style transactions and the two-phase commit protocol are frequently turned off by these phrases, which sound like hype and consultant-speak to those who are more comfortable working with languages like C++, Java, or Visual Basic than a business-process modeling language. But if you think business-process automation is hocus-pocus or hype, you might be surprised at how far the field has come as a pragmatic, implementable discipline. Programmers can now model and develop complex business processes in much the same way they write stand-alone applications, using both text and visual tools.

Business Processes

As discussed in the previous chapter and illustrated in Figure 12-1, transactions manage and coordinate multiple tasks.

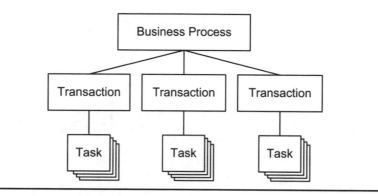

Figure 12-1: The Business-Process Hierarchy

In turn, a business process consists of multiple transactions and *workflows*, or specifications for routing documents to the applications and users that implement the business process. *Orchestration,* an even newer term, more accurately describes the way web services coordinate complex multi-party business processes.

Ten key concepts support loosely coupled inter-organizational business processes. We've already discussed some of them earlier in this book, but the following definitions describe how they fit into the context of orchestration:

- **Loose Coupling**. More than any other single factor, the understanding and practice of loose coupling by architects and developers determines the success of external business-process integration. Aside from the technical advantages, there's a business reality that mandates loose coupling: A company can't trust its partners' systems to behave themselves if granted tightly coupled access to its internal resources. Very few companies allow even a long-time trusted business partner to directly lock or otherwise control local resources—nor should they.
- **Document-style interaction**. Chapter 9 showed the importance of moving from the remote procedure call (RPC) mod-

el of interaction to one based on self-contained documents. In this chapter, we'll see even more convincing examples of the value of documents.

- **Reliable asynchronous messaging**. When we give up the simplicity of synchronous communications, we also lose the ability for participants to be promptly informed of software, hardware, and communications failures. Without notification, the participants can't take responsibility for handling such errors, so they depend on a reliable asynchronous messaging system.

- **Compensation**. Long-lived, loosely coupled asynchronous transactions provide a foundation for external business-process integration, but they can't use the resource locking typically employed in ACID-style transaction systems. Compensating transactions are therefore critical for successful orchestration.

- **Representing processes in XML**. Just as XML is key to the success of the fundamental web-services protocols, business processes will also be represented in XML. It may take some time, however, until XML-based business-processes standards can be agreed to and widely adopted. Chapter 9 discussed the importance of moving business logic out of hard-coded applications, and instead expressing it either within self-contained XML-based documents or via reference to such documents available to all parties.

- **Routing**. A method of routing documents (as described in Chapter 10) is needed to support the many potential participants and interactions in a complex, real-world business process. The routing must also be flexible enough to be established at runtime, so that it can support ad-hoc changes to business processes.

- **Dynamic processes**. Not only can document routing be specified on-the-fly, but so can the business logic of processes as represented in XML.

- **Complex outcomes**. In tightly coupled, ACID-style transactions, either all participants succeed or all are instructed to abort. But in the real world, things aren't always so black and white. Complex business processes require transactions that can complete successfully, despite the failures of some participants.

- **Negotiated commitments.** All participants in traditional tightly coupled transactions must make their commitments at roughly the same time, at least within the same phase of a multi-phase transaction. We'll see how this constraint can be relaxed in a loosely coupled business-process transaction, so that transactions can map onto real-world needs more accurately.

- **Distributed state.** A complex business process may not be under the control of a single entity, which implies that the current state of a process may not be known centrally, and certainly not by all participants in real time.

In the sections that follow we'll explore the pieces of the business-process automation puzzle that we haven't already introduced.

Process Representation in XML

The business logic of traditional applications is embodied within the software. The decisions that must be made and the actions that must be taken are coded by programmers during development. But if a business process invokes many applications that run on separate systems, the logic of the overall business process is actually distributed among all of those applications and systems. Not only is this a maintenance nightmare, but a complete sense of the business process exists only to the extent that each of the participants maintains its own view of it. There's no centralized way to understand, manage, or modify such a distributed business process; it's based on conventions and implicit understandings that are hard-coded into each of the co-operating applications. It's tightly coupled, inflexible, and brittle.

As explained in Chapter 9, document-style messaging allows business logic to be moved out of applications and into self-contained documents. Orchestration does this in two ways. First, it uses XML documents to describe business processes in terms of the *public behavior* of the individual participating systems. These documents are essentially scripts, or executable, structured-text representations of traditional flowcharts. These scripts specify activities, such as *invoke* (interact with a web service), *receive* (wait to be invoked by another process), *call* (start a process and await its completion), *spawn* (start a process that runs in parallel with the current one), and *fault* (signal an error). This means that one participant, acting in the role of a *coordinator*, can transmit a scripted behavior to another participant at runtime. The receiving participant only needs a generic *business-process engine* that can parse the XML-formatted script, and follow the instructions it contains.

Second, orchestration uses XML to define the entire multi-participant business process, including all of the messages that pass from one participant to another. Such *business-protocol documents* allow all participants to have a common understanding of the big picture, without the need to share the details of their internal private behaviors—in other words, while remaining loosely coupled.

Although the orchestration coordinator is not privy to the internals of every participant, its awareness of the components of the overall process being executed by each participant enables it to monitor those remote activities. This isn't possible without the common understanding of the overall process, or *shared context,* that's achieved by exchanging the business protocol in XML format.

Dynamic Processes

The goal of traditional business-process modeling is to arrive at a well-documented, thoroughly understood process. Unfortunately, this encourages static business relationships in an era when the desire for business agility is skyrocketing. By removing business-process definitions from within applications and instead expressing them as external, sharable XML documents, process definitions no longer need to be static. A complex multi-party business process can be altered and customized merely by modifying its XML description. In fact, if the definition of a business process is contained within the associated documents, the process can be different every time it's executed. Orchestration provides the ultimate agility by allowing business processes to be created and modified on the fly, thereby enabling loose coupling at runtime.

Complex Outcomes

In simple transactions, all of the participants experience the same results; a transaction either succeeds or fails. But in real-world processes, some participants may succeed while others do not. Such multiple-choice processes require extra steps, which can only be modeled by using an orchestrated process and not via simple transactions.

Consider a travel reservation that includes the following rules for airline bookings:

- There are two possible itineraries. The first is preferable because it's cheaper, but it requires flying on two different airlines (A and B) with a stopover and change of planes. The second itinerary is a non-stop flight on airline C, and should be booked only if the first is unavailable.
- If either reservation on airline A or B fails, then both should be aborted.
- Alternatively, if the segments on both A & B are available, then the reservation on C should be aborted.

Imagine another example in which a participant requests five separate resources, but only three of them are available. Using traditional techniques, the entire transaction and all component tasks would be aborted. But using orchestration, it's possible to specify, for instance, that only two are required—either a particular two, or any combination that can be specified using Boolean algebra. The two that are never committed are ignored, and the one that's committed, but not used is released. Orchestration allows applications to express such arbitrarily complex business rules for complex outcomes.

Negotiated Commitments

Participants in orchestrated-process transactions may *offer* to commit resources even when no such commitments are requested in advance. For example, an airline's system can voluntarily reserve a seat early in a more complex travel-booking process, before the stage where it's required to do so. Such early commitments can even be made with *caveats* or *reservations*. If a participant offers a resource without pre-committing it, an additional step is then required to secure that commitment. Any resource committed early depends on a compensating transaction in case the resource ultimately isn't required.

Distributed State

If you think of a business process in terms of a flowchart (or an XML representation of a flowchart), you can imagine the equivalent of a *You Are Here* marker marking your place in the process at any given point in time. Ideally, all participants should consistently, unambiguously, and at all times know the position of that marker indicating the current *state* of the overall process. When systems are tightly coupled, this is a reasonable objective. But when systems are loosely coupled, linked asynchronously, and controlled by different entities, often it's not possible to know for certain which tasks and transactions have been completed and which have not at any given instant.

Orchestration solves this problem by supporting a shared *coordination context* in which the state of the business process is distributed among participants. At any one moment, the state of a business process may not be known at a single location or within a single system. Each participant may have a different understanding of the workflow's state, potentially for long periods of time, but they can depend on a reliable asynchronous messaging infrastructure to not lose the documents that maintain state. Among the key benefits of orchestration are the coordinator's ability to manage distributed state, monitor the participants, and initiate orderly cancellations and compensations in such a complex environment.

State of the Art

Inter-company business processes have been an elusive goal for many years, and they'll remain bleeding-edge technology for some time to come, with relatively few enterprises attempting to implement them. But web services will ultimately change all that. For the first time the goal is achievable, and not just for large companies who are desperate for inter-company business-process management. Once we get past the immaturity of the protocols and software and other obstacles common to many web-services technologies, automated business processes via web services will become practical even for companies of modest means and requirements.

At the time of this writing (early 2003), the standards for workflow, orchestration, and business-process modeling in a web-services environment were evolving rapidly. By the time you read this, the associated protocols may well have been adopted, and the software toolkits made available. But there's still another gating event: that lack of definition of business semantics mentioned repeatedly in this book. All of the great web-services technology for linking business partners is for naught, unless and until the parties can agree on the structure of the business documents that will be exchanged as part of the business process. In most industries, it's these lagging semantic definitions and not the orchestration technology that will delay the adoption of inter-company business-process management.

Even if the orchestration technologies aren't yet mature and the business-semantics problems haven't yet been solved for your industry or application, don't let that keep you from deploying simpler web services for more humble applications. Basic request/response (synchronous) web services can use traditional ACID-style transaction management today, and it's only a matter of time before you'll be able to move up the evolutionary tree from transactions that encompass tasks to long-lived, loosely coupled asynchronous transactions—and eventually to fully orchestrated business processes.

Keep the concepts of orchestration in the back of your mind as you embark on simpler, more pragmatic web-services projects, and reflect on this long-term vision as you evolve your service-oriented architectures. The complete orchestration of multi-party business processes—such as automating the workflow of complete value chains—will eventually deliver tremendous return on your web-services investment, so it's crucial that you, your systems, and your applications get in a position to take advantage of it when the time is right.

Chapter 13

Security—The Challenges

"The stuff that keeps you up at night is security."
—Tony Scott, CTO, General Motors[19]

When a group of software development managers was asked to identify the obstacles to the deployment of web services, nearly half (47 percent) pointed to security. That was more than twice the percentage of other challenges mentioned, such as bandwidth and access issues (21 percent) and interoperability problems (13 percent).[20] While managers justifiably fear hackers and loss of confidential customer information such as they've experienced with their e-commerce web sites, web services present even greater security challenges that managers haven't previously encountered.

The good news is that Internet security technologies for both the World Wide Web and web services have progressed beyond the rocket-science phase. The Ph.D.'s have completed their work, leaving us with well-understood technologies for encryption, authentication, non-repudiation, and trust. The bad news is that we've now got to figure out how to stitch these technologies together into an end-to-end security quilt that meets the needs of complex web-services applications. What keeps IT managers up at night is wondering when that quilt will be completed—and whether they should try to move forward with piecemeal solutions in the meantime.

In this chapter, we'll explore the unique challenges of security for web services. We'll begin with the concept of *security contexts*, highlighting the variations in security requirements among different types of web services and the more familiar security technologies of the World Wide Web. Then we'll introduce the building blocks of Internet security, followed by a detailed analysis of the security requirements for web services. In the following chapter, we'll explore the various solutions to these web-services security challenges.

Security Contexts

You'll recall that in Chapter 5 we segregated web services according to their complexity. One of the starkest distinctions between simple and complex web services is the difference in their security requirements. What works well for simple web services (most notably those that are synchronous) doesn't come close to solving the security problems encountered by more demanding asynchronous services.

To get a handle on the differences in requirements between these categories of web services, let's look at the *security context*, or the environment in which a system's security technologies must function. The security context includes two properties or dimensions: space and time. The table in Figure 13-1 summarizes the differences among three security contexts: those of the World Wide Web, simple web services, and complex web services.

	World Wide Web	Simple Web Services	Complex Web Services
Space	In-Transit Only	In-Transit and Multi-Hop	In-Transit, Multi-Hop and In-Storage
Time	Seconds or Minutes	Seconds or Minutes	Perhaps Years

Figure 13-1: Security Contexts

Let's take a few moments to explore this table in more detail, so that we can understand the fundamental differences in the security requirements of the three environments.

Space

Each security context has certain physical boundaries that create a defined space within which information must be secured. As you can see from the table in Figure 13-1, there are three possible locations to consider: in-transit, multi-hop, and in-storage.

In-Transit

While data is being transmitted from one system to another, it's said to be *in transit*. For example, on the World Wide Web the Secure Sockets Layer (SSL) protocol is used to encrypt data as it moves between web browsers and web servers, as illustrated in Figure 13-2.

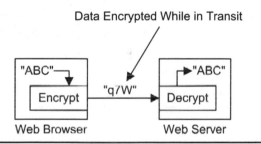

Figure 13-2: In-Transit Encryption via SSL

Using SSL, data is encrypted at one end of the connection just prior to transmission and decrypted immediately upon receipt at the other end. SSL is a *transport-layer* security technology that provides a *point-to-point* encrypted transmission path between two systems. In other words, the security provided by SSL only exists while information is in transit between systems, not while it's stored on the systems themselves. The web's standards and protocols don't address the security requirements of the computer systems on which the browser or server software run—only the links between them, so the web's security context is limited to in-transit security, as illustrated in Figure 13-3.

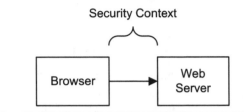

Figure 13-3: In-Transit Security Context for the World Wide Web

The simplest synchronous web services operate in a security context that's essentially the same as that of the World Wide Web, so SSL is often sufficient to meet their security requirements.

Multi-Hop

More elaborate synchronous web services and all asynchronous web services operate in a security context that's substantially broader and more complex than that of the World Wide Web. Specifically, such web services may communicate through *intermediaries*, in which case messages will make multiple *hops* between systems or hosts. This is where we begin to see a divergence between the security contexts of the web and those of web services, and in the ability of SSL to meet the needs of those web services. In a multi-hop topology, as illustrated in Figure 13-4, SSL encrypts and decrypts data each time it's sent over a point-to-point link.

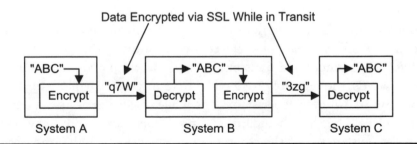

Figure 13-4: SSL for Web Services

There are two problems with using SSL in this application. First, unlike topologies that consist of only two systems, the exchange of XML documents between complex web services may involve a number of stops along the way. Some data should be able to be seen, interpreted, and optionally modified by these intermediate nodes (e.g., System B in Figure 13-4), while other data must remain encrypted and unreadable by the same intermediate nodes. SSL only encrypts data while in transit, so the data is fully decrypted on each intermediate node and is no longer secure. The second problem with using SSL in this case is that if the objective is to deliver data securely from System A to System C, twice as many encryption and decryption operations will be performed than are required.

In-Storage

Complex web services present yet another challenge not shared with either simpler web services or the World Wide Web: the need to secure information while stored as well as while it's in transit. Consider a confidential document, such as a medical record, sent from System A to System C as shown in Figure 13-4. The medical record may need to be stored on System C for later retrieval. For that matter, the record may need to be securely stored on Systems A or B as well. But SSL explicitly decrypts data as it arrives at each new system, so if received data is to be stored securely on any system, it must be re-encrypted via a technology other than SSL.

If a document used in a web-services transaction must be confidential, the web service's *security context* encompasses the various systems on which that document may reside even temporarily, as well as the infrastructure that connects those systems. The greater the number of systems that have access to the document, the broader the spatial scope of the security context, and the more demanding the security requirements.

Time

The security contexts shown in Figure 13-1 are also defined according to time, or how *long* security must be preserved. For the World Wide Web and the simplest web services, data must only be secured during transmission from one system to another. But for complex web services, data must also be protected during the time it's stored—potentially for very long periods. The complexity of the security requirements increases with a corresponding increase in the time dimension of a security context.

On the web and for simple web services, the time component ranges from a few seconds to a few minutes, so security requirements are comparatively simple and short-lived. A web browser sends a request to a web server, then waits for and receives a response—and that's the end of the relationship between the two entities. If it takes more than a minute or so, a timeout occurs, and the entire process must begin again. Since the time dimension of the web's security context is so short, the security technologies can be relatively simple.

Underlying SSL is the web's HyperText Transfer Protocol (HTTP). Although this is a *connection-oriented protocol*, it only supports very short-lived connections—those that consist of no more than a single request/response exchange. Yet because the security contexts of both the web and simple web services also exist for such short periods of time, both can be based on the primitive security features of HTTP and SSL. The short-lived transport-layer connections between browser and web server or between web-services requestors and providers are sufficient for the brief duration of these applications.

When a somewhat longer-term relationship is required on the web, it can be managed through the use of *cookies* or other means, but no comparable standard exists for web services. And truly long-running asynchronous web services require that security be *persistent* and maintained over an extended period of time. This is a challenge rarely encountered in simpler World Wide Web applications, which is another reason why the security requirements for complex web services exceed the solutions offered by the web's existing standards and protocols.

Security for Asynchronous Web Services

The security context matrix has helped us see that the security requirements of simple web services are similar to those of the World Wide Web, and that many simple web services' security requirements can be met by using standard web protocols. HTTP and SSL provide a shortcut for simple web services that have the following attributes:

- They involve only two entities or endpoints.
- The entities are only connected for relatively short periods of time (seconds or minutes).
- All that needs to transpire between the two entities can be accomplished within the context of those short-lived connections.

For the remainder of this chapter, we'll take on the more difficult security challenges of external, asynchronous, and aggregated web services, beginning with an analysis of the building blocks of security.

The Building Blocks

Security is a broad topic, but it can be broken down into five very specific elements or building blocks, as illustrated in Figure 13-5. These building blocks are applicable to virtually all data-processing environments, including the World Wide Web and web services.

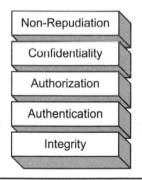

Figure 13-5: The Building Blocks of Security

- **Integrity** ensures that documents, messages, and their components have not been altered.
- **Authentication** guarantees that an entity (a person or system) is who or what it claims to be.
- **Authorization** determines the privileges available to an authenticated entity.

- **Confidentiality** ensures that unauthorized parties can't read documents, messages, or their components.
- **Non-repudiation** prohibits an entity from denying that it sent or received a message.

Integrity

Perhaps no other concept is as fundamental to security as our ability to know for certain that the documents and messages we receive haven't been altered, either maliciously or due to technical errors such as packets damaged in transit. Credentials presented by a consumer or business partner can't be trusted unless you're confident they haven't been forged. Likewise, a digital receipt is of little value unless it can be shown to be tamper-proof. Without integrity there can be no authentication, authorization, confidentiality, or non-repudiation.

SSL is a sufficient solution for the integrity of simple synchronous web services where the security context consists of only a single pair of endpoints, and the relationship between them lasts for no more than the time it takes to exchange a single pair of request/response messages. But SSL is inadequate for complex web services, whose unique requirements include both *end-to-end integrity* and *component-level integrity*.

End-to-End Integrity

SSL can ensure the integrity of information between a single pair of entities, but not if the information must pass through one or more intermediaries. Once data has been decrypted on an intermediate system, SSL can no longer guarantee the integrity of the original data. This is the fatal flaw of using transport-layer encryption to try to guarantee the integrity of data in any but the simplest of web-services architectures. Even some synchronous web services make use of intermediaries, so SSL may not be adequate even for them.

Component Integrity

Transport-layer encryption provides all-or-nothing integrity. In this case, a stream of data containing packets, messages, and documents is decrypted in its entirety, so there's no way to allow an intermediary to modify one portion of a message or document while prohibiting that intermediary from modifying other portions. In other words, if any of the data can be altered, there's no way to keep other data from being altered as well.

Intermediaries can be used to perform *transformations* that intentionally modify portions of messages or documents. For instance, a transformation service might convert an invoice amount from US dollars to Euros. However, this intermediary should not be allowed to modify other components or elements of the message. Web services must be able to guarantee the integrity of information at multiple levels, such as the following:

- **Documents**. In some applications, integrity should be maintained at the document level. For example, a contract or other traditional document should be guaranteed intact.
- **XML elements**. Some applications require that the integrity of individual elements within an XML document be maintained separately. This allows some elements of the document to be modified by intermediate processes, yet guarantees protection to elements that must not be changed. For instance, as documents are routed through various stages of electronic approval, the documents may accumulate digital signatures, but the original content should not be altered.
- **SOAP messages**. XML payloads may be carried within SOAP messages, and in some instances integrity must be maintained at the SOAP level rather than for each individual document.
- **Digital credentials**. The integrity of usernames, passwords, and digital certificates must also be guaranteed, sometimes independently of the documents and messages to which they apply.

Authentication

After a foundation of integrity is established, authentication is the next building block for web-services security. Authentication allows web-service requestors and providers to verify the identity of the entities with which they interact.

Usernames and passwords are by far the most common form of authentication on the World Wide Web, and this web-based approach to authentication may meet the needs of particularly simple web services. But many web services have requirements that exceed what's available from the web's security mechanisms. Five authentication requirements for web services go beyond what we typically encounter on the web:

- Loosely coupled authentication
- Bi-directional authentication
- Credential consolidation
- Multi-party authentication
- Durable authentication

Loosely Coupled Authentication Models

Web-services endpoints that are owned by different entities will probably have their own models, systems, and standards for authentication. One system may be based on Kerberos (an authentication system developed by MIT and used within Microsoft's .NET), while another may use *public-key infrastructure* (PKI). In order for these web services to work together, there must be a trusted mechanism by which the disparate models can exchange identities. And because authentication models can vary so greatly, such a system must be loosely coupled just as web services themselves are loosely coupled. Well-designed web services must be flexible in their expectations of other systems' authentication models.

Bi-Directional Authentication

Authentication is accomplished when one entity presents its *credentials* to the other, as illustrated for the World Wide Web in Figure 13-6.

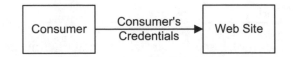

Figure 13-6: Consumer Use of Credentials

E-commerce web sites authenticate consumers through a combination of usernames, email addresses, passwords, and other schemes, and many simple web services can use these same techniques. But authentication in the opposite direction is rare on the web. Although server-side digital certificates are always used in conjunction with SSL, few web-site visitors bother to check them. In fact, few consumers know how to verify the identity of the sites they visit, and even fewer do so as a matter of course.

There have been many cases where high-visibility sites have been hijacked, and web-site content delivered from unauthorized servers. Sometimes going to the wrong web site is a simple user error—for example, www.whitehouse.gov is an official site of the President of the United States, whereas www.whitehouse.com is a porn site. In the case of consumer e-commerce, the risks due to weak authentication are mostly embarrassing rather than costly.

For web services the need for bi-directional authentication (as illustrated in Figure 13-7) is more critical.

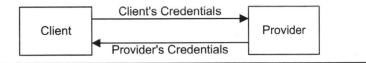

Figure 13-7: Bi-Directional Authentication

There are three reasons why this bi-directional authentication is required for web services. First, the consumer-protection laws that apply to individuals using their credit cards online don't similarly protect businesses that utilize web services. A US consumer's liability for fraudulent purchases made using his or her credit card is limited by statute to US$50. No such limits exist in the US for businesses-to-business transactions.

Second, the values of business-to-business web-services transactions are typically much greater than those in business-to-consumer commerce. Such values can be either monetary or derived from the confidential nature of information being exchanged, since the unauthorized or inadvertent publication of a trade secret can be very expensive.

Third, web services are based on unattended automated systems, so there's an increased risk that damage may go undetected. Whether due to an error or a malicious attack, automated web services that run amok can create substantial liabilities. When using web services, bi-directional authentication can be critical.

Credential Consolidation

In the typical multi-tiered architecture used by e-commerce web sites and web services alike, consumers and requestors don't interact directly with back-end systems such as databases or legacy applications. Instead there's typically at least one intermediate system—often an application server or *portal*—that accepts requests from consumers and communicates with the database or other back-end system on their behalf. In this sense, the application server is acting as an *agent* of the requestor or consumer, as illustrated in Figure 13-8.

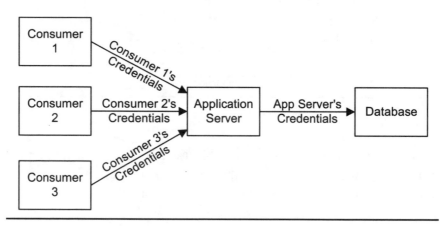

Figure 13-8: Credential Consolidation

For its own protection, a back-end database system must authenticate its users—but in the above example, the actual *user* of the database is the application server rather than a consumer. The typical solution to this problem is to develop business logic within the application server to perform both the authentication and authorization functions (in other words, to authenticate the consumers and also to determine their privileges). The application server must have broad *superuser* privileges on the database system, and then parcel out these privileges on a consumer-by-consumer basis. In this instance, the authorization logic is located within the application server—which is not particularly appropriate if authentication must be performed in other locations as well. This also creates an additional vulnerability: If a hacker can gain access to the application server, he or she will then have superuser privileges to read and modify the database.

Furthermore, this architecture destroys the ability of the database to discriminate or even identify individual consumers. The application server can pass along the consumer-identifying data to the database, but this requires a custom application on the database system to enforce consumer-specific authorization and authentication policies. Such one-off applications can be difficult and expensive to maintain.

Multi-Party Authentication

When web services are aggregated, it results in a problem similar to the one faced by aggregators on the World Wide Web, such as travel-reservation services. When an individual consumer uses a web browser to visit a travel aggregator's web site and make airline reservations, there are actually three authentication operations required, as shown in 13-9.

Figure 13-9: The ID-Passthrough Problem

Not only must the consumer authenticate him- or herself to the travel site (to guarantee payment, for example), but the travel site must also present credentials for itself *and* pass-through the consumer's credentials to the airline. The travel site must provide the consumer's name, address, and frequent-flyer numbers, and it must authenticate itself in order to receive its commission. When aggregated web services are built upon many such relationships—linearly or hierarchically—the challenges of multi-party authentication become increasingly complex.

Where to Provide Authentication Services

After deciding what to authenticate, the second question an implementer of web services must answer is: At what point in the architecture should authentication be provided? Previously, we looked at a model where the application server was responsible for authentication. On the World Wide Web, this function is performed either in the transport layer (using the authentication facilities built into HTTP) or within the custom-written web applications. Neither of these solutions is ideal, even for e-commerce web sites. But although we've become accustomed to them both as consumers and as developers, a better and more standardized solution for web-services authentication is required. (We'll look more closely at the question of *where* to provide security solutions in the next chapter.)

Durable Authentication

Another requirement for web-services authentication is *durability* or *persistence*. Using the mechanisms built into HTTP, authentication is valid only for a single request/response exchange. Although usernames and passwords need not be re-entered, they're re-transmitted by the browser or web-services requestor each time a request is made. Due to the *stateless* nature of the HTTP family of transports, there is no association of one request/response exchange to the next, and each subsequent request must therefore include the authentication credentials.

When it comes to asynchronous web services, there's a need for authentication to persist far longer than the time during which two endpoints are communicating. In our example of the online bookstore in Chapter 8, the session during which the customer's credentials were presented was terminated once the order had been placed. However, those credentials must be accessible for as long as the merchant retains the order information, perhaps for many years.

This presents two challenges. First, the authentication credentials must be retained along with the documents and messages that move through the web-services pipeline. (In some cases, the credentials will be contained within the documents.) Second, there must be a mechanism for verifying credentials long after they're initially presented, and it must work for an appliation that may not be able to connect to the system that originated the transaction.

A web site's server can query a user for additional authentication information at any time, because the browser and server remain connected for the life of the session. But asynchronous web services often need to verify credentials or perform other authentication tasks long after the consumer or web-services system involved with the transaction have been disconnected. This is also a requirement for non-repudiation, since it may be necessary to re-establish the authenticity of the parties months or years after a transaction has been completed.

Authentication is made even more difficult when there's a break in the chain of trust—for instance, when a digital certificate expires or an intermediate *certificate authority* goes out of business. These are very real challenges in situations where credentials must be stored and retained for extended periods.

Authorization

Once an entity's identity has been authenticated, the next step is to determine what that entity is authorized to do. Some of the authorization challenges faced by web services include the need for loosely coupled authorization models, authorization durability, identity consolidation, and service-level authorization.

Loosely Coupled Authorization Models

Two endpoints controlled by different entities will probably have their own models and systems for authorization as well as authentication. One system may simply associate usernames with directory and file privileges, while another might depend on a more elaborate rules-based system for authorization. In order for these web services to work together, there must be a mechanism by which the multiple models can exchange identities and mediate their authorization concept differences.

Durable Authorization

Because complex asynchronous web services may involve long-lived transactions—particularly those supporting external business processes—it's quite possible that authorizations and permissions will change over a transaction's lifetime. This presents a number of challenges that can be difficult to resolve. For example, when a customer's purchasing limits are lowered, is that customer allowed to increase the quantities on already-approved orders? It's one thing to code the business logic that implements such policies within a stand-alone application, but it's far more difficult to do so in the distributed asynchronous environment of web services.

Identity Consolidation

From our discussion of credential consolidation, you'll recall that in many application environments, the identity of the individual user is lost when back-end system access is performed through an agent. The problem is compounded for authorization, as it's no longer possible to make decisions about user privileges once a user's identity has been lost or consolidated.

Service-Level Authorization

Ultimately, web services will require an authorization model of their own, beyond what currently exists for the World Wide Web. Such a system must determine who has access to what services, and within the context of an individual service, what those individuals are allowed to do. Evolving web-services protocols address these unique requirements, determining which specific individuals or other services are allowed to execute certain methods and which are authorized to modify specific XML elements.

Confidentiality

By combining the building blocks of integrity, authentication, and authorization, we can create confidentiality: the ability to ensure that documents, messages, or their components can't be read by any other than authorized entities. Integrity gives us the knowledge that information hasn't been intentionally or otherwise altered; authentication allows us to identify entities; and authorization lets us determine whether those entities should be allowed access to the confidential information.

Confidentiality is often confused with integrity, and it's true that the two are very closely related. But integrity only allows us to determine whether information has been modified, and only coincidentally keeps that information out of the hands of unauthorized entities. Encryption guarantees integrity while prohibiting information from being understood by unauthorized entities, but it's quite possible to guarantee the integrity of data without encrypting it. One such example would be when a digitally signed document is sent as clear or unencrypted text, which can be read by anyone who intercepts it but can't be altered without detection.

On the World Wide Web and for simple synchronous web services, transport-layer encryption (SSL) is the most common way of maintaining the confidentiality of information in narrow and short-lived security contexts. But as we've seen before, the limitations of SSL quickly become apparent when applied to the broader, long-lived security context of asynchronous web services.

Using SSL, once data is received at its ultimate destination or at an intermediate location, it's restored to its unencrypted format. Data stored on disk or even retained in RAM can no longer be considered confidential, except to the extent that it's protected using additional methods.

For example, if you download account information from a banking web site using SSL, it will be protected while in transit. But if you save that information on your disk drive, it becomes as vulnerable as any other data stored there. Protecting data stored on users' systems or on a web server falls within the domain of security techniques that are beyond the scope of SSL, and hence require more sophisticated solutions.

Web services have confidentiality requirements that extend beyond what SSL provides and fall into four categories: end-to-end encryption, transport independence, encrypted storage and element-level encryption.

End-to-End Encryption

This challenge is similar to the problem of integrity. In the same way that SSL can't guarantee that data hasn't been modified on intermediate systems, it also can't protect that data from unauthorized access. Data is unencrypted—and therefore accessible—on each intermediate system between the endpoints.

As we saw in Figure 13-4 earlier in this chapter, any data flowing from A to C is temporarily decrypted while on B. A and C can't depend on SSL for confidentiality, since SSL doesn't support end-to-end encryption. The solution is true end-to-end encryption, as illustrated in Figure 13-10.

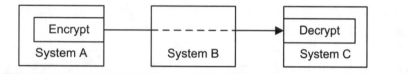

Figure 13-10: End-to-End Encryption

End-to-end encryption can't be implemented in the transport layer. Instead, it must be implemented either within the applications that run on Systems A and C—or better still, in standard software libraries or hardware or software firewalls. (We'll look at these options in the next chapter.)

Transport Independence

The World Wide Web uses HTTP(S) over TCP/IP as its transport protocols, but web services aren't tied to a single transport protocol. Since a web service might use HTTP for one exchange and SMTP or FTP for another, it's inappropriate to implement encryption uniquely within each of these protocols. The solution should be moved up the protocol stack, so that encryption is applied to web-services documents and messages rather than to the transport protocols that carry them.

Encrypted Storage

Because SSL only encrypts documents and messages while in transit, those messages must be re-encrypted using another technology if they're to remain confidential while stored. Looking again at Figure 13-4, let's suppose B acts as a third-party auditing web service, maintaining a log of messages between A and C. While it's important for B to store copies of the messages, it may be inappropriate for B to be able to read them. An end-to-end encryption scheme will prohibit B from decrypting the messages, but allow it to store them in their encrypted form.

One common mistake is to assume that storing information in an encrypted form is the same as limiting access to that information. Encryption is a helpful tool, but it isn't the complete solution. If hackers can reach your information, encryption can keep them from reading it, but there are also two important reasons why you should take reasonable steps to keep the hackers from getting to the information in the first place.

First, even if they can't exploit the encrypted information, they might be able to do harm in other ways, just by virtue of being inside your systems. For example, they might find a way to delete an important document, even though they can't read it.

Second, allowing hackers to gain the knowledge that a document or file exists may be enough to cause you serious harm. For instance, a personnel document may be encrypted, but if the file name happens to be the employee's US Social Security Number, hackers can identify employees and collect valid SSNs. (But no one would be so foolish as to design a system that used SSNs as filenames, right? Wrong! It happens.)

Element-Level Encryption

Because simple web services involve only two endpoints (the requestor and the provider), there's no need for the individual elements within the messages that pass between them to be encrypted individually. These web services can use SSL or a comparable transport-layer encryption scheme, even though such a scheme has no awareness of the structure of the data it encrypts. Transport-layer encryption indiscriminately makes *all* data inaccessible to third parties. It's a brute-force approach, with no way to let selected participants gain access to some portions of a message but not to others. 13-11 illustrates a web-service message *envelope*, which in turn contains a *header*, a *body*, and (within the header or body) individual *elements*.

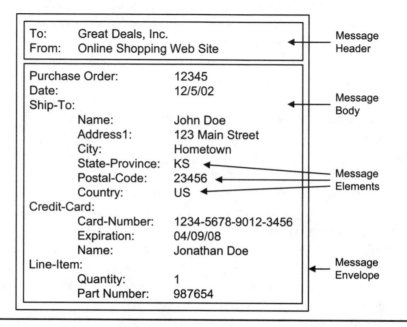

Figure 13-11: Web-Service Message

Using SSL or another transport-layer encryption scheme, a message such as this would be encrypted in its entirety, but only while in transit between two nodes. This is a problem for multi-hop web services, which often need to protect the elements or fields of web-service messages individually. Consider the requirements of an aggregated web service, as illustrated in Figure 13-12.

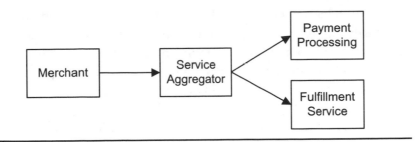

Figure 13-12: Web-Services Message Flow

The merchant's system creates an order such as the one shown in Figure 13-11, and forwards it to the service aggregator. The aggregator's system must be able to read and understand most of the message, but there's no reason it should have access to the consumer's credit-card information. The aggregator should merely forward that data as-is to a payment-processing service. Therefore, the merchant uses *element-level encryption* to keep the consumer's credit card data confidential end-to-end, or all the way through to the payment-processing service. Element-level encryption protects the individual elements or fields within a web-services message, as illustrated in Figure 13-13.

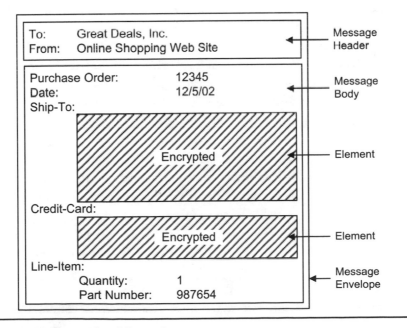

Figure 13-13: Element-Level Encryption

The merchant encrypts the ship-to data in a manner that it can be read by the aggregator (who perhaps handles customer service, and therefore needs to know the shipping address), by the fulfillment service, and by the payment processor. However, it encrypts the credit-card data in such a way that it can be decrypted only by the payment-processing service. The message passes through the aggregator's system, and can even be safely stored there in case it's required at some time in the future. Likewise, the aggregator forwards the message to both the fulfillment and payment services, but only the payment processor has access to the credit-card data.

Non-Repudiation

SSL or other transport-layer encryption schemes can be used to meet many of the security needs of simple web services, much as they do on the World Wide Web. But SSL has no built-in capability for non-repudiation: proof of events, such that (for example) buyers can't deny placing orders, and sellers can't deny receiving them.

The existing non-repudiation methods on the World Wide Web have been implemented by custom applications or in some cases using proprietary packages. The most familiar non-repudiation technique would be a printable receipt delivered as a web page, although this isn't particularly strong in a legal sense because it can easily be forged. Receipts offer a degree of protection for consumers, but most merchants simply rely on credit-card fraud detection to minimize risk and absorb the cost of whatever fraud can't otherwise be prevented.

Some web services can get by without a non-repudiation strategy. For instance, web services that don't include commercial transactions typically don't require non-repudiation. If you query Amazon.com for the price of a book, there's no need for either you or Amazon.com to be able to prove that the event occurred. But many commercial transactions—even those conducted over simple synchronous web services—require non-repudiation for the legal protection of the business entities involved.

The techniques for establishing non-repudiation using digital certificates are well understood, although they haven't yet been universally and consistently adopted. We'll explore these solutions in the following chapter.

Defensive Security

We can't conclude our discussion of web-services security without considering the vulnerability of web services to attacks, and the measures required to defend against such attacks. Although web-services systems are susceptible to many of the same attacks as those that occur on e-commerce web sites, we'll focus our attention on the vulnerabilities unique to web services.

Denial of Service (DoS)

Network firewalls and other tools can be used to detect and block DoS attacks—attempts to disable a service by flooding it with traffic—at the network and transport layers. But web services are also vulnerable to application-layer DoS attacks. It's not enough to merely watch for packets sent to particular ports or carrying payloads based on one protocol or another. Web-services defensive systems must employ application-layer logic, such as looking for sudden increases in the number of transactions per unit time or tracking high-level business metrics (e.g., the total dollars per hour that are processed by a service).

Replay Attacks

Another application-layer attack is referred to as a *replay attack*, and occurs when a hacker captures and then repeatedly re-submits a transaction request. The damage can be similar to that caused by a DoS attack, when the system rejects the forged transactions but gets bogged down doing so. Worse still, the forged transaction may actually be accepted and acted upon. The best protections against this are strong authentication, document or message integrity, and the unique (and encrypted) identification of all transactions.

Downgrade Attacks

Security downgrades aren't attacks in the traditional sense, but they pose a risk similar to that of any explicit attack. In its simplest form, a downgrade attack occurs whenever you interact with a business partner whose security policies or practices are less robust than your own. Once you send data to a partner, the information is only protected to the extent of the partner's own security policies and practices—even if that information is encrypted. If your partner's environment isn't as secure as yours, the level of security will effectively be *downgraded* simply by virtue of your data being shared with a less robust partner. Furthermore, what guarantees do you have that your partner's security policies or practices won't change over time? A partner that meets your security requirements today may not do so tomorrow.

Now consider a scenario where your data passes through a middleman or aggregator, such as illustrated in Figure 13-12. Even if you have agreed to strong levels of authentication, encryption, and so on, the aggregator may have far less robust relationships with other entities with whom your data will be shared (such as the fulfillment service or the payment processor). Again, you may be subject to a security downgrade attack, and this may occur without your knowledge or approval.

Given all the challenges of web-servies security, perhaps it's no wonder it keeps IT managers up at night. As complex as this landscape may appear, there are solutions on the horizon, and now that we've detailed the security challenges for web services, we'll turn our attention to exploring and comparing the variety of security solutions in the chapter that follows.

Chapter 14

Security—The Solutions

Like many other mid-level supporting technologies of web services, the solutions to the security challenges are still evolving and will probably continue to evolve for a number of years. This volatility creates temporary opportunities for vendors to offer non-standard (or more accurately, *pre-standard)* workarounds to security problems, which allow their customers to deploy web services before the standardized solutions are available.

Because the security technologies are rapidly moving targets, the goal of this chapter isn't to compare the evolving competing security protocols, but rather to understand the general categories of platforms on which to deploy them, regardless of which protocols and standards are ultimately adopted. In other words, we'll be answering the question, *"Where* should I implement security?"

A complete security solution includes multiple platforms, such as network and application/XML firewalls, discrete security services, web-services networks (WSNs), and of course security code within the web-services applications themselves. We'll explore the strengths and weaknesses of these various platforms in solving the challenges posed by each of the security *building blocks* introduced in the previous chapter. The five platforms we'll consider are the following:

Network layer security includes the *Secure Sockets Layer* (SSL) protocol used by secure web sites and browsers, which offers simple and effective transport-layer encryption for temporary, point-to-point connections. Also in the category of network-layer security are *virtual private networks* (VPNs), which can link pairs of web-service endpoints.

Host-based security is implemented within a web-service application, or at least runs on the same system as the application.

Peripheral-service security solutions run on systems other than those on which the applications run, and offer security services to multiple applications within an enterprise or beyond. A peripheral-service solution is so named because it's the one option that's not part of the web-services message path. It sits on the side, and the messages between endpoints don't pass through it. A peripheral service provides functionality on an as-requested basis.

XML firewalls or proxy servers are delivered either as software products or bundled with hardware as self-contained *security appliances*. In either case an XML firewall typically runs on hardware that's separate from that on which the web-services applications it protects are running.

Web-services networks (WSN) are like EDIs' *value-added networks* (VANs), in that they offer security features as shared, centralized third-party services. But unlike VANs, WSNs are typically accessed over the Internet via VPNs or SSL rather than through dedicated circuits.

The matrix in Figure 14-1 compares how well each of the five platforms for security solutions meets the requirements of the five security building blocks introduced in the previous chapter. The ratings are approximations, and we'll explain why each solution is rated as it is in the sections that follow.

	Network Layer	Host	Peripheral Service	XML Firewall	WSN
Integrity	◒	●	○	●	◒
Confidentiality	◒	●	○	●	◒
Authentication	◒	◒	●	●	●
Authorization	○	●	●	●	●
Non-Repudiation	○	◒	◒	◒	●

● Complete solution included
◒ Partial solution included
○ Solution not included

Figure 14-1: Web-Services Security Platforms

Network-Layer Security

Network-layer security is typically implemented within *network firewalls* such as those regularly used to protect traditional IT systems. They're the foundation of security for most e-commerce web sites, but they solve only a portion of the web-services security challenges. One reason is that network firewalls are intended to *prevent* access to application servers, databases, and legacy systems rather indiscriminately, whereas web services require a different type of firewall that *enables* access.

With the exceptions of basic business-infrastructure components such as email and remote LAN access, your only applications that currently require visibility from the outside world are probably those supporting web-based e-commerce. And if you outsource your e-commerce web hosting, then there's no reason to allow *any* external access to internal systems through your Internet network firewall. As far as outbound traffic is concerned, your internal users need to reach external web sites via browsers, but that's about it. The security policies are comparatively simple, and network-layer firewalls are capable of handling a large percentage of your security needs.

Web services present an entirely different challenge, because they expose to the outside world those very same systems you've been trying to hide. In fact, you may even advertise your internal systems' web-services interfaces, possibly in public directories. Suddenly you'll have a new set of problems that your network firewalls were never intended to solve.

Ironically, some of the web-services protocols (e.g., SOAP over HTTP) were designed specifically to bypass the very protections enforced by network firewalls. At the network and transport layers, a web-services request is intentionally indistinguishable from a request for a web page because they both use HTTP through TCP/IP ports 80 and 443 by default. If the standards makers had it to do over again, they might at least use different ports—and indeed, some implementations do just that. But SOAP and HTTP over ports 80 and 443 are by far the most commonly used combinations. In fact, the only way to distinguish between a web-services request or response and one from the World Wide Web is to look inside the XML payload carried by HTTP—a task beyond the capabilities of most network firewalls. Web-services messages can therefore sneak through the same firewall holes opened to access the World Wide Web.

Network firewalls also come up short when evaluated according to the web-services security building blocks introduced in the previous chapter. Although network firewalls are necessary, they're incapable of providing authorization or non-repudiation, and can only play supporting roles for integrity, authentication, and confidentiality. Using SSL or VPNs, network firewalls can establish simple point-to-point links (such as those used by web services without intermediaries) and support exchanges between endpoints and WSNs. SSL is the most widely used security protocol on the Internet, and we explored its strengths and weaknesses in detail in the previous chapter.

A VPN is conceptually the same as a connection using SSL—a VPN can even be based on SSL—except that a VPN is persistent, while most uses of SSL are not. A VPN isn't initialized and torn down in a matter of milliseconds like most SSL connections. Instead, creating a VPN requires substantial business and technical negotiations between the parties, both of whom must manually configure their firewalls and routers to establish the VPN link.

Figure 14-2 illustrates two VPNs, each linking a separate web-services requestor to a single provider.

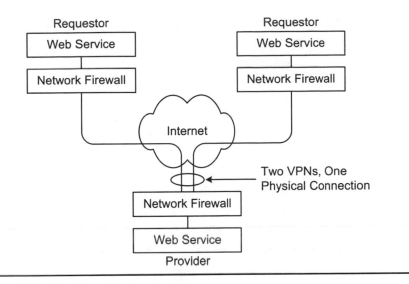

Figure 14-2: Virtual Private Networks

Note in the example shown in Figure 14-2 that each of the three parties has a single *physical* connection to the Internet, but the web-services provider's network firewall is configured for two *logical* VPNs over its Internet link.

You can think of a VPN as extending your corporate LAN to outside partners and locations, thereby making external web services appear as though they're internal. While this simplifies deployment, it's not without its downside. SSL and VPNs will successfully keep hackers out of your systems, but only so long as the hackers don't breach the systems owned by your business partner at the other end of the connection. A VPN or SSL connection is only as strong as its weakest endpoint, and if a hacker does manage to get into a system at the far end of the connection, he'll be able to exploit the tunnel you've established, and through it gain relatively unobstructed access to your systems.

Let's see how the network-layer technologies of SSL and VPNs solve the challenges of web-services security:

- **Integrity**. SSL and VPNs encrypt all traffic at the transport layer, and therefore offer a simple integrity solution—but only for point-to-point applications. What goes in one end is guaranteed to come out unchanged at the other, but there's no element-level encryption or support for end-to-end integrity in multi-hop architectures. (In the single-hop environments where VPNs and SSL are used, there are no intermediaries and hence no need for end-to-end integrity.)

○ **Confidentiality**. Likewise, VPNs and SSL maintain confidentiality over their links. However, they can't provide end-to-end confidentiality in a multi-hop architecture, nor do they address the confidentiality of stored data.

○ **Authentication**. In conjunction with HTTP, SSL includes three mechanisms for authentication: *basic authentication, digest authentication,* and support for *digital certificates.* Basic authentication is by far the most common; it's the World Wide Web's username/password scheme we all know. Since passwords are notoriously easy to crack, password-based SSL is far from robust. Still, it's an effective solution for simple web services that require only moderate levels of requestor authentication. Authentication via digital certificates over SSL can be used for more demanding applications.

A VPN authenticates the firewalls at either end (i.e., bi-directionally) when it's initialized, but it provides no support for the authentication of users, applications, services, and other finer-grained entities. Authentication at these levels remains the responsibility of the applications or other authentication systems. Since SSL and VPNs are network-layer technologies, they don't address requirements for durable authentication (that is, authentication that can be verified at a later time).

○ **Authorization**. SSL provides no support for authorization, which must be handled by other components of the web-services environment. The only authorization provided by a VPN is the approval or rejection of access to the link itself at the system level only, not for individual applications or users. There are no considerations for loosely coupled authentication models, the consolidation of identities, or individual services authorization.

○ **Non-repudiation**. Since they're based on network-layer technologies, SSL and VPNs are blind to the data they carry, and hence can't examine it to provide non-repudiation. Again, this is left to the applications or other tools.

Given that network-based security fails to meet so many requirements for web-services security, what good is it? VPNs and SSL play two important roles in web-services security. First, they fill a very specific niche for point-to-point, synchronous web services. SSL is so ubiquitous that it's nearly guaranteed to remain the standard for securing these simple, one-hop web services that don't require persistent connections, particularly those available to a large number of authenticated or anonymous parties. SSL can also be used without authentication, in which case it still provides in-transit integrity and confidentiality. Second, as we'll see in more detail shortly, VPNs and SSL can be used to provide secure links between endpoints and web-services networks.

More complex web-services security challenges require a better platform. In web services, the general goal is to move security out of the network layer and into the *messaging layer*. This allows security concepts to be implemented independently of any particular network or transport protocol. For example, if all or part of a SOAP message is encrypted, that encryption will endure regardless of whether the message is sent using HTTP, SMTP, or any other protocol. Network- and transport-independent security is required for any message that will be routed over more than one protocol on the way to its final destination.

Host-Based Security

Network-layer security may satisfy your requirements for simple, private point-to-point web services, or to secure a link to a WSN. But if you need to communicate over multiple hops, or if you require more than the most basic authentication and authorization schemes, you'll need a more sophisticated approach. If you're starting small and neither scalability nor support for a wide variety of remote requestors are at issue, a good-enough solution may be provided by *host-based security* as illustrated in Figure 14-3. As we'll see, certain security components should always be host-based, even for complex, high-volume web services.

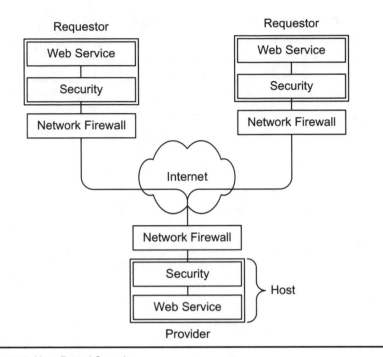

Figure 14-3: Host-Based Security

Host-based (or *application-based)* security doesn't mean actually writing security code from scratch, but rather using libraries and utilities provided by software vendors, and deploying them on the same systems that run your web-services applications, as illustrated in Figure 14-3. General-purpose connections to the Internet allow any system to communicate with any other, unlike the dedicated VPN tunnels shown in Figure 14-2. Let's see how host-based security meets the requirements established in the previous chapter:

- **Integrity**. By performing encryption and decryption as close to the application as possible, data is protected against modification over the greatest percentage of its route. By comparison, when encryption is performed in a network firewall, the host sends data *in the clear* to the local firewall where it's then encrypted. As illustrated in Figure 14-2, the data remains unencrypted and vulnerable between the application and the firewall.
- **Confidentiality**. Certain data that is financial or highly personal in nature should be encrypted *before* it leaves the applica-

tion environment. Not only does this protect the confidentiality of the data within the corporate infrastructure, but it also keeps the data confidential all the way from one endpoint to the other, and prevents it from being decrypted by intermediaries.

- **Authentication**. You can implement authentication within your web-services applications, but that's perhaps not the best approach. Given that at some time in the future you'll have more than one such application, you'll then need a decentralized instance of your authentication logic for each application. Not only does this increase the cost of development and maintenance, but the coordination of identities can become a massive problem. Consider what happens in the classic example of an employee leaving a company. If authentication is distributed among the applications, disabling a user's accounts requires an interaction with each of them. A superior alternative is to deploy a separate authentication service, as we'll consider shortly.

- **Authorization**. Authorization requires the interpretation of complex rules, such as, "Employees in group ABC are allowed to issue purchase requisitions for up to US$5,000 for pre-approved vendors, or up to US$1,000 for other vendors." And in the days before distributed systems, authorization was considered to be one of the essential roles of applications. Since authorization isn't addressed in any way whatsoever by network-layer schemes such as SSL or VPNs, host-based authorization is a reasonable first step. Utilizing a separate authorization service would be better still.

- **Non-repudiation**. While it's possible to implement non-repudiation logic within an application using digital-certificate technologies, it isn't as valuable as having an independent third party providing such a service.

The above seems to paint a generally rosy picture for host-based security. But while this approach offers many theoretical advantages (such as the data's proximity to encryption/decryption), in practice there are a number of less-obvious disadvantages that must also be considered:

Future-Proofing

One reason not to relegate security to applications is the rapidly evolving state of security standards in web services. When a new protocol is announced or an old one is modified, any software in which security technology has been implemented will probably need to be updated. If security is implemented in an XML firewall, a WSN, or on another platform external to the applications, no applications will have to be modified in order to keep the overall system up-to-date.

Loose Coupling

In a multi-party web-services environment, not all partners can or will want to implement identical security capabilities. If security is embedded within your web-services applications, you're more likely to be stuck with a single security model and one implementation, and there's no guarantee they'll be the same as those selected by your partners. Even if you know the security needs of your partners today, they may change in the future as you use your web services in unexpected ways and communicate with currently unknown partners. Centralizing security and keeping it out of your individual web-services applications makes it easier to adapt to new and different security models and technologies.

Internal Security Risks

It's well known within security circles that most attacks (particularly those that are the most damaging) aren't initiated by anonymous hackers in foreign countries, but rather by insiders who know about and already have access to your internal systems. In addition, few application programmers are trained in the specialty of security. Many tend to be security-ignorant and dangerously motivated to "get something working" and "worry about security later." Security is often postponed forever.

As web services become simpler to develop and deploy, even less-skilled programmers will be using them—all the more reason to implement security concepts external to the applications themselves, possibly even under the control of a department separate from software development. It's often valuable to keep security out of the hands of programmers, and instead make security the responsibility of a separate team or independent third party. Security is a difficult problem that's become a specialty all its own, just as programming has been for decades. Like programming, security is generally best left to its specialists.

Peripheral-Service Security

One alternative to deploying security solutions within the same hosts on which applications run is using separate (peripheral) systems that provide security as services—even as web services. For example, this is a very common solution for managing usernames and passwords for an organization with multiple, disparate systems. Figure 14-4 illustrates a peripheral service that can be reached by multiple web servic es participants over the Internet. For internal web services, a similar service can be provided over a corporate intranet.

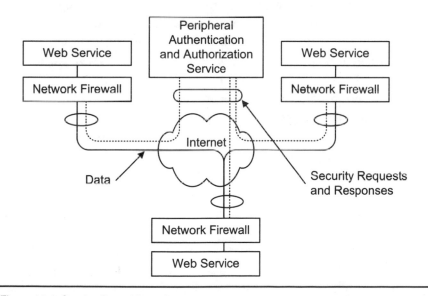

Figure 14-4: Service-Based Security

How does peripheral-service security meet our requirements?
- **Integrity**. Because the service is peripheral to the message stream and messages don't pass through the service, periph-

eral-service security plays no role in the encryption required to maintain the integrity of the messages.

○ **Confidentiality**. Since messages pass from one endpoint to another without passing through the security service, it doesn't have the opportunity to perform encryption or decryption.

● **Authentication**. Identity management can be performed in one place by using a peripheral authentication system accessible to all participants. For example, a departing employee's credentials can be disabled from a single location using a shared authentication system. Centralized identity-management systems—such as those based on the *Lightweight Directory-Access Protocol* (LDAP)—are well-suited to this application, and are readily available. Other more elaborate schemes such as Microsoft's *Passport* and technology from the Liberty Alliance[1] support *single sign-on* and sharing of identities among business partners.

● **Authorization**. Using a peripheral-service based scheme, it's possible to express authorization rules in standardized XML outside of the applications that use them. This allows the use of general-purpose *authentication engines* that support arbitrarily complex rules. Such a solution is a viable—and in some cases, superior—alternative to host-based authorization.

◐ **Non-repudiation**. The key to non-repudiation is the involvement of a third party that can objectively certify transmission and reception. If messages pass through a service, it has the ability to log them and hence provide some degree of non-repudiation. However, such an intermediary can't guarantee to the sender that a message has been received by the ultimate receiver. Doing so requires some cooperation from the receiver, acknowledging receipt of the message. A service that's not in the message path isn't in a good position to perform non-repudiation, but it can still play the role of a logging server if it receives notifications of events to be logged from the endpoints.

XML/Application Firewalls and Proxies

A traditional network firewall deals with packets. It understands the supposed source and destination of the traffic at the system-to-system level, rather than at the application-to-application level. Network firewalls are also aware of the general nature of the traffic according to the protocols used (FTP, HTTP, etc.), but most network firewalls can't distinguish a web-services packet from one that's part of a World Wide Web browser/server exchange. An *XML firewall* or *application firewall* operates at the application layer, examining the XML content of packets rather than just their addresses.

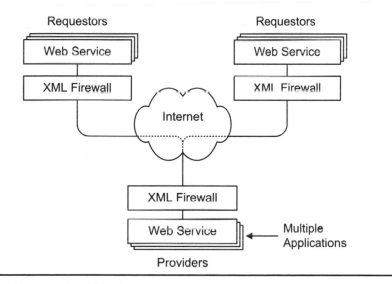

Figure 14-5: Application/XML Firewalls

The architecture using XML firewalls is very similar to that of host-based security, shown earlier in Figure 14-3, except that XML firewalls are physically separate from the systems that run the web-services applications. Because an XML firewall is separate from the web service, the firewall is able to provide security for multiple web-services applications, as illustrated in Figure 14-5. This is a significant advantage of separating the security software or appliance from the applications.

Yet another term used to describe this category of software package or appliance (the functionality can be delivered in either form) is

XML proxy, which emphasizes the enabling functionality that sets this technology apart from the merely defensive technologies implied by the word *firewall*. An XML proxy serves as a stand-in for the applications it protects, performing a number of services on behalf of those applications and thus lightening their load. For example, an XML proxy can perform *transformations*, converting data from one format to another. Other features include *XML acceleration*, which improves the performance of web-services applications.

When an XML firewall receives a message destined for one of the applications it protects, the firewall looks within the message and within its *envelope* to examine the XML data contained in the message's header and body. The XML firewall can decrypt selected data, off-loading this responsibility from the application and allowing the firewall to examine the decrypted content. The XML firewall can then verify the authentication and authorization, validate the XML, and perform problem diagnosis, billing, and intrusion-detection tasks. All requests sent or received can be logged by the XML firewall for later analysis, if needed.

XML firewalls can be used to solve many web-services security problems:

- **Integrity**. By handling all encryption and decryption tasks, XML firewalls provide a complete set of integrity services including component-level integrity and end-to-end integrity for multi-hop systems. However, they can't take responsibility for the integrity of data once it's stored or passed on to local applications.

- **Confidentiality**. Not only do XML firewalls handle the encryption and decryption tasks of SSL (assuming they include the functionality of network-layer firewalls), they also support SOAP-based element-level confidentiality, as described in Chapter 13. However, one disadvantage is that some highly confidential data should still be encrypted and decrypted within applications, so that that information never appears unencrypted outside the application's host.

- **Authentication**. XML firewalls can perform authentication tasks at multiple levels, including bi-directional and multi-party authentication and management of digital certificates. They can also link to the peripheral authentication and single sign-on systems that are becoming common within many corporate environments. XML firewalls can't directly provide durable authentication since they aren't part of storage or database systems.

- **Authorization**. Given their ability to read the contents of web-services messages and to authenticate the authors of those messages, XML firewalls are ideal points at which to implement authorization. Most XML firewalls include sophisticated rules-based engines allowing companies to express complex authorization logic. XML firewalls can also support loosely coupled authorization models.
- **Non-repudiation**. Although they can't provide a complete non-repudiation service on their own, XML firewalls can assist third-party services with non-repudiation by acknowledging their receipt and processing of messages and reporting those activities to the third-party service.

XML firewalls are sometimes referred to as *application proxies* because they offer features that go beyond merely solving the major problems of web-services security. These additional features include the following:

Management

To provide the redundancy necessary for both high reliability and scalability, a company may deploy multiple XML firewalls. These systems can be linked to one another and managed centrally to guarantee synchronization and consistency of security policies and business rules across an enterprise. This can even be extended to XML firewalls owned and operated by other participants in multi-party web-services environments.

Virus Protection

Encryption has the unfortunate side effect of hiding or masking viruses, since it's not possible to examine XML messages for viruses while the messages are encrypted. An XML firewall can handle the decryption of arriving messages, so it has the first opportunity to check those messages for viruses. The earlier the checking is done, the better, since it lessens the chance that viruses will interact with downstream applications. An XML firewall also performs the encryption of outgoing data and is the last point at which the unencrypted data can be read, making it the ideal place to check for viruses in the outbound direction as well.

Security-Policy Auditing

Implementing security either in a centralized location or in a system that can be centrally managed allows an organization to perform automated security audits, which prove to the organization and to others that a given security policy has been implemented correctly.

Service-Managed Proxies

Figure 14-6 illustrates a variation on the XML-firewall theme, in which a third-party service manages its customers' XML firewalls.

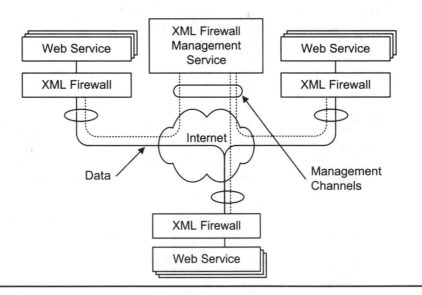

Figure 14-6: XML Firewall Management Service

Because such a service manages firewalls for a large number of organizations, it can often do so more robustly and cost-effectively than the organizations could themselves. Since the management service

has control over the firewalls, it can perform independent audits and
provide non-repudiation.

Web Services Networks

A WSN acts much like a value-added network (VAN) in the EDI
world, but a WSN isn't actually a network. A WSN is just a *hub* that
uses the public Internet for connectivity, as illustrated in Figure 14-7.

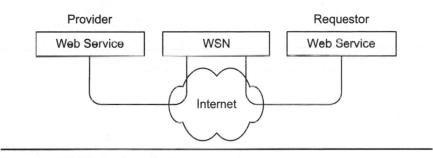

Figure 14-7: Web Services Network

A request from one endpoint is sent via the Internet to the WSN,
rather than directly to the provider. The WSN performs its operations then forwards the request via the Internet to the provider. The
reverse occurs for the response sent from the provider to the request-
or. In reality, the architecture of a WSN may be far more complex
than as shown in Figure 14-7, including geographical distribution
of the WSN's components. But from the endpoints' perspectives, a
WSN appears as merely an overlay to the Internet or an extension of
it.

Endpoints link to WSNs using a variety of protocols, but the
most common techniques are to use SSL or to create a VPN link between each endpoint and the WSN.

XML firewalls and WSNs provide comparable, but not quite
overlapping solutions to web-services security problems. As we'll see
shortly, it often makes sense to combine the two to get the best of
both worlds. WSNs provide more than just security, and we'll explore
them in greater detail in Chapter 15. For now, let's just consider a
WSN an intermediary that sits logically between the participants (requestors and providers) in a web-services topology.

Let's see how well WSNs stack up against the other solutions we've explored:

- **Integrity**. Because of their remoteness from the applications, WSNs can't perform the initial data encryption necessary to guarantee integrity, either single-hop or end-to-end. The endpoints must use host-based security or XML firewalls to encrypt data before its initial transmission, unless the network-layer protection provided by SSL or a VPN connection is considered sufficient. If the data isn't encrypted by the sending endpoint, there's no guarantee the data will be unmodified when it's received by the WSN. But since WSNs are able to decrypt and re-encrypt data, they can support the more advanced component-level integrity requirements, such as encryption applied to documents, entire SOAP messages, or individual XML elements.

- **Confidentiality**. Although data that doesn't need to be read by the WSN can be protected using end-to-end encryption, data on which the WSN should act must obviously be readable by the WSN. While WSNs can be expected to go to extraordinary lengths to guard against the loss of confidentiality, any intermediary that has access to unencrypted data in a web-services architecture increases the risk that confidentiality will be breached. Data will pass through and reside on these third-party systems, so it will be accessible to more people and vulnerable to more misuses. WSNs would argue that their security practices are superior to those of their clients—which may be true, but that doesn't alter the fact that WSNs do introduce an additional point of vulnerability. WSNs can't take the primary responsibility for confidentiality, since the endpoints must ultimately perform encryption and decryption to ensure that data remains confidential in transit between the endpoint and the WSN (or vice versa). And although their own storage may be secure, WSNs can't provide encryption for endpoint storage. The endpoints must do that for themselves.

- **Authentication**. WSNs implement a broader array of authentication schemes than are likely to be implemented at any single endpoint, and can therefore deal with a number of authentication challenges that are difficult to solve at the endpoints. They also can map authentication schemes onto one another, or transform them. For example, if one participant uses digital certificates and another relies on usernames and passwords, the WSN can moderate authentication between them according to rules of trust established by each participant to protect itself.

WSNs can also manage credential consolidation and multi-party authentication. But due to their remoteness, WSNs can't provide durable authentication for data located in endpoint storage systems or databases.

- **Authorization**. WSNs also offer robust rule-based authorization schemes, including the ability to map the scheme used by one participant onto the scheme of another. A WSN is a good place to implement such loosely coupled authorization models, and to perform identity consolidation.

- **Non-repudiation**. As a legally independent third party, a WSN can provide non-repudiation services that are superior to those managed by a web-services endpoint. As is the case with an EDI VAN, a WSN's ability to log and retain transaction records is critical in certain business environments. After all, when it comes to non-repudiation, you want to have something that will hold up in court.

Web-services networks are a form of outsourcing, like web hosting or co-location. WSNs provide important benefits to their customers, allowing them to focus on their core businesses and reducing time-to-market for the deployment of web services. WSNs are particularly helpful for keeping up with still-evolving standards in security and other areas, and for adapting to business partners who have implemented non-standard interfaces. WSNs can monitor web-services endpoints to ensure that the security policies of one are, in fact, adhered to by the others.

On the other hand, there's always a downside to introducing intermediaries, no matter how robust their infrastructures may be. WSNs utilize message queuing (as discussed in Chapter 9) to support long-lived web services, but any additional hops and links will always increase the likelihood of a communications failure. The same is true for security: Passing messages through an intermediary will always increase the risk that integrity or confidentiality will be compromised.

All of the Above

By now it should be obvious that there's no single best location to implement all of the solutions to web-services security problems. The ideal solution is therefore some combination of the solutions considered in this chapter. Figure 14-8 illustrates such a hybrid configuration.

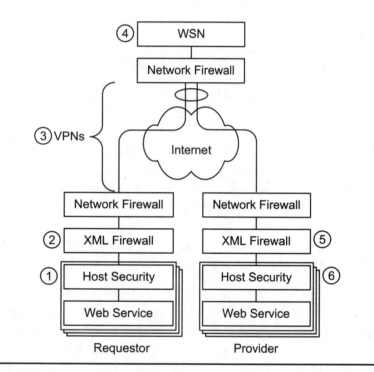

Figure 14-8: An Integrated Security Solution

Let's follow the path of a web-services request message in this sample configuration:

1. Personnel records, credit-card numbers, and other highly con-fidential data should be encrypted at the first opportunity us-ing host-based, element-level encryption.
2. The encryption of less confidential data can be deferred until it reaches the XML firewall, which should be the default loca-tion for such operations. The XML firewall is also an excel-

lent point for verifying XML syntax, checking documents against business rules, and authenticating and verifying the authorization of entities submitting outbound requests.

3. The VPNs implemented between the network firewalls of the web-services endpoints and the WSN have the primary responsibility for the integrity of data as it passes through the Internet and back again.

4. The WSN provides the mapping or transformation services that make one endpoint compatible with another. Such services require the WSN to selectively decrypt received data, modify it, re-encrypt it, and re-transmit it to the destination endpoint. The WSN is also the ideal place to log data for the purposes of non-repudiation and accounting. In some cases, the WSN will also perform authentication and authorization functions, particularly if the two endpoints use different models and therefore require mediation.

5. When the message continues on its journey from the WSN to the provider's web-services endpoint, the receiving endpoint's firewall manages its own end of the VPN link to the WSN to guarantee the integrity of the data it receives. The receiving XML firewall also handles authorization and authentication to the extent that these weren't already performed by the WSN, and decrypts any data that doesn't need to remain encrypted until it reaches the application.

6. Finally, the host-based security mechanisms are used to decrypt the most critical elements and perform more granular authentication and authorization than is possible in the XML firewall.

The above step-by-step scenario isn't intended to dictate the only way to distribute the responsibilities of security solutions, but it illustrates some of the opportunities to do so.

The introduction to this chapter explained that although the security challenges posed by web services are substantial, no new inventions are required—just the hard work of combining proven components, creating standards, building consensus, and gaining experience.

The standards for web-services security solutions will continue to evolve for a number of years, until they reach a point where they're as stable as those of the World Wide Web. In the meantime, deploying a web-services project with significant security requirements will take a fair amount of finesse and planning.

We've already considered some of the platforms for solving web-services security problems, such as WSNs and XML firewalls. In the next chapter we'll look at these and a variety of other deployment options in more detail, from their security functions to the other services they provide as well.

Chapter 15

Deployment Options

When it comes time to develop and deploy your web services, where will you obtain the required pieces of technology? Should you license software from a major vendor or an independent software vendor (ISV)? Would you be better off buying an XML proxy or gateway? Or should you do as little as possible in house, and outsource virtually everything to a web-services network (WSN) or web-services provider (WSP)?

In this chapter we'll evaluate these and other options available for the deployment of web services. Unfortunately, we can't start with a simple matrix and directly compare each of these deployment solutions, because their relative strengths and weaknesses are still changing. Instead, we'll use the *solution-evolution timeline*, which will help us understand how the various technologies of web services are evolving and how their implementations will be available from different sources at different times.

The Evolution of Solutions

If you were to deploy a simple networking project today (not necessarily one based on web services), where would you obtain your TCP/IP protocol-stack software? The answer: You wouldn't obtain it at all—you've already got it. Just as will be true for web-services protocols at some time in the future, most modern programming languages (such as Java, C#, Perl, and Python) directly support networking concepts, and the TCP/IP protocol stack is now built into virtually every computing platform that supports a network interface.

But this hasn't always been the case. Thirty years ago, anyone wanting to use TCP/IP had to first *implement* the protocols—that means write the code, not merely install a software package. If you were planning a TCP/IP-based project in 1975, your buy-versus-build deployment recommendations probably would have been very different from what they'd be today.

In 1985, TCP/IP software entered the solution-evolution timeline as an expensive do-it-yourself technology, and emerged a decade later as a technology we now expect to be bundled with every operating system. During that ten-year period, implementations of TCP/IP were available from a variety of sources, and the quality and performance continued to improve as costs declined. If you were planning a TCP/IP project between 1985 and 1995, you were aiming at a moving target. The successful outcome of your project, financially and otherwise, depended a great deal on its timing and your source for TCP/IP software at that given moment.

The technologies of web services are now at the same critical point that TCP/IP was fifteen years ago. Your ability to successfully implement a complex web service today depends upon your understanding of the many deployment options, and where they are on the web-services solution-evolution timeline, as illustrated in Figure 15-1.

When a technology is new (far to the left on the timeline), the only way to deploy it is through a home-brew or do-it-yourself implementation. As the need for that technology becomes more widespread, web-services networks (WSNs) offer the first commercial implementations. WSNs specialize in solving problems of cutting-edge technologies, particularly those for which the standards have yet to be adopted or widely deployed. Once the standards for a particular technology appear (as illustrated in the timeline by the vertical dashed line), specialty ISVs enter the market. The ISVs initially release their software as part of gateway or proxy packages, and later bundle it with hardware as standalone *appliances*. Soon after that, the ISV solutions become available from another breed of service provider: *web-services delivery networks* (WSDNs). Eventually, the technology becomes

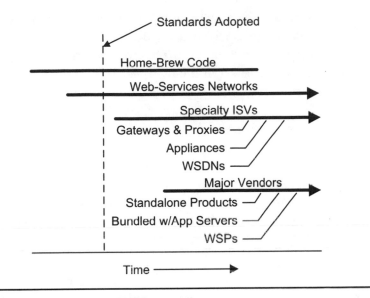

Figure 15-1: Solution-Evolution Timeline

so common that the major software vendors release their own solutions. They also begin by delivering standalone software packages, but later bundle their solutions with application servers and even operating systems. Finally, as the solutions become universal and clear favorites appear from among the crowd of vendors, *web-service providers* (WSPs) offer outsourced hosting of the most popular solutions.

Note that the timeline in Figure 15-1 applies individually to each of the component technologies of web services, which means that at any moment in time, specific technologies will be at different points on the line. The fundamental technologies such as SOAP are far to the right, since SOAP tools are available from virtually all vendors (including the major ones). Security and other less mature technologies may still be far to the left, since they're typically only available as pre-standard solutions from WSNs. Over time, all technologies move to the right, as their solutions become available from a wider rage of sources.

Mixing Metaphors

The timeline illustrates how a technology evolves over its life cycle, and how it's delivered by various categories of vendors over time. By comparison, the *web-services pyramid* introduced in Chapter 5 shows the web-services technologies and their relationships to one another, but captured at a single point in time. As technologies move through the timeline, they also sink lower in the pyramid. For example, in early 2003 most security solutions were not yet standardized, and therefore remained in the middle tier of the web-services pyramid. They were only available as home-brew code or from WSNs.

The pyramid illustrates three separate layers of web-services technology components. The standardized horizontal components in the lowest layer of the pyramid tend to be those that have either worked their way through to the end of the solution-evolution timeline, or (as in the case of XML and SOAP), skipped the earlier stages altogether. The horizontal but not yet standardized components in the middle tier are still working their way through the timeline, while industry-specific components in the top layer of the pyramid haven't made it very far along the timeline. In some industries, standards for business semantics will be adopted slowly, perhaps never advancing along the timeline beyond the home-brew segment.

It's going to take many years—if not forever—before all the technologies are codified in standards. Even then, there will always be a need for ad-hoc solutions. In the meantime, where should companies turn for solutions to their urgent web-services technology problems? And where will they turn tomorrow? In the sections that follow, we'll explore each of the web-services deployment options suggested by the solution-evolution timeline.

Web Services Networks (WSNs)

In Chapter 14, we introduced the first commercial-deployment option on the timeline, web-services networks, as a solution to security problems. Indeed, WSNs are a good way to deal with many of the youngest and most immature of web-services technologies. WSNs excel as solutions where standards have yet to be set, let alone widely implemented. WSNs can certainly implement standardized technologies, too—but they specialize in solving problems in which the parties involved aren't able to agree on the use of a single protocol, whether standardized or not.

The architecture of a WSN is illustrated in Figure 15-2. Note that all of the traffic between the web-services endpoints travels *through* the WSN. As shown, each endpoint uses the Internet (typically via a VPN or using SSL) to reach the WSN, but private lines that bypass the Internet are also sometimes used.

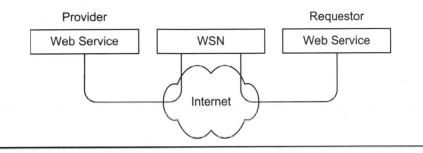

Figure 15-2: Web Services Network

Mediation

A WSN is an intermediary that provides *mediation* services. It allows you to implement as little as possible within your own infrastructure, and handles your web-services facilities and management. Rather than requiring all participants to adopt the same protocols, a WSN allows each participant to use whatever technologies it has already implemented. The WSN mediates and transforms each participant's protocols and formats into those of the other parties.

The mediation capabilities of a WSN are particularly valuable when there's a significant discrepancy among the sophistication, technology, or skill sets of the participants. For example, one party may have extensive networking and web-services capabilities, and prefer to use SOAP and HTTP. But if that party wants to communicate with another that can only support rudimentary tools such as FTP, a WSN allows them to interoperate without either party's having to adjust to the other's technologies or skills. Mediation also means that new participants can be added to the community without the need for any of the participants—old or new—to make changes.

However, if one participant is an 800-pound corporate or governmental gorilla that can mandate technologies to be used by all the other participants, the mediation value of the WSN is not as obvious.

In such cases, there is less of a need to mediate various protocols and standards. The gorilla can often dictate the specifications for connectivity, security, and so forth, and all the smaller primates will probably follow the leader with little resistance.

WSNs are better suited to projects that are more democratic, where the parties are closer in terms of size and clout. There may even be a bit of a standoff between them over who should incur the expense of adapting their practices to be compatible with the others'. A WSN allows every party to win such a standoff, since no one is put in the position of having to yield autonomy.

Transformations

Another scenario in which WSNs provide value is with *transformations*, such as the simple example of a currency converter that translates monetary units used by any participant into those of any other (US dollars to Euros, and so on). WSNs provide transformations in two ways: They develop and maintain the transformation software themselves, and they act as aggregators of external transformations. In some cases the difference between these two functions may not be apparent to a WSN's customers. For example, if your data passes through a transformation at the WSN's hub, you can't tell whether the WSN used its own software or issued a web-services request to a remote service to perform the transformation on your behalf. But you might want to know if your data is sent out over the wire to a third party to be transformed, in case doing so violates your corporate security policies.

When considering a WSN, you've got to ask yourself whether you really need a fourth party (the WSN) to invoke third-party transformations on your behalf. On one hand, if you've implemented a standardized web-services environment of your own, there's no reason you can't utilize third-party transformation web services directly. You don't need to go through a WSN to reach them. If you have the skills, tools, time, and money to do so, you may want to do your own aggregation of currency converters and other transformation services rather than pay a WSN to do this for you. On the other hand, if you're already committed to using a WSN, you may find it simpler and even more cost-effective to use it as a broker for such transformations. Alternatively, you might even build your own WSN using software products and appliances from specialty ISVs and the major vendors, as described later in this chapter.

Service Switching

If you decide to forego using a WSN and link directly to independent transformational web services, not only will you have to select your vendors, and code to their interfaces, but you'll also have to deal with any service-level problems that may occur. For example, suppose your application is linked to one of the many credit-card processors' web services. How can you protect yourself from the risk of the vendor's service being down or otherwise unavailable? One solution is to create your own software *service switch* that will fail-over to an alternative service. But this requires that you develop the switch, deal with the differences in the vendors' interfaces, and initiate and maintain business relationships with two processing services.

Since a WSN acts as a broker or gateway to such third-party services, you could choose instead to develop a single interface to a WSN's generic credit-card processing service and let the WSN provide the switching. Because the WSN delivers this best-of-breed, switched multi-vendor service to many of its customers, it can usually do so for less than it would cost you to develop and maintain the service switch yourself.

Closed Community

WSNs are closed systems, which means they don't support web services to anonymous partners or to the public and thus can support proprietary compression schemes. This can potentially reduce the transmission time of XML documents—but keep in mind that any proprietary technologies you utilize tend to lock you into your vendor, making it increasingly difficult to switch should that become desirable.

Since all participants in a common business process must become customers of a single WSN, basing a web-services project on a WSN only works for restricted-membership communities, such as a consortium of suppliers to a single large manufacturer. This may not be a problem if all of your web-services links are within a single closed community—but eventually, most companies will use web services to communicate in multiple domains. For example, a distributor will communicate with its suppliers as well as with its customers, and there's no guarantee that these two domains (suppliers and customers) will overlap, both use the same WSN, or use any WSN whatsoever. Even if you work with a WSN in one domain, you may still need to deploy your own infrastructure to communicate in another. You may end up working with multiple WSNs, each acting as your broker or mediator for a different community of web-services partners.

Topology

A WSN will always introduce an extra *hop* in your web-services architecture. If your design already includes multiple hops, one more may not make a significant difference. But if your web service would otherwise require only a single hop, going from having no intermediaries to having one makes a huge difference and can substantially and unnecessarily increase the cost and complexity. That's because there are many security shortcuts available for single-hop topologies, such as using SSL or a VPN, as discussed in Chapter 14.

Inserting a WSN into the middle of a web-services architecture will also increase the latency at all levels. There are extra transmission paths, additional encryption/decryption operations, and extra processing steps. For many asynchronous web services, the increase in latency is inconsequential. For synchronous services, however, it can be unacceptable. The message queuing employed by most WSNs is typically too slow for synchronous services, and these services rarely require a WSN's advanced mediation and transformation features anyway.

Outsourcing

But when all is said and done, the question of whether or not to use a WSN is essentially an outsourcing decision, and many of the advantages and disadvantages are similar to those in other outsourcing situations. The benefits include reducing capital expense (trading upfront investment for recurring costs), improving time-to-market, and retaining your internal resources for core-competency projects.

The unique characteristic of the WSN-outsourcing option is that it's a decision made not just for one company, but for all of the companies participating in the project. This makes the decision more difficult, because it may be optimal for some participants but not for others. In some cases this requires a consensus, whereas in others it's up to the first one or two parties that enter into the WSN outsourcing agreement. Those that join later have little say in the matter—which can be good or bad, depending on your point of view.

The optimal situation for using WSNs exists when the number of parties is still small, and when one is not dominant or otherwise able to mandate the technologies to be used. A WSN reduces the number of parties with which you must *directly* communicate by funneling all traffic through a hub, but it does nothing to reduce the number of business relationships that must be created, monitored, and maintained. A WSN is a good solution for inter-company projects in which it's not politically or economically feasible for all the parties to invest in their own development and deployment.

The Future of WSNs

When standards are written and adopted, technologies advance to the next stage on the timeline. Solutions then appear from specialized ISVs, and eventually from the major vendors. As each component technology works its way along the timeline, fewer problems remain that can only be solved by WSNs. WSNs specialize in solving problems for which no standardized solutions yet exist, so their role will certainly diminish as standards are adopted and implemented and the web-services world becomes increasingly homogeneous. This begs the question: Is there a long-term role for WSNs, and if so, what is it? Won't the success of web services and the commoditization of technology eventually put them out of business? .

As technologies become available from other sources at lower prices than WSNs can afford to charge, WSNs will be forced to evolve. If we look at the web-services pyramid in Chapter 5, we can see that the middle layer of horizontal non-standard technologies will continue to shrink as the technologies in this layer become standardized and move towards the bottom of the pyramid. WSNs live and breathe in this middle layer of the pyramid, and they'll have to track and anticipate technological changes very carefully in order to be successful long-term.

But there is one area of services where WSNs will perhaps remain protected from solution evolution and the downward-moving technologies in the middle layer of the pyramid. WSNs may remain the preferred solution when it comes to logging, auditing, monitoring, and non-repudiation, services that are better provided by third parties.

Vertical Hubs

Another possible evolutionary path for WSNs is for them to morph into *vertical hubs*, which meet the needs of specific industries. Initially, all WSNs were horizontal (i.e., non-industry-specific) because the markets for most verticals were either already controlled by pre-web services hubs (EDI VANs), or they weren't mature or lucrative enough on which to base such a business. As the WSNs are forced to work their way up the pyramid looking for new opportunities, some of them will offer vertically oriented services and actually become dedicated to one or more vertical markets. Whether they're operated by WSNs, former WSNs, or entirely independent companies, these vertical hubs will offer centralized services in direct competition with those offered by horizontal WSNs. And once there's a vertical hub in your industry, you'll be hard-pressed to make use of a more generic horizontal WSN instead.

Distributed Web-Services Networks (DWSNs)

Rather than develop centralized WSN-like hubs, some suppliers of early-stage technologies have chosen to deliver their solutions via a distributed architecture, as illustrated in Figure 15-3. Instead of deploying functionality as a WSN does in the form of a centralized service, a *distributed web-services network* (DWSN) packages most of its features into an *XML proxy* that's located on the DWSN's customers' premises. An XML proxy (also known as an *application proxy*, *XML firewall*, *application firewall*, or *gateway*) is a software package or a

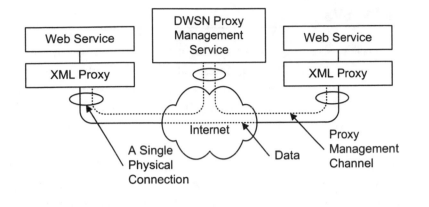

Figure 15-3: Distributed Web-Services Network

hardware/software appliance that provides services on behalf of one or more web services within an organization.

The DWSN hub is linked to the proxies using secure channels over the public Internet, and certain management services are provided there—but only select services that are most appropriately located at the hub. A DWSN is like a WSN in which the non-management functionality has been pushed out to the participants' sites, thereby allowing them to communicate directly with one another without the latency or other topological implications of an intermediary. For this reason, DWSNs can be used for synchronous web services, unlike WSNs. With DWSNs, data isn't routed through an intermediate hub as it would be with a WSN.

Although a DWSN looks somewhat different from a traditional WSN (compare Figures 15-2 and 15-3), the two models have one characteristic in common. Like a WSN, a DWSN is designed to meet the needs of a closed community with a limited number of participants. It's not intended to provide web services to the public, to anonymous partners, or to any participants who need to join the community on an ad hoc basis.

WSNs don't generally consider themselves to be software vendors, but some DWSNs will license their software allowing you to build and operate your own DWSN. Of course, you would then lose the advantages of third-party audits, monitoring, management, and non-repudiation.

Specialty ISVs

Commercial WSNs and DWSNs make substantial investments in pre-standard solutions. Their greatest value comes from being able to solve problems that require expertise (such as professional services) and some degree of customization. But as web-services technologies mature—and particularly as they become standardized—solutions are more likely to be delivered in the form of packaged software from independent software vendors. These early packaged solutions don't at first come from the large, old software companies like Microsoft or IBM, but rather from smaller, younger, and more technically aggressive companies in the business of delivering the latest cutting-edge solutions. Specialty ISVs package their software in four forms: gateways, proxies, appliances, and components of web-services delivery networks.

Gateways, Proxies, and Appliances

We introduced the idea of XML proxies a few pages back as part of the DWSN concept. Specialty ISVs also deliver their solutions in the form of XML proxies, but specialty ISVs deliver no centralized management services of their XML proxies as DWSNs do. Instead these functions are provided by the customers themselves, as suggested by Figure 15-4.

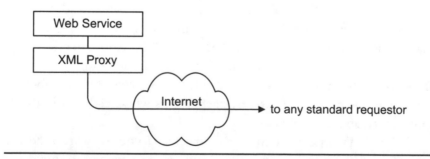

Figure 15-4: An XML Proxy

Let's compare the XML-proxy solutions from specialty ISVs to the solutions offered by WSNs. In the sections that follow, we'll explore the specific pros and cons of customer-managed XML proxies.

Vendor Independence

Because they're centralized, and often use proprietary solutions, WSNs require all members in a community of participants to use the same vendor. In contrast, solutions from specialty ISVs are based on standards, and are therefore the first solutions on the timeline that allow each participant to select its own vendor. Thanks to standards, one party can use software from ISV A, and still interoperate with a partner who chooses solutions from ISV B. This also means that the selection of vendors can be deferred for the benefit of late-joining participants. When working with a WSN, the vendor selection must be made up front, and all future participants must use the same WSN. Since using a specialty ISV allows you to defer vendor selection, solutions from specialty ISVs can be used to deploy public web services or even services for anonymous requestors—whereas WSNs are limited to use by populations of known partners.

First-Mover (Dis)Advantage

Just because the technologies are standardized and the solutions are available doesn't necessarily mean that everyone will deploy them at the same time. You've got to decide whether you want to be the proverbial first kid on your block to deploy standardized web-services, or wait until your partners or competitors have already done so. Standards compete with one another, and early winners can ultimately lose. Perhaps no example in recent memory (if you were thinking about such things in 1975) is as vivid as the battle between VHS and Betamax. Being better and first didn't guarantee ultimate success for Betamax.

Synchronous and One-Hop Services

WSNs (but not DWSNs) unavoidably add latency to any web-service path. In fact, most WSNs are based on sophisticated message-queuing systems that intentionally trade latency for improved reliability and capacity. WSNs are always part of a multi-hop architecture by definition, and therefore best used for asynchronous web services. XML proxies don't typically add additional hops to web-services architectures, because they're deployed as part of the endpoint infrastructure.

Up-Front Costs

If your web services are deployed via XML proxies, you'll have to make greater commitments of time, skill building, and non-recurring capital expense than you would using a WSN. In other words, it will take longer and cost more up front to deploy web services using your own XML proxies than if you depend on a WSN to provide them. But over the long term, your total cost of ownership using the products of an ISV may well be lower than they would with a WSN.

Control and Responsibility

By deploying an XML proxy, you'll probably have more control than if you rely on a WSN. However, you'll also be taking on more of the responsibilities. When there's a problem with the XML proxy software, an ISV may deal with it as part of a relatively lengthy bug-fix process. A WSN might take a professional-services oriented approach instead, digging in to solve unique problems quickly. Of course, it's entirely possible that a specific ISV might provide better service and support than a particular WSN, or vice versa. But in general, a vendor with a services-based revenue model tends to be more responsive—albeit more expensive—than one trying to leverage products.

Mix and Match

An XML proxy can be combined with a WSN to take advantage of the strengths of each. For example, technologies that are fully standardized can be deployed within an XML proxy, while problems that still require one-off transformations, links to non-standard partners, and other ad hoc solutions can be solved by a WSN. Such a configuration also allows fully standardized interactions—for instance, those that don't require transformations—to bypass the WSN, and operate directly between the parties via their XML proxies.

The key to success is to pick and choose which components to deploy through a WSN, and which to deploy through an XML proxy that you install in house. In general, it's wise to leave non-standard tasks that are likely to change or even disappear over time to the WSN, and deploy the more standardized components in a proxy.

Business Risks

Like some of the WSNs, many specialty ISVs won't be in business a decade from now. The cost of switching ISV platforms isn't as great as switching WSNs due to more standardization in ISVs—but it still represents a very real risk. Even before a weakened specialty ISV goes out of business, it's likely that its support will wane, and you won't be able to count on its products to keep you up-to-date with the latest changes in technology. The only solution is to remain vigilant, and to be aware that a reduced level of service and support can sometimes be a leading indicator of more serious problems to follow.

Web-Services Delivery Networks (WSDNs)

Perhaps you'd like to outsource your web-services infrastructure, but you need to be able to communicate with unknown partners. In other words, you want the economics of a WSN, but the flexibility of an ISV's solution. One option is a *web-services delivery network* (WSDN), as illustrated in Figure 15-5.

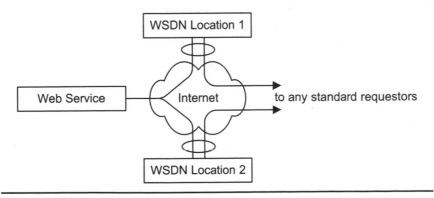

Figure 15-5: Web Services Delivery Network

WSDNs evolved from *content delivery networks* (CDNs) that were created to optimize the performance and reliability of static- and streaming-content delivery on the World Wide Web. Both CDNs and WSDNs achieve improvements over traditional single-location delivery by operating servers and proxies at multiple locations throughout the world, and thereby deliver content and services from as close to the end user as possible. WSDNs are most appropriate for synchronous performance-sensitive web services. For example, Figure 15-5 shows that requestors located closer to WSDN Location 1 would normally be served from that location, and likewise for Location 2. But in the case of an outage or communications bottleneck, either location can serve either requestor.

Instead of operating your own XML proxy (or using one supplied by a DWSN), you can use an XML proxy in data centers operated and managed by a WSDN. This gives you most of the benefits of a WSN, plus some additional ones. The proxy services are fully standardized to the point where they're essentially identical to those of a specialty ISV's normal proxies, enabling you to communicate with any standards-based third parties. You're not limited to those partners that must join your club, as you would be using a WSN or DWSN.

Major Vendor Support

With most technologies other than web services, the major hardware and software vendors are the last ones to jump on any new technology bandwagon. IBM invented the PC in 1982, well after upstart Apple created the market with its release of the Apple II in 1977. As we've discussed, Microsoft finally included TCP/IP—then a 20-year old protocol—with the 1995 version of Windows. Innovation usually comes from small independent vendors, not from the majors. As the technologies mature and become standardized, and—most importantly—as large markets appear, the major vendors finally roll out their offerings.

So it's highly unusual that when it comes to web services, much of the initial work has been done by such major vendors as IBM, Microsoft, and Sun. Not only did these players jump onto the web-services bandwagon early, but they're the ones who built the bandwagon and are pulling it forward.

What is it about web services that caused these traditionally conservative, post-innovation-phase companies to make such early-stage investments in technologies with no proven market and not even a hint of customer demand? You can bet they didn't do so out of the goodness of their hearts, or to make a better world where all vendors could interoperate in blissful harmony. No, they were motivated by the need to create new markets.

The dawn of the Internet and e-commerce were huge boons for all of the major vendors. As some have said, during the late 1990s it was hard *not* to make a lot of money as a vendor in this business. But the Internet bubble had to burst, and what many thought was the new economy turned out to be only a one-time opportunity to profit from the creation of a new medium and its infrastructure. As the demand flattened and the economy weakened, the major vendors' only source of new business was to steal customers from their competitors.

As the Internet rush came to an end, the major vendors needed to create new opportunities—ideally, new markets where they could again snatch up fresh low-hanging fruit before having to take it away from competitors. The obvious opportunities were automated business-to-business transactions, but the vendors realized they first had to create this new business-to-business playing field. After all, it wouldn't do IBM much good to come out with a solution that only allowed IBM customers to communicate with others of the same persuasion. The e-commerce world built on the competing Windows and Java platforms had become polarizingly heterogeneous, so the new market had to embrace vendor and technology independence.

Since the major vendors recognized this from the very beginning, they collaborated just enough to develop a vendor-independent platform consisting of the XML, SOAP, WSDL, and UDDI protocols. These standards were rolled out in near-record time, and all of the major vendors quickly delivered their initial web-services developer's toolkits to support them.

Today, these are the protocols and technologies that make up the lowest layer of the web-services technology pyramid. They're the standardized horizontal technologies that are the foundation for all types of web-services transactions across all industries. By creating those standards, the major vendors didn't just create a new playing field. They built a new mega-stadium, a Coliseum-like arena where they can now do battle for a prize that's even greater than the consumer-oriented World Wide Web: Internet-based business-to-business transactions.

But with the stadium in place and the competition underway, there isn't as compelling a reason for the major vendors to come to agreement quickly on additional standards. This is why we see more competition and debate surrounding the efforts to standardize the middle-layer technologies. In order to bootstrap this new market, the major vendors jumped in early, skipping the early segments of the timeline. Now that the market is open, the major vendors are free to return to competition as usual, and the remaining technologies will once again evolve through the stages of the solution-evolution timeline.

The first-version products from major vendors are often lacking in areas such as compatibility, performance, and reliability. Aggressive ISVs can continue to sell their products because they can remain one or two steps ahead of the major vendors. But eventually the major vendors always win. Their products improve, and as they continue to gain market share the ISVs have an increasingly difficult time competing. In some cases the major vendors acquire the independents, and the issue becomes moot. Those ISVs that remain independent must sell to increasingly conservative, late-to-adopt customers who prefer not to take risks on specialty ISVs' products, even though the ISVs' products may be superior.

Web Services Providers (WSPs)

Ultimately, every web-services technology will make its way through the solution-evolution timeline, at which point the technology becomes stable, standardized, and universally adopted. Once that occurs, you can usually find multiple implementations of the technology, and you'll frequently hear the phrase *best-of-breed*. It's at this stage that the *web-services providers* (WSPs) finally step in.

WSPs are similar to *managed service providers* (MSPs) in the context of the World Wide Web. They're generally conservative vendors who get involved with technologies only after most of the issues of standardization, implementation, and acceptance have been resolved, and clear winners emerge from among the competing solutions. In fact,

WSPs and MSPs both wait until it's obvious what their prospective customers are buying before offering to manage those solutions for them.

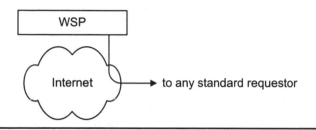

Figure 15-6: Web Service Provider

WSPs handle virtually every aspect of web-services outsourcing, including hosting and managing back-end systems. Note in Figure 15-6 that there's no longer a web-services box on the left side. All of the servers and other systems are located within the WSP's facilities.

Outsourcing

The benefits of using a WSP to deploy your web services include those of other outsourcing arrangements: focus, time-to-market, trading non-recurring capital expense for recurring costs, and leveraging the expertise and staff of a third-party specialist. Unfortunately, some customers look for and even enter into such relationships expecting the outsourcer to handle everything, including all the decision-making. Rarely does it work out that way, since conservative-by-nature WSPs and MSPs tend to take on only the standardized, easy 80 percent of web-services and web-site management tasks, respectively. This leaves the customer with responsibility for the most difficult 20 percent of the tasks, which according to the 80/20 rule will probably account for 80 percent of the cost. Outsourcing can certainly be worthwhile, but it's important to enter into such relationships with realistic expectations.

The WSP model is better suited for web services that can be outsourced in their entirety, just as MSPs typically take responsibility for all the components of e-commerce web sites. If your web-services architecture includes back-end systems that must remain in house,

WSPs may not be a particularly good solution. Yes, it's possible to run a link such as a VPN from the WSP's facilities back to your corporate data center, but then you'll have created a topology that's essentially the same as that of a WSDN.

Software-as-Service

Outsourcing to a WSP is particularly attractive to software publishers who want to repackage their products as services, but lack the experience required to operate the high-availability sites required by this new distribution and business model. Software publishers are adept at manufacturing and distributing their intellectual property on CD-ROMs, and even offering products and updates via Internet download. But since the World Wide Web is only their secondary medium, traditional software publishers aren't out of business if their web sites briefly go down or slow down. Still, publishers will need help when they switch to a software-as-service model, where their customers depend on the Internet and publishers' infrastructures for the real-time operation of applications. We'll discuss the issues surrounding software-as-service in greater detail in Chapter 20.

———

Selecting the best deployment option for web services is a bit like jumping onto a moving train—it's all about timing and relativity. Getting it right requires that you develop a sense not only of where things are at the moment, but also the direction in which they're headed, and the speed with which they're moving. The keys are to understand the web-services pyramid as a snapshot of the technology state-of-the-art, with all of the technologies moving towards the lower layers of the pyramid as they evolve along the solution-evolution timeline. This understanding of the rapidly evolving nature of web services will allow you to create an overall strategy for web services within your organization—which is the topic of Part IV of *Loosely Coupled*.

Part IV

Strategies

Chapter 16

Strategies and Projects

In 1985, when the IBM PC was barely three years old, many companies asked, "Should we build networks to link our computers?" By 1995, most organizations with more than one computer in a single location had installed local-area networks (LANs), and the networking quandry had been replaced by the question, "Should we get involved with the Internet?" A mere five years later, that question had become irrelevant. From Fortune 100 companies down to the local pharmacy, virtually every organization now has email and some presence on the World Wide Web.

Today, organizations are asking, "Should we get involved with web services, and how?" But this won't be a question for long. Web services will soon become as ubiquitous as LANs and the Internet. We'll accept web services as a matter of fact, and there will be a new data-communications question on the tip of everyone's tongue.

Web services will eventually permeate every nook and cranny of your company, just as computers have done. You'll use web services behind the firewall and beyond, to communicate with customers, vendors, and employees. Web services will run on your largest systems and your smallest mobile devices. Eventually, web services will even become the standard interfaces to your microprocessor-controlled appliances and vehicles.

Since everyone will eventually use web services, the real issues now are how your organization should think strategically about web services, and how individual web-services projects should be planned and managed. These are the questions we'll answer in Part IV, *Strategies*.

But first we'll consider two often-recommended, yet very distinct strategies for the adoption of web services: the *stepping-stone* and the *fast-track* approaches to web-services adoption. Then we'll sort web-services projects into simple and complex types. In the following chapters, we'll see how to plan for each type.

Adoption Strategies

There's an ongoing argument over the best way for an organization to get started with web services. Virtually all of the opinions voiced fall into one of two categories: the stepping-stone approach, or the fast-track approach. Proponents of the stepping-stone approach suggest you get started by seeking out opportunities for simple web-service projects, learn as you go, and cautiously work your way into more complex projects. This is an appealing approach because it's a common-sense, low-risk strategy that's inherently simple.

But supporters of the fast-track approach argue that visionary companies should instead dive in and begin with complex web services, most notably those that link companies with customers or suppliers for strategic business advantages. Rather than waste time with low-return, non-directed experiments and opportunistic utilization of web-services technologies, they suggest you immediately get to work on the web services that will increase your company's revenues most quickly. This approach implies that you'll get started with relatively complex and expensive projects—which means you're in for higher risks, but also potentially higher returns.

Both of these approaches seem logical. They make intuitive sense. But one urges you to act quickly, while the other cautions you to walk before you run. Which is right? The answer is…both, depending on the project. As we'll see in the remainder of this chapter and those that follow, both of the approaches are valuable, but for different types of projects. There's no single approach that's right for all organizations or for all projects, so you need to scope your projects carefully and select the best approach for each.

Grass Roots

The stepping-stone approach may already be in use within your organization, whether you're aware of it or not. Because web services are the hot new technology, your programmers may already be using them to solve simple day-to-day problems. If a programmer is responsible for internal or external application integration, that person may already be well-versed in web services if not actually using the technology in production work. The advantages are just too compelling, and improvements in development tools continue to make web services simpler.

Such grass-roots, stepping-stone projects may not be identifiable as *web-services* projects per se. They're probably the usual run-of-the-mill integration projects, with the exception that the programmers happen to be making use of web-services technology. They're simply switching to the latest tools, just as carpenters would upgrade from handsaws to power saws. But although your company may already be developing basic, grass-roots web services, these simple projects shouldn't be confused with more strategic, complex web services. The two are very different indeed.

Complexity

A simple web service project is one that can be implemented and deployed easily without the need for a formal plan, such as a grass-roots integration effort. Such simple projects fit well into the stepping-stone approach.

A complex web service project is one that requires significant investments of people, time, and money, and therefore demands strategic planning. For web-services projects of this type, a modified version of the fast-track approach will yield the best results.

We could have used a terminology other than "complex versus simple." We could have said "large versus small," for example, but the complex/simple distinction works because a simple web service may be strategic and important to your business. But as long as it won't take much effort to build and operate a web service, we'd still refer to it as simple. The complex/simple distinction makes it clear that web services in one group require strategic planning, while those in the other group do not.

How do you determine whether a particular web service project is simple enough to qualify for the stepping-stone approach, or complex and therefore requiring a strategic plan? Here's a good guideline. If a project meets *any* of the following three criteria, treat it as complex:

- It's based on the asynchronous-interaction model.
- It requires high availability of the application or the infrastructure.
- You'll be *providing* the service to one or more external systems (i.e., not under your control and outside your firewall), rather than merely subscribing to it as a requestor.

If a project qualifies as none of the above because it's synchronous, doesn't need to operate 24/7, and doesn't require you to provide an external service, you can probably treat it as simple and skip formal strategic planning.

QoS Asymmetry

The second point on the list above refers to *high availability*, a generalized term that refers to a high *Quality of Service* (QoS). In the world of those who measure and manage web services, QoS is the umbrella term covering a number of specific ways to track the performance of a web service. For example, QoS includes measurement of response times, availability, and downtime. But for strategic planning purposes, QoS boils down to one simple question: How important is this web service to your business?

At one extreme of the QoS spectrum are mission-critical web services, and at the other extreme are web services that are not at all critical. Why the distinction? As you develop your project plans, you've got to consider the robustness requirements of your services. It will take much more time and money to build and run a robust web service that must operate 24/7 and handle severe peak loads than it will to build and run a service that's not critical to your business. We'll use the terms *commercial-grade* to describe web services that are mission-critical or must otherwise be implemented and operated robustly, and *basic-grade* to define web services at the other end of the spectrum.

The QoS requirements are not an attribute of a web service itself, but rather are determined by its importance to the requestor or provider organization. What's commercial-grade to one organization may be basic-grade to another. QoS is, therefore, *asymmetrical.*

Consider the example of a package-tracking web service. FedEx needs this service to be commercial-grade. If the service is unavailable, tens of thousands of customers each hour will be affected. While a failure of its package-tracking system may not be as critical to FedEx as an air-traffic delay at its Memphis hub, the impact on customer relationships for a multi-hour outage could be substantial.

But what about the requestors to that service? If a FedEx customer's application that queries the FedEx web service is unavailable for a few hours, only that customer is affected. For many businesses, the temporary lapse in web-service package tracking might be no more than a minor inconvenience. After all, if you need to track only a few packages and the service is down, you can still call FedEx on the telephone or use its web site via a browser. For some individual customers this might be a problem, but probably not on the same scale as it would be for FedEx to lose the entire service and be unable to help all of its customers. FedEx considers its package-tracking web service to be commercial-grade, whereas it's probably only a basic-grade web service for most FedEx customers. This distinction has a significant impact on effort and cost, and hence on the planning process.

Mapping Complexity to Strategy

Understanding QoS and other requirements that determine complexity is important for any web service you're considering developing and deploying. You could easily spend $300,000 to $1 million to deploy a complex web service, in addition to the cost of developing the underlying application. On the other hand, you may be able to put together the pieces of a simple web service using free open-source tools, and run it on hardware you already own.

Let's return to the example of a FedEx package-tracking web service. The requestor side of such a web service for most businesses would be neither commercial-grade nor complex. The task qualifies as simple, and fits well into the stepping-stone approach. This is a fairly straightforward project: One person can implement it in a day or two, and it doesn't require a strategic plan.

Now consider the same web service from FedEx's perspective. Creating the provider side of this web service isn't particularly difficult—but since FedEx is playing the role of provider and the service must be commercial-grade, it's clearly complex. Considerable thought, time, and money should go into developing a web service such as this one, so the iterative stepping-stone approach isn't appropriate. This project needs a strategic plan that will allow the service to be launched at the optimum time to deliver the best return on investment.

Critical Components Revisited

Unfortunately, segregating simple and complex web services isn't always as easy as the three-point list we considered above. This list is only an approximation, because it doesn't take into consideration one important fact: All technologies become easier and less expensive to deploy over time. A project that would be complex in the early days of a *critical technology* (see Chapter 5), will become simpler and less expensive to implement as the technology becomes commonplace, and better tools for deploying it are widely available. The short list of criteria doesn't allow you to consider the evolutionary effects introduced in the *technology pyramid* in Chapter 5 and the *solution-evolution timeline* in Chapter 15. To optimize the timing of your web-services projects, you need to understand the basic criteria for segregating simple and complex projects, and take into consideration the current and future availability of the critical components involved.

———————

Simple and complex web service projects must be approached quite differently from one another. Each type requires a very different plan and time table as we'll see in the following chapters.

Chapter 17

Simple Projects

By definition, simple web services are relatively easy to design, implement, deploy, and support. For example, a skilled programmer can probably get a basic-grade requestor utilizing FedEx's packaging tracking service up and running in far less time than it would take to complete a detailed strategic plan for the same project. Simple web-service projects like this are prime opportunities to get your feet wet first, then gradually expand your usage of web-services technology until you're implementing complex strategic projects. You can begin with synchronous, basic-grade web services and work your way up to commercial-grade asynchronous web services, linking to your external business partners. This is the essence of the stepping-stone approach that we'll consider in detail in this chapter, assessing its usefulness for different types of projects.

A Stepping-Stone Template

The stepping-stone approach has become conventional wisdom for how to get started in web services. The stepping-stone mantra goes something like this:

Identify opportunities to deploy simple web services in order to gain experience and over time, work
your way towards increasingly more ambitious web-
services projects.

You create a stepping-stone plan by identifying the individual tasks
or stepping stones that will get you to your desired destination, one
step at a time. As with stones in a river or along a garden path, the
tasks should be closely spaced, so that only a small, incremental step
is required to get from one stone to the next.

Only a single new feature or concept should be introduced at each
step. For example, don't make a web service more complex in the
same step where you change its environment from internal to external. Complete one change before embarking upon the next, and use
two steps rather than combine them into one.

Think of the following list of simple web-services tasks as a template for a stepping-stone approach to web services. This list isn't
intended to be taken verbatim, since the whole idea of this approach
is to learn and adapt as you go. Develop your own list of stepping-
stones and update it frequently. Note that each stepping-stone has a
formal *objective* that explains the purpose of the step and provides a
goal by which you can measure your success. As you create your own
stepping-stones, make sure you include an objective for each one.

1.   Begin by implementing a few read-only, basic-grade re-
     questors that query someone else's external web services.
     You can find databases of such services at XMethods
     (www.xmethods.com) and SalCentral (www.salcentral.com).
     *Objective: Have your programmers learn about the development environ-
     ment and how to code a simple web-services requestor.*
2.   Unless your development environment already supports such
     a feature, add a logging facility to your simple services. *Objec-
     tive: Learn the subtleties of the web-services protocols and how to debug
     a web-services exchange.*
3.   Build a simple *portal*—a web site that delivers web pages com-
     posed of the results from multiple web services. Use this por-
     tal from now on as a user interface to the new web services
     you develop. *Objective: Learn how to develop a portal, which is also a
     great debugging platform.*

4. Make your portal available to others within your organization (i.e., behind the firewall). Take your portal seriously: Use version-control software and staged-development methodologies. Get into the habit of publishing new releases to the portal as you would for a software product. *Objective: Learn software management and how to support a portal—before it becomes popular, and even mission-critical.*

5. Verify your portal's security. Have someone who knows what he or she is doing try to break into the system. Pick an insider with strong internal knowledge—after all, you can't assume all hackers will be outsiders. Make sure your portal can't be used to reach internal assets from outside the firewall, but that it's available to all users, including those accessing information via any virtual private networks (VPNs). *Objective: Learn basic web-service security now, before mistakes become more costly.*

6. Write simple web-service queries to some of your company's existing web-services-enabled software packages, such as ERP, CRM, and accounting. Don't publish them on the company-wide portal just yet. *Objective: Learn how to link to enterprise applications.*

7. Add authentication and authorization controls to your portal, enabling access to your read-only enterprise-application web service. Configure various roles with different permissions, and test them to ensure your restrictions are working. *Objective: Continue to learn more about web-services security, and gain experience with secure access to legacy systems.*

8. Write your first simple web-service provider from scratch, and enable in-house access via the portal. Begin with a trivial service, such as one that merely returns the date and time, then move on to those that query live databases. Continue to use your portal as the web-services requestor. *Objective: Learn how to develop web-services providers.*

9. Prepare your portal for commercial-grade use with high availability using redundant hardware and software. *Objective: Learn the issues associated with commercial-grade infrastructure.*

10. Build a query-only aggregated web service. Identify two applications with overlapping queries. For example, build a web service that can look up a customer name in two different databases or applications, and return a joined result for dis-

play on your portal. This may be your first web service that performs a valuable function that your organization can't already do. If so, it could quickly become very popular with your employees and unexpectedly develop into a mission-critical application—and you'll be glad you preceded this step with experience in deploying commercial-grade infrastructure. *Objective: Learn to build an aggregated web service.*

11. Make an internal web service available to a trusted external party using SSL or a virtual private network (VPN). *Objective: Learn how to use SSL and VPNs to deliver secure web services.*

12. Build a second portal, but this time for external use. Publish a web service that *doesn't* link to your internal systems for reasons of simplicity and security. Make it available to the public, but only via the portal user interface, not as a directly accessible web service. *Objective: Take a small step towards external web services.*

13. Permit access to an external web service *as a web service*, rather than via the portal. Your first external web service should have no requirements for authentication or encryption, so make sure it can't be used to access internal systems. You may have to enlist the help of business partners or other departments to test this service under realistic conditions. *Objective: Gain experience with external web services.*

14. Provide another external web service that uses authentication, but still can't reach internal databases for security reasons. *Objective: Learn how to deploy external authentication for web services.*

15. Perform a security audit of the external portal. *Objective: Learn how vulnerable you are.*

16. Make use of an asynchronous web service offered by another company or department. *Objective: Learn how to develop and deploy an asynchronous web service.* Note: This is a very large step that you may be able to break into smaller ones.

17. Create your own asynchronous web service. *Objective: Expand your knowledge of asynchronous web services.*

Journey or Destination?

The stepping-stone approach is more about the journey than the destination. Rather than focusing on long-term strategic objectives, the stepping-stone approach embodies the learn-as-you-go philosophy. It's ideal for simple web-services projects, because decisions about what to do next are made according to the successes and failures of the previous steps.

The stepping-stone approach is opportunistic. Each subsequent project is subject to change according to new opportunities and requirements that arise. The stepping-stone approach is also adaptive, since it reacts to such environmental changes as improvements in technology and the evolution of business requirements.

But as useful as the stepping-stone approach may be, it's only effective as long as you remain in the world of simple web services. As an intentional path to more complex web services, it fails miserably. In fact, the stepping-stone approach isn't a strategy at all. It's an iterative and purely tactical process in which each decision is based upon the outcome of the previous one. You'll learn as you go, but you may change directions at each step and ultimately follow a very inefficient, purely reactive path to your ultimate strategic destination.

Most organizations following the stepping-stone path find that their ultimate destination actually changes along the way. This is both the advantage and the disadvantage of the approach. If your destination is as clearly defined as it should be in a strategic project, the stepping-stone approach won't be the best way to get there. On the other hand, as the old adage goes: If you don't know where you're going, any path will get you there. So use the stepping-stone approach for simple web services, but don't make the mistake of expecting simple web-services experiments to achieve your larger strategic objectives as well.

———————

That said, there's no doubt you'll receive some residual benefits to your strategic objectives from your stepping-stone efforts. You'll gain experience as you complete increasingly sophisticated projects, some of which will certainly be applicable to your strategic projects. Even though the stepping-stone path doesn't lead directly to a strategic goal, some of the knowledge and experience gained from implementing simple web services will stick. You can even take advantage of this in your strategic planning, possibly shortening the estimated development times of strategic projects to reflect the shortened learning curve. But it's important that strategic projects should drive the simple ones, and not the other way around.

Chapter 18

The Timing of
Complex Projects

As we've learned from the previous two chapters, complex web-services projects are those in which the web services themselves are complex, they must be deployed via commercial-grade infrastructure, or they're provided to external business partners. Complex projects require a degree of planning, along with substantial commitments of money and human resources, and optimizing the ratio of costs to benefits to maximize the return on investment becomes the primary objective of project management.

In this chapter, we'll focus on one element of strategic planning: the *timing* of complex web-services projects. We'll begin by determining whether a project's critical components are in the top or middle layer of the web-services pyramid introduced in Chapter 5. This matters because the timing of a project depends upon the availability of its critical components. Then we'll explore technology-adoption life cycles and their effect on a project's optimum start and launch dates.

Here's a preview of where we're heading: If a project's critical component is evolving rapidly, as manifested by rapidly falling deployment costs, you can reduce the cost of the project by delaying its start. But if you wait too long, you'll miss out on the project's benefits. We'll see what factors help us track declining costs for web-services deployment, and how to use these indicators to determine the optimum launch and project-start dates.

Business Semantics

From our look at the web-services pyramid in Chapter 5, you may recall that the timeline of a project's critical components actually determines the timeline of the project overall. Since simple projects never require providing services to external business partners, their critical components are always in the middle layer of horizontal but not-yet-standardized technologies. In other words, simple web-services projects are never dependent upon business semantics as their critical component. On the other hand, complex web-services projects may depend upon critical components in either the middle layer or the upper layer of business semantics.

To get a handle on the critical component for your project, consider the scope of the business-semantics problem. If specifying the business semantics will require extensive negotiations among multiple parties, then it's likely that this will be the critical component. This isn't a technological issue, but rather a political one. Getting a consortium of more than two parties to agree on business semantics is a major undertaking that dwarfs most middle-layer technical challenges. On the other hand, if there are only two parties or the business-semantics standards already exist, then you're likely to find that the most critical component does indeed lie within that middle layer of horizontal, not-yet-standardized technologies.

The 800-Pound Gorilla

In addition to the two-parties-or-less rule, there are two other cases where the lack of an existing business-semantics standard isn't necessarily a problem for complex web services projects. These cases involve so-called 800-pound gorillas and first movers.

Organizations like General Motors, Cisco, and the U.S. federal government are 800-pound gorillas, at least within their supply chains. If General Motors wants its suppliers to adopt a particular technology, for instance, G.M. has the clout to "make it so." The suppliers have little say in the matter. Either they comply, or General Motors will buy elsewhere. When dealing with its suppliers, G.M. is the 800-pound gorilla. If G.M. desires, it can skip the complex negotiations for business-semantics standards when dealing with its suppliers. The company doesn't need to secure the consensus of a consortium. So while business semantics will still be required for any web services G.M. chooses to implement, development and acceptance of the business semantics aren't likely to be a critical component to such efforts.

A similar advantage accrues to so-called first movers, or parties that take it upon themselves to develop and deploy business-semantics standards on their own. First movers may not have the clout of an 800-pound gorilla. Often a first mover will take the initiative precisely because it isn't an 800-pound gorilla. The first-mover believes that being the first kid on the block to offer a web service will deliver a competitive advantage: clout that it doesn't otherwise have.

In some cases, the first mover won't actually be one of the business partners directly involved with the web service project. For instance, a value-added reseller (VAR) with expertise in a particular vertical market might decide to invest in the development of business-semantics standards for that vertical. A VAR specializing in software for doctors' offices might develop an XML schema for scheduling referral appointments with other doctors, or perhaps develop standards for the ordering of medical supplies. The VAR's motivation is the enhanced positioning it would ultimately receive if its ad-hoc standards were to be accepted by a large number of physicians and their partners. Many VARs with expertise in such verticals are in ideal positions to invest in such efforts, and like the 800-pound gorillas, these first movers can bypass the political overhead of having to build consensus.

Identifying the Critical Component

We can now determine whether the critical component for a web-services project will be the business semantics, or whether it will instead lie in the middle layer of horizontal, not-yet-standardized technologies. The critical component for a complex web-services project lies among the horizontal technologies in the middle layer of the web-services pyramid if any of the following are true:

- The web service is internal.
- It involves no more than a single external business partner.
- It's based on an already-existing business-semantics standard.
- An 800-pound gorilla or a first-mover will mandate the web service's business semantics.

If none of the above four conditions is true, the business semantics will most likely be the project's critical components.

Strategic Timing

In Chapter 16, we described two versions of conventional wisdom for web-services adoption strategies: the *stepping-stone* approach, recommended for simple web services; and the *fast-track* approach, which we suggested might be more appropriate for complex web services. Progressive companies focus their attentions on complex web services, for these are the web services that will grow their businesses. Simple web services, by comparison, tend to merely reduce costs. If your company is part of a highly automated industry in which others—perhaps even your competitors—are planning to deploy complex web services, you can't afford to merely dip a toe into the web-services pond to check the temperature. You need to dive in and get started immediately, before it's too late.

But notice we said "If." Not every company is part of a highly-automated industry, and web services—particularly complex, expensive strategic web services—aren't yet right for everyone. The fast-track approach is no panacea. Even if there's a clear business case for complex web services in your company, now is not necessarily the best time to begin. While some companies can benefit from deploying complex web services immediately, most cannot.

Many small- and medium-sized enterprises won't feel the impact of web services for many years to come. Most companies will never even know they're using web services; the technology will be embedded within the products they acquire, and will therefore be invisible to them. There's no point for such companies to develop in-house expertise in web services. It would be a waste of their money and resources. Far too many companies dive into expensive and aggressively scheduled web-services projects without first seeking answers to two fundamental questions: When should we launch those services, and when should we begin their development?

Planning for complex web services is mostly a matter of timing. For some specific types of web services for certain types of companies, now *may* be the right time to begin. But development costs for web services are declining rapidly, so delaying the start of a complex web-services project could substantially reduce its cost and thereby increase the return on that investment.

Launch Dates

Whether simple or complex, every project needs a target completion or launch date. But launch dates for simple and complex projects are determined quite differently. You plan simple projects in *forward order*. Beginning with a *start date*, you identify the tasks, apply the available resources, and the launch date appears as a result of the project-management processes. Within limits, you can add or remove resources to the project in order to shift the launch date earlier or later.

IT projects are often expected to launch "as soon as possible," but that may be inappropriate for projects based on complex web services. The reason has to do with the network effect: It won't do any good to launch an external web service if there won't be any business partners capable of using it. Complex web-service projects, should therefore be planned in *reverse order*. You begin with a *fixed launch date* as determined by legitimate and realistic business objectives, then map the tasks and resources backwards in time to determine the start date. If the start date has already passed or will arrive too soon, within limits you can apply more resources so that the project can be completed on time.

How do you determine the launch date for a complex project? First, apply the same criteria we used to identify the critical components. If a complex web service will be used internally or to communicate with only a single business partner, the optimal launch date can be determined according to the opportunity. The decision for a two-party service may be made tactically—as in, "When do you think you can have it done?"—but it's still true that the longer you wait, the lower the costs should be. Of course, you'll lose the benefit of the web service in the meantime, so you need to balance the tradeoffs. Selecting a launch date for a multi-party complex web service is a far more difficult task that should be based on an understanding of the adoption life cycles of technologies.

Adoption Life Cycles

The bell curve shown in Figure 18-1 will be familiar to any business-school graduate. Originally developed to portray the adoption rate of new strains of seed potatoes by farmers, the graph gained new fame when Geoffrey Moore applied it to high-tech marketing in his 1991 book *Crossing the Chasm.*[22]

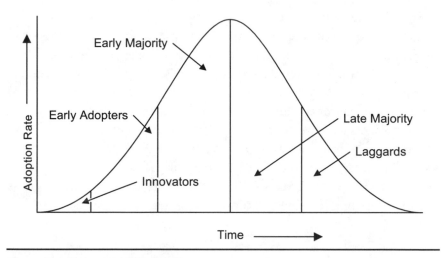

Figure 18-1: Technology Adoption Curve

The curve illustrates how adoption rates increase then decrease over time. A new technology first *ramps up*, meaning it's adopted at an increasing rate. Once the technology begins to be widely accepted and its market starts to reach saturation, the adoption rate slows.

The vertical divisions in Figure 18-1 separate five groups of technology adopters and are roughly equivalent to where the standard deviations would fall. The early and late majority are within one standard deviation of the mean, and the early adopters and the laggards each fall within two standard deviations. The relatively few innovators are in the leading third standard deviation.

The groups are based on *psychographics*—a combination of psychology and demographics. For example, *innovators* aggressively seek new technologies, often adopting them before the technologies are even known to most potential users. Innovators are looking for technological advantages.

Early adopters are more interested in the business and competitive advantages of a new technology rather the technology itself. But they're still risk-takers, since they're willing to adopt a new technology before it has been proven or widely accepted.

Those in the *early majority* group are the pragmatists. They don't want to take the risk of adopting a technology too early, but they also recognize that waiting too long can put them at a substantial disadvantage. They want to make sure the technology works for others before they invest.

The *late majority* are even more conservative. Not only do they want to be certain the new technology works, they also want to wait until it's been widely adopted and standardized. They don't consider the technology to offer them any competitive advantage, but they recognize that they can't live without it once their partners or competitors have adopted it.

Laggards are those that only adopt a technology when they have no choice. In fact, many laggards don't explicitly adopt technologies at all, but rather acquire them accidentally when a technology is a component of a packaged solution. For example, a laggard might purchase a computer-based telephone system, but has no interest in its computer per se.

Moore's breakthrough was the recognition that adoption is not continuous. As illustrated in Figure 18-2, he discovered a gap—which he called the *chasm*—between the early adopter and early majority phases, across which many technologies never jump. When the early majority never adopts a technology, that technology never becomes widely accepted and is condemned to languish or die. There have been some classic cases of products that never quite *crossed the chasm* such as the NeXT operating system and the original pen-based computers.

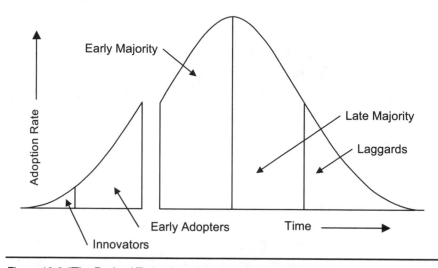

Figure 18-2: "The Revised Technology Adoption Life Cycle" (Chapter 1) from "Crossing the Chasm" by Geoffrey A. Moore. Copyright ©1991 by Geoffrey A. Moore. Reprinted by permission of HarperCollins Publishers Inc.

If a technology has crossed the chasm, we say it has *achieved critical mass*. In other words, enough people or organizations have adopted the technology that its long-term viability is assured. It has caught on, and come too far to sink into oblivion.

Timing is Everything

It's easy to imagine beginning a project too late, but have you ever started one too early? This happens frequently. Many dramatic examples occur near *tipping points*, when major technological changes take hold. For example, consider a programmer struggling with the design of a user interface (UI) under DOS, only months before Microsoft shipped the first Windows developer's toolkit. Had the developer waited six months, his development time would have been cut in half and he would have launched a more marketable product. No matter what the application did, its success was dependent on a critical component, the UI.

You can't wait forever, of course. If you do, you'll never accomplish anything. But when a technology is evolving as rapidly as web services and the development costs are falling, you can save your company a bundle by putting some thought into the timing of your entrance into the fray. To determine the best time to launch a complex web services project, you'll need to answer the following questions:

1. Where are the critical components in their own adoption life cycles? Are they still bleeding-edge, high-risk technologies, or stable and widely adopted?

2. Where is *your industry* relative to the adoption life cycle of the critical components? When will your competitors deploy complex web services based on them—this year, or two years from now? Or have they begun already?

3. Relative to others in the same industry, where is your company positioned? Are you an innovator? An early adopter? A technology laggard?

Let's see how to answer these three sets of questions.

Adoption of the Critical Components

Where do web services sit on the technology adoption life-cycle curve? Overall, there's little risk that web services won't make it across the chasm into the early-majority phase. As pointed out in Chapter 1, the adoption of underlying web-services standards by all the major software vendors has essentially built a bridge across the chasm already.

But for strategic-planning purposes, we must consider each web-services component technology's position on the curve. For each web-services project, it's important to know where on the curve the project's critical component lies. If the critical-component technology is new, you'll be taking a number of risks, including the possibilities that it might change substantially or even fail altogether. You also may be forced to work around a number of early-adopter problems that won't exist later in the critical component's life cycle. On the other hand, if the technology is mature, your competitors may be way ahead of you and planning to roll out web services based on that technology any day now. Whether the critical component technology is new or mature, your strategy will be greatly affected by its adoption-cycle context.

The components in the bottom layer of the web-services pyramid have generally crossed the chasm and are at least into the early majority phase. Most analysts and consultants agree that the basic web services technologies (SOAP and WSDL) moved from the innovator phase into the early adopter phase sometime during 2002. On the other hand, security protocols were still in the early adopter phase in 2003, and transaction management protocols hadn't even made it beyond the innovation phase.

Positioning Your Industry

The next question you need to answer is: How far along is your industry in the web-services adoption life cycle for your critical component? For example, companies in the financial-services industry might consider their critical component for an industry-wide web-services project to be the business semantics, and they might expect adoption to peak in late 2005 as shown in Figure 18-3.

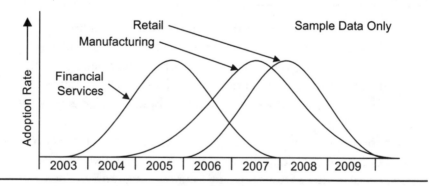

Figure 18-3: Industry-Specific Critical-Component Adoption Curves (sample dates only)

By comparison, a manufacturing business might expect its industry's adoption of a critical component to peak in mid 2007, while a retail consortium might expect the same in early 2008. These dates aren't meant to be accurate, but they illustrate that the timing and shape of the technology adoption life cycle curve varies according to the industry, the specific web-services project, and the project's critical component.

Your challenge is to assign dates to the curve that are appropriate for your project, given the context of your industry. Start with the most progressive company in your industry. It could be a competitor, or it could be your own company. When will that company deploy a web service comparable to the one you're considering? Whatever that date is, align it with the early-adopter segment of the curve.

Figure 18-4 shows what a curve might look like for an industry in which associated standards will be adopted and the first complex web services will be launched at the beginning of 2005. In this sample case, the middle of the early-adopter phase runs from mid-year 2004 through mid-year 2005.

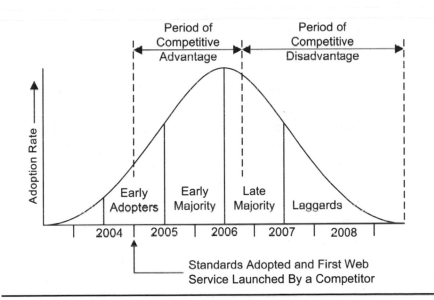

Figure 18-4: Period of Competitive Advantage (sample dates only)

Now consider your own situation. Is there already a consortium of companies in your industry working to develop semantic standards for the exchange of information via XML? When do you expect such standards to be adopted? Perhaps they're already in place. The adoption of standards for the type of web service you're planning would indicate you're in the early-adopter phase.

The time during which you think there may be a competitive advantage for your company to have a web-services implementation typically extends from the middle of the early-adopter phase into the start of the late-majority phase. For the sample industry shown in Figure 18-4, this period is through the third quarter of 2006. At some time early in the late majority phase, having an implementation ceases to offer any competitive advantage, and *not* having an implementation begins to be a problem. This shift is a *lagging indicator*, an after-the-fact hint that the late majority phase of adoption has begun.

Your Adoption Profile

You now have a web-services technology adoption curve that's specific to your industry, and to the particular web services you plan to deploy. The next question you need to answer is: What type of adopter is your company? Are you an early adopter, or part of the early majority? After taking a good hard look at your company, you may find that you're actually in the late majority or even a laggard.

That sounds horrible, doesn't it? Why would anyone purposely identify his or her company as a laggard? But your company may be a laggard for some web-services projects, and not for others. For example, when it comes to communicating with your customers, your company may be particularly progressive. You may be an early adopter in this area. But at the same time, you may be in the late majority when it comes to ordering office supplies, managing your payroll, or other non-revenue business processes.

The key is to identify your position on the curve—your adoption profile—for each complex web-service project you're considering. This will allow you to determine your target launch date for that project.

Finding Your Launch Date

Once you've got an adoption curve for your industry, and you've determined where your own company belongs after some sleepless nights of soul searching, you can determine the launch date for your web-services project.

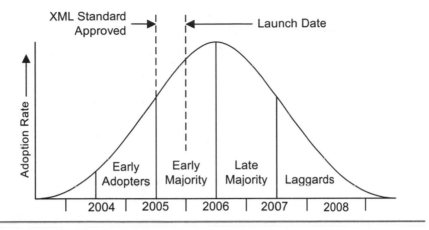

Figure 18-5: Your Position Relative to Your Industry (sample dates only)

An example is shown in Figure 18-5. This is the adoption curve for an industry where a particular type of web service will cross into the early-majority phase in the middle of 2005. Perhaps that's the date by which an XML-based standard for the business semantics of the web service is expected to be adopted. In any case, this particular company believes it should be within the early majority of companies to adopt this standard, and will release a web service based upon it. According to the curve, the company should launch the web service at the end of 2005 or early in 2006, roughly six months after the XML standard has been adopted.

Finding Your Start Date

There's only one more question to answer: How long will it take to develop the web service? In other words, what's the *lead time* required to meet the desired launch date?

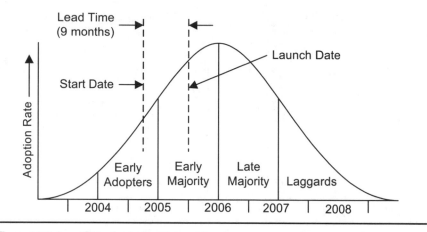

Figure 18-6: Lead Time (sample dates only)

Figure 18-6 is an example of a company that estimates it will require a nine-month lead time in order to develop and deploy a particular web service. In this case, it wants to launch at the end of 2005, so it must begin the project at the end of the first quarter of 2005.

The graph in Figure 18-6 highlights an interesting challenge. If the standards upon which this web service will be based won't be adopted until the middle of 2005, the company will be starting its efforts three months before that occurs to achieve its launch-date objectives. The company will therefore need to obtain an advance copy of the proposed specification. If it waits until the official publication date, the company's launch will be at least three months late. Since development must begin before the protocols are finalized, it's possible that significant changes may be required during development. Perhaps those nine months are therefore too optimistic. The company should consider tacking a few more months onto the project schedule, and therefore starting even earlier to allow the time needed to hit a moving target.

Ultimately, it may even be necessary for the company to participate in the standardization effort, possibly by taking an active role in the organization that's performing that task. Companies that are in the late majority or are laggards don't have this problem, and don't need to incur the expense associated with starting a project before the associated standards are finalized. They have the luxury of letting their competitors deal with the most difficult issues. They can wait until competing interests and technologies shake out, and the standards activities settle down. As you can see, it costs more to start early.

The Decreasing Cost of Implementation

This last point is a critical one, and fundamental to the strategic-planning process. Most executives and IT managers are aware that the cost of implementing software-based systems decreases over time. But few of them understand the implications, the most important of which is this: *You can always reduce cost by delaying the start of any development project.* There are many reasons for this, but the most important is that nearly everything associated with the technology becomes less expensive over time. We've illustrated this concept by the *decreasing cost curve*, as shown in Figure 18-7.

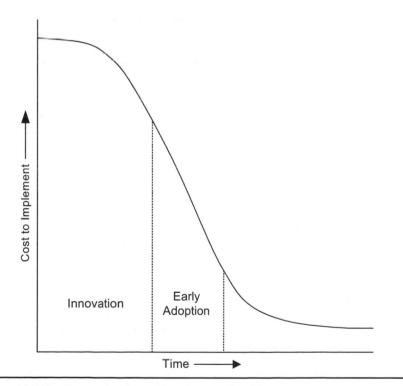

Figure 18-7: The Decreasing Cost of Development Over Time

Put simply, the cost of implementing a technology drops rapidly during the early phases of the technology's adoption life cycle. This curve illustrates this important point, but it's lacking any specific events or milestones that help us pinpoint the state of emerging technologies, such as web-services critical components. Are we in the early-majority phase? Early adoption? The graph doesn't give us a clue. As a solution to this problem, consider the *software-evolution timeline*, which shows the ten milestones that precede widespread adoption of any new software technology. The timeline is shown in Figure 18-8.

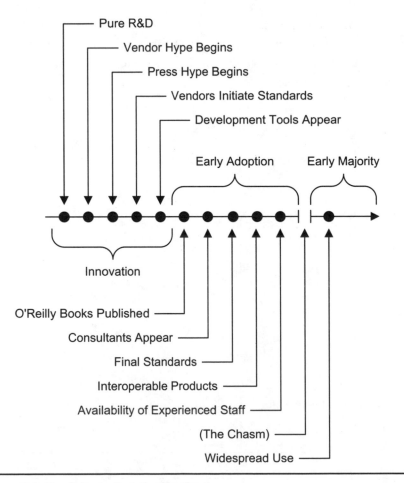

Figure 18-8: The Software Evolution Timeline

Borrowing from Geoffrey Moore, note that the chasm falls very late on the timeline in Figure 18-8, just before early-majority adoption appears. This occurs for two reasons: First, the timeline isn't linear or to scale. For instance, more time typically elapses between the appearance of consultants and the adoption of final standards than between the start of vendor hype and its coverage by the press. Second, all of the milestones identified in the timeline occur during the innovator and early-adopter phases of the adoption life-cycle curve. Once a technology crosses the chasm and is accepted by the early majority, it has become relatively stable, complete with the infrastructure and trained individuals required to support rapid adoption and growth.

The timeline has proven to be a useful tool to help managers and executives pinpoint the current state of adoption for new software technologies. As an example, the publication of an O'Reilly book covering a particular software technology, protocol, or tool marks the shift from the innovation phase to early adoption. Likewise, when companies can readily hire experienced staff who have already implemented, used, or deployed a technology at least once before, those companies know the technology is close to crossing the chasm into adoption by the early majority.

We can visualize this concept by projecting the software implementation timeline onto the decreasing cost curve. The result is the *software implementation cost curve* as shown in Figure 18-9.

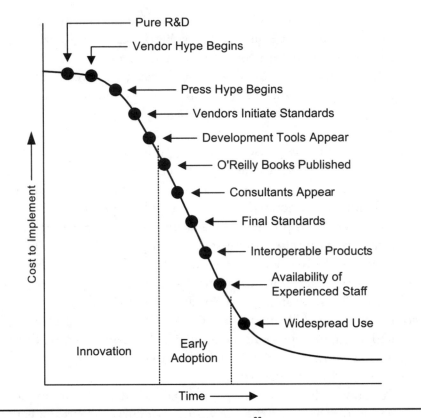

Figure 18-9: The Software Implementation Cost Curve [23]

The diagram illustrates that it's less expensive to develop an application once third-party tools become available than when the press hype begins. Likewise, it's more expensive to hire contractors and consultants in the early stage of a new technology (before it's a common skill set) than to hire employees later who have learned the required technology at a previous job, or perhaps even in school.

Lead Time

It will take time to develop the web service, so we need to work backwards as discussed earlier to determine the point in time when we must begin development. This process is illustrated in Figure 18-10.

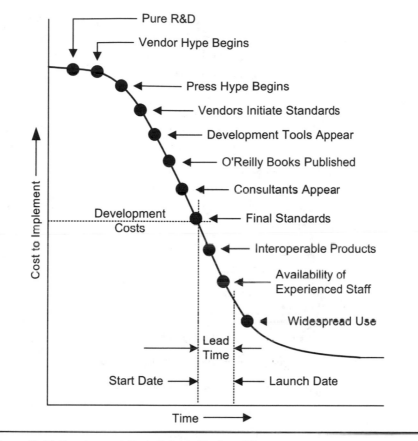

Figure 18-10: Development Costs Adjusted for Lead Time

We move backwards in time from the desired launch date by the amount of lead-time it will take to develop the service. This gives us the start date when development must begin in order to launch on schedule. Note that the development cost on the Y-axis is the point at which the start date intersects the cost curve. It appears that in order to launch the example web service prior to widespread use of similar services, the organization must begin development immediately upon the publication of the final standards for the underlying technologies. If the web service is an external business process, for instance, development should begin as soon as all of the required protocols and standards have been finalized.

Note also that at the time development begins, a number of important issues will not yet have been resolved. Because the associated milestones will not have been reached, the development team should be prepared for problems with product interoperability, and the company should not expect to hire employees who have previous experience with the recently standardized technologies required to build the web service.

Using an analysis such as shown above, it's possible to avoid starting a web-service implementation project too late. But it's also possible to avoid starting too early. That's critical for minimizing IT waste and maximizing ROI. Consider what would happen if the company in the above example were to begin development as soon as the first developer tools became available. The effect on implementation costs can be seen in Figure 18-11.

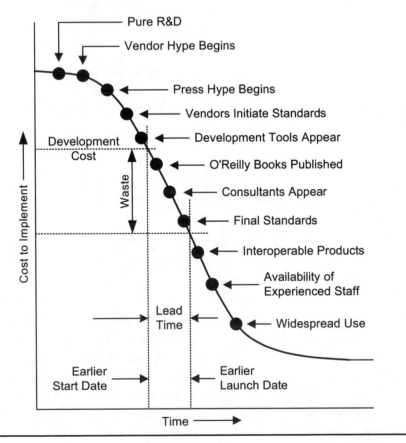

Figure 18-11: Waste Due to Early Development

Because the start dates is earlier, it intersects the cost curve at a higher (more expensive) point. The excess development cost or *waste* is shown as the difference between the optimal and premature development costs. Rather than starting just after the final standards appear (as shown in Figure 18-10), the project will begin just after the development tools first appear. Look at the milestones that will occur *after* the project is underway. Due to the early start, the project will not have the benefits of certain documentation, the availability of outside consultants or final standards. Books regarding the technology won't be published at the time the project commences, either. The company will have no choice but to do everything in house without consultants, and without the benefit of final standards. The development team may well have to re-design and re-code substantially before launch.

Postponing the Critical Component

Astute managers may have noted yet another option: not to delay the entire project in anticipation of the optimal start date, but instead just to begin work on the critical component later in the project. That component will become dramatically less expensive over time, so putting it off could reduce the cost of the entire project, and therefore increase its profitability. If a security component is most critical, for example, you could implement the web service's security concepts late in the project when simpler, more reliable, and less expensive solutions have hopefully become available.

This would be a good idea if not for the fact that the critical component is usually also the one with the greatest risk. Most of a project's unknowns are associated with its critical component, so the risk of the overall project remains high until those unknowns are resolved. Good risk management requires that unknowns surrounding high-risk components be resolved as early as possible in the project schedule, in order that confidence in the project increases over time. If high-risk unknowns are delayed, the risks remain constant, and confidence that the project will be completed on time and within budget actually decreases over time.

We've covered many theories and looked at a lot of charts and graphs in the past three chapters. But at the end of the day, you've got to reduce the philosophical to the practical, and figure out exactly how and when to start your web-services projects. From all of the information we've covered, here are the steps that have worked for others in distilled form:

- Segregate your simple and complex web-services projects. (See Chapter 16.)
- For simple projects, determine the critical components using the web-services pyramid, as shown in Chapter 5. Create milestones for these, and then use the stepping-stone approach to achieve them.
- Apply dates to the technology-adoption curve as appropriate for your industry (Figure 18-3).
- Determine the appropriate adoption profile for your company.
- Combining the above, determine the launch date for your web-services project (Figure 18-5).
- Estimate your project's development time.
- Working backwards from the launch date, determine the project's start date (Figure 18-6).
- Apply the software-implementation cost curve (Figure 18-10) to identify the milestones for the critical components required to create your web service.
- Based on the milestones and the estimated start date, determine if you should start now, wait for the development costs to decrease, or instead get extra help (e.g., from consultants) because you're already late.

Chapter 19

Service-Level Agreements

Other than those you've developed in house, virtually all of the applications you use today are licensed from software-product vendors. You're accustomed to the packaged-software distribution model, and you probably have your own guidelines for pre-purchase evaluation, perhaps including formal testing to whatever degree of rigor your company can justify and afford. You've also learned how to deal with software vendors, and to read and understand software license agreements and warranties.

You have a high degree of confidence that the software you've evaluated before purchase will continue to operate as it did when tested because it will be used in an environment that's reasonably under your control. The applications will run on your company's computers, not someone else's. The performance of the programs won't be affected by outside influences, such as the financial stability of the software vendors from whom you obtained them. If a vendor experiences business difficulties or even bankruptcy, you may have trouble getting support or updates, but the software won't suddenly stop working. The operation of the packaged software you've obtained is relatively immune to external events.

Compare this to the new world of web services, where the deliverables are no longer products but services, and the quality of those services can change day to day, hour to hour, and even second to second. A web service that works today may fail tomorrow or the next day. Pre-purchase evaluations and due diligence remain important in this new world, but the requirements for on-going monitoring and management far exceed what you've been used to up until now.

Managing the quality of web services requires all-new procedures, tools, and skills. Just as testing and warranties are key to managing the quality of packaged software, monitoring and *service-level agreements* (SLAs) are key to managing web services.

An SLA is just what its name implies: an *agreement* between a customer and a provider about what *services* will be delivered by the provider, and the measurable *levels* of those services the provider is expected to achieve. SLAs are not typically standalone contracts, but tend to be exhibits or attachments to more general agreements that contain boilerplate and other terms and conditions. As attachments, they're as legally binding as the rest of the contract.

A good SLA will describe a web service in great detail by answering the following questions:

- What *exactly* is the service to be provided?
- How will the quality of the service be measured?
- Based on those measurements, what are the *service levels* the provider is expected to achieve?
- How will the provider's performance be reported to the customer?
- What corrective actions will the provider take if the service levels are not met?
- What financial remedies or penalties will compensate the customer when the service levels are not achieved?
- What exclusions (if any) exist to the terms of the SLA?

Communications

The most important function of an SLA isn't technological, but to express and document the true understanding of the provider and customer. Even with SLAs in place, parties often embark on business relationships on the basis of implicit rather than explicit expectations—handshakes that later become misunderstandings.

Would you be satisfied if a provider's web service that was mission-critical to your business went down for nearly one full, eight-hour business day each and every month? Or suppose it failed for 22 minutes every day, or continuously during two consecutive 40-hour workweeks. Then would you be able to say, "That web service meets our expectations"? In fact, if you've accepted a 99 percent uptime service-level guarantee, that's what you've agreed to. There are 168 hours in a week, so one percent downtime is equal to 1.68 hours per week, or 7.25 hours per month. If the service is unavailable as often as this, don't be surprised if the provider thinks everything is just fine even though you don't. You'll be on record for having agreed that such a level of service is sufficient.

Providers often claim they actually deliver higher service levels than they're willing to put into their written SLAs because they've got to be conservative with their promises. But that argument isn't legitimate. We don't do that in our other contracts and warranties. We put into writing exactly what will happen in case something goes wrong. So why should we expect web-services providers to deliver levels of service that are higher than promised in their SLAs? Whether you're a provider or a customer, you shouldn't accept an SLA that doesn't accurately describe the level of service you'll find satisfactory. Too many web-services relationships are built on unwritten expectations. The greatest cause of disputes is the gap in understanding between what the web-services provider intends to provide and the results expected by the customer. A good service level agreement will align these expectations by clearly expressing up front the levels of services to be provided.

The Realities of Parity and Clout

After reading the above, you may wonder about the reality of SLAs in other aspects of your life. Consider the SLAs offered by your telephone company or your electric utility. Most likely, you've never read them—at least not those for your residential services. As compared to large companies, you pay relatively little for those services, and service outages are generally inconveniences rather than disasters. But for a hospital, for example, loss of electricity can be a life-threatening event. Likewise, if a call center loses telephone service, its business will be severely affected. In these examples, you can bet the customers have paid close attention to—and possibly negotiated—their SLAs.

Whether or not an SLA is even offered and you have the opportunity to negotiate it depends a great deal on the business relationship between you as the customer and the provider. For example, FedEx isn't likely to offer an SLA for its package-tracking web service to small customers, but it might do so for major accounts. At the other extreme, a high-value service that supports real-time financial transactions between peer institutions might well include an SLA as part of its fundamental service definition.

The discussions and explanations put forth in this chapter reflect the realities of high-value web services between parties with similar clout, which is the area where the most interesting SLAs are written and negotiated. At the other end of the spectrum where the value of the service is low and one party is a monopolistic provider, the guidelines presented here are academic. But for any situation in between, these examples offer important lessons.

Guarantees and Due Diligence

Does the existence of an SLA guarantee you'll get the service it describes? Not really—no more than a warranty on a new car can prevent it from breaking down. The SLA merely specifies what will happen if something does go wrong. While an SLA should give you some degree of confidence, the document itself can't perform the service. It's just a piece of paper. An SLA also isn't a substitute for your due diligence. For example, you shouldn't select a provider solely on the basis of which one has the best SLA any more than you would select application software packages by reading their license agreements. You need to evaluate which provider is most likely to be able to *achieve* the service levels you need, and at a fair price.

For example, some providers advertise 100 percent uptime. Sounds good, doesn't it? Better than 99.9 percent or 99.999 percent for sure. But, as common sense will tell you, 100 percent just isn't realistic, and as you might expect, providers that make this claim rarely achieve it except within the caveats and exceptions of their contracts. When you compare actual performance, you may find that a provider offering 99 percent uptime has a better track record than one offering 100 percent.

An SLA can't make a good web service out of a bad one. It's one thing to have a clear expression of mutual expectations, but it's quite another to have confidence that the provider you select can actually deliver on its commitments. Don't begin your search for a web service by reading SLAs, and don't impart too much significance to SLAs during the first round of your evaluation process. Like any other contract, an SLA should be addressed somewhat later. On the other hand, don't wait until after you've selected a vendor to evaluate its SLA. Make the SLA an important criterion of your final vendor-selection process.

For the purpose of analysis, we've divided SLAs into three categories: performance SLAs, reactive SLAs, and proactive SLAs. We'll look at each of these types of SLAs in the sections that follow.

Performance SLAs

Performance SLAs address ongoing availability, throughput, and other aspects of Quality of Service (QOS). These SLAs set expectations for web services based on objective measurements and baseline values that establish acceptable service levels. At the very least, all web-service contracts should include or refer to a performance SLA.

SLAs written for web hosting, ISP connectivity, and most other Internet-based services tend to focus on network performance measurements such as packet loss, latency, and uptime (usually expressed in some number of nines: 99 percent, 99.9 percent, 99.99 percent, etc.). While these data are fairly easy to measure, they aren't as applicable or valuable as metrics for web services. They don't typically address the customer's business needs or the experience of the end user, who is the ultimate consumer of many real-time web services. Web-services customers aren't so much concerned about performance at the network or transport layer as they are about the higher-level performance issues, such as the following:

- **Availability**. Is the service operational and ready to process requests? At what frequency, of what duration, and at what time of day are outages acceptable? What *scheduled maintenance* is acceptable, if any?

- **Transactional Throughput and Latency.** How many transactions can be completed per second, per minute, or per hour? How long does it take to complete submitted requests?

The following is a sample performance SLA for a web service. Like the others that follow, this SLA is just an example, appropriate only for particular types of web services and business relationships. The real-world range of SLA styles and content is as broad as the range of web services themselves. These examples have been fabricated to illustrate the concepts of each type of SLA, rather than to serve as templates for any particular web service.

SLA (Type)	Average Transaction Latency (Performance)
Description	The purpose of this SLA is to ensure performance of the XYZ web service.
Measurement	The elapsed time of each transaction shall be measured and logged by the Customer's systems.
Targets	So long as transactions are submitted at a rate not to exceed 10 transactions in any 5-second period (the Maximum Submitted-Transaction Rate and the Sampling Period, respectively), the following thresholds shall apply:
	Threshold A: 80 percent of all transactions submitted each day shall be correctly processed within 3 seconds. 100 percent shall be correctly processed within 6 seconds.
	Threshold B: 80 percent of all transactions submitted each day shall be correctly processed within 7 seconds. 100 percent shall be correctly processed within 15 seconds.
	Transactions submitted during periods of unavailability or connectivity failure (as defined in and covered by a separate SLA) shall be ignored for the purposes of calculating performance hereunder.

Reporting   Customer's systems shall log all transaction-latency times, and submit such logs to Provider daily in a format and via methods to be mutually agreed upon.

Responsibilities   Provider shall compute and credit Customer's account for all penalties due hereunder.

Remedies   Provider shall credit Customer's account 1.0 percent of fees paid in any month for each day during that month in which Threshold A service levels are not achieved, and an additional 2.0 percent for each day in which Threshold B service levels are not achieved. The total of all credits due under this SLA, when combined with those of other SLAs for this service, shall not exceed 100 percent of the fees paid to Provider by Customer in the associated month. If the number of transactions submitted during any Sampling Period exceeds the Maximum Submitted-Transaction Rate, no calculation shall be performed for the purpose of computing penalties hereunder.

Reactive SLAs

Reactive SLAs define the actions that a provider will take when a problem occurs. Reactive SLAs are based on the provider's reactions to *events*, and the principal measurement is *time*. This is quite different from performance SLAs, which describe expectations for ongoing, continuous services such as availability and throughput. Their principal measurement isn't time, but the quality of the service.

One important issue with reactive SLAs is the distinction between *time to initiate*, or respond to the problem, and *time to complete*, or resolve the problem. A weak SLA contains a provider's commitment to respond, initiate, or begin working on a problem within some period of time. That's all well and good, but if service is down, it's not the response that counts—it's the completion of the task or the resolution of the problem that matters.

Some providers insist that all they can do is promise to start their diagnostic efforts within a given timeframe. After all, they argue, how can they promise to solve a problem within any time limit until they know what caused it? One would expect this attitude from a provider that's seeing every problem for the first time. But a well-designed, well-operated service should present few new challenges to its provider. In fact, such experience should be among your criteria for evaluating service providers.

If a web services fails, the provider should know fairly accurately how long it will take to restore it. The provider should have more than enough statistical experience to know what it can promise. Look for SLAs that commit to resolving problems, not merely initiating responses.

SLA (Type)	Service Outage Resolution (Reactive)
Description	The purpose of this SLA is to establish expectations for the restoration of the XYZ web service in case of outages.
Measurement	An outage shall be considered to have begun when the XYZ service does not respond within 15 seconds to requests from *both* the Customer's facility *and* the monitoring facilities of independent service ABC. A restoration shall be considered effective as of the time the XYZ service responds within 15 seconds to requests from *either* the Customer's facility or from those of ABC.
Granularity	An outage event shall be noted when the XYZ web service fails to respond to three attempted requests (i.e., two retries) over a 60-second period.
	Outages separated by less than 10 minutes of availability shall be considered as a single outage, which shall include the intervening time.
Reporting	Customer's system shall transmit notifications of all outage and restoration events to independent service ABC, which shall compare them with its

own event log. ABC shall provide monthly reports to both Customer and Provider.

The duration of each outage shall be rounded up to the next full minute.

Responsibilities   Customer shall report its detection of service outages and restorations to ABC within one minute of such events. ABC shall report outages, restorations, and unconfirmed Customer-supplied outage reports to the Provider within one minute. The Provider shall compute and automatically credit Customer's account for all penalties due hereunder.

Remedies   Provider shall credit Customer's account 0.50 percent of fees paid in any month for each minute of outage during the hours of 1600Z (universal time) and 0200Z on days during which US banks are open for business.

Provider shall credit Customer's account 0.25 percent of fees paid in any month for each minute of outage during other times.

The total of all credits due under this SLA, when combined with those of other SLAs for this service, shall not exceed 100 percent of the fees paid to Provider by Customer in the associated month.

Proactive SLAs

The first two categories of service level agreements, *performance* and *reactive*, addressed ongoing services and responses to problems. The third and final category, *proactive* service level agreements, includes those that describe services intended to prevent problems from occurring in the first place.

Proactive SLAs are conceptually simpler—although not necessarily shorter—than those in the other categories. One reason is that the basis for measuring whether a proactive service has been delivered as expected is typically just a matter of determining whether the task was completed on time and error-free.

SLA (Type)	Archiving (Proactive)
Description	This SLA ensures availability of most-recent data in case of failures or disaster. An archival copy of each transaction shall be recorded on removable media upon completion of the transaction. The format used shall be appropriate for rapid recovery of complete databases (via roll-forward techniques), as well as individual transactions indexed by *transaction-ID* or *customer number*.
Measurement	The service levels are defined in terms of error-free backups as calculated each month. Measurement of these criteria shall be via review of entries in the backup log files.
Targets	80 percent of all transactions each day shall be archived within 10 seconds of the completion of the transaction. 100 percent of all transactions each day shall be archived within 30 seconds.
Reporting	Provider's systems shall log all archiving activities. Provider shall provide Customer with web-service-enabled access to such logs, which must include the timestamp of each transaction and the timestamp of each transaction's verified archive.
Responsibilities	Provider's systems shall automatically compute and credit Customer's account for all penalties due hereunder.
Remedies	Provider shall credit Customer's account 1.5 percent of fees paid in any month for each day during that month in which the target service levels are not achieved. The total of all credits due under this SLA, when combined with those of other SLAs for this service, shall not exceed 100 percent

of the fees paid to Provider by Customer in the associated month.

Beware of Weak SLAs

While in your role as a web-services customer, you'll find many one-sided issues favoring providers. If you're a provider, don't be surprised when an astute customer brings these to your attention. Many SLAs contain outrageously weak time commitments, for example. One SLA might promise to initiate a response to a critical outage within an hour. Another might guarantee a resolution within two days. What's wrong with this picture?

Providers offer weak SLAs because customers let them get away with it. Many weak SLAs come from providers that have jumped onto the bandwagon just so they can claim they *have* an SLA. Customers might be tempted to brush off weak SLAs as merely worthless. In fact, they can actually cause more harm than if they didn't exist at all.

If the parties end up in arbitration or litigation, someone (an arbitrator, judge, or jury) will need a basis for determining the level of services to which the customer is entitled. Lacking anything in writing, an arbitrator will probably use some vague criteria such as "industry standard practices" or "reasonable efforts," which may or may not be appropriate. But if there's something in writing, such as a document entitled "Service Level Agreement" that purports to express the original intentions of the parties, that document will most likely supercede other criteria.

If that SLA doesn't express your understanding of the service-level expectations, it may be too late. If a contract includes a weak SLA, the customer as well as the provider must be willing to live with it. When push comes to shove and the provider holds an SLA up in front of an arbitrator, it's too late for the customer to claim it expected something more than was written into the agreement.

Customers should be careful not to include or even reference an SLA in a web-services agreement unless it expresses the levels of service they'll accept. If the parties can't agree on the wording of an SLA, it may be best for the customer not to have one at all. Better

yet, the customer should find another provider who will put acceptable service levels in writing.

Service-Level Measurements

The next obvious question to arise is: Who is to perform the measurements, and make the determination of service-level compliance?
This is a classic problem that shows up in virtually every outsourcing agreement, aggravated by the asymmetric nature of the relationships. In web hosting, for example, the systems are usually owned
and operated by the vendor, who therefore has the systems and skills
required to monitor performance. Furthermore, the web-hosting customer can't directly evaluate the quality of the web-hosting vendor's
services, because the customer isn't the ultimate recipient of those
services. Instead, it's the experience of the consumer or end user that
matters—and that consumer could be located anywhere in the world.
This is why third-party measurements performed by monitoring systems strategically placed in dozens of locations worldwide are so important in managing web-hosting SLAs.

But web services aren't as asymmetric as web hosting for two reasons. First, the customer of a web service does have an investment in
technology, and can therefore make its own measurements. Second,
the customer *is* the direct recipient of a web service, so measurements made at the customer's location are more valid than measurements made anywhere else.

A third-party measurement service as is used for web hosting is
actually a proxy for users. It can't tell you exactly what any single user
experiences, but it can approximate the experiences of many. With
web services, it's quite reasonable to expect that measurements taken
at the customer's location reflect the actual experience of the customer. In fact, a third-party measurement will provide a less accurate
measurement than one performed at the customer's location. Third-
party measurements thus play a less important role in web services
than in web hosting—although in our example of a reactive SLA, a
third party did serve a purpose.

How, then, can you achieve the objectivity afforded by third parties in web-services monitoring? One way is for web-services transactions to pass *through* a third-party intermediary such as a web-services

network (WSN), which we explored in Chapter 15. If third-party objectivity is important, the provider and customer should consider using such an intermediary, even if it's not strictly required for any other reason.

An alternative is for both the provider and the customer to measure the performance of the web service at their own locations, and to agree in advance on a method by which variations between their measurements will be mediated. This can be done by a third party that's not an intermediary within the message-routing path, but which has access to the raw data collected at the provider and customer locations. In our example of a reactive SLA, a third party (ABC) played yet another role: that of an objective observer to validate and complement the experiences of the customer.

In any case, it's rarely a good idea for a single non-objective party to be entrusted with determining compliance with an SLA. If it's not possible to distribute the responsibility to the endpoints and to mediate observed differences, then a third party should be used.

The Devil in the Details

In addition to watching out for weak SLAs, here are some other issues to be aware of when reviewing or negotiating SLAs and web-services contracts.

Claims

The SLA must specify which party has the responsibility for identifying, reporting, and verifying service-level deficiencies. With web hosting, responsibility is commonly assigned to the service provider to monitor service levels and determine whether a deficiency has, in fact, occurred. But then it's the customer's responsibility to issue a claim. If the customer doesn't present a claim promptly, the vendor is off the hook.

For web services, it's quite reasonable for both the provider and the customer to monitor the service levels, so it's not unreasonable to place the burden for problem identification and notification (including initiating a claim) on the shoulders of the provider. Credits for missed service levels are thus generated automatically. The customer's role is merely to monitor service levels and review the credits issued.

Maintenance

Years ago, Internet SLAs typically included exclusions for periods of planned outages or scheduled maintenance. But because many web services are expected to be available 24/7, such exclusions often aren't appropriate in web-services SLAs. State-of-the-art Internet and e-commerce infrastructure allows virtually all web services—particularly those supported by reliable asynchronous messaging—to operate all day, every day. The only exceptions might be older legacy applications that have substantial batch-processing components or must be taken offline for backup. Other than such cases, scheduled or preventive maintenance should be counted as downtime when calculating an availability service level.

Acts of God, Force Majeure, and Insurance

Virtually all service-level agreements contain exclusions for acts of God (e.g., fire, flood, and earthquakes) as well as for other instances of *force majeure*, such as labor strikes, connectivity outages, and so on. As web services play an increasingly important role in business operations, however, both providers and customers must consider the appropriateness of such exclusions. After all, Class A Internet data centers (IDCs) are expected to be impervious to earthquakes, fires, floods, and the like. Certainly, that's what the vendors suggest in their literature and sales pitches.

More and more, the operators of IDCs are offering "no-buts" 24/7 uptime SLAs, where acts of God and force majeure are often mitigated by insurance paid for or arranged by the vendor. Over time, customers of business-critical web services will demand such levels of service, and progressive providers will deliver them. In the meantime, all customers of mission-critical web services should explore their own options for insurance to mitigate these risks.

Granularity and Consecutive Periods

Customers should watch out for service-level definitions that include language such as, "To be considered unavailable, the service must be unusable for a continuous 60 minutes." If after 59 minutes there's a brief period during which the service is available, but it then goes down again, the "consecutive minutes" counter is reset to zero. In theory, there could be short bursts of availability only once an hour for an entire month, and the customer wouldn't be entitled to any compensation.

SLAs for Aggregated Services

Whereas traditional IT service-level agreements typically aren't passed through from one provider to another, such aggregation is common in web services. But how can an SLA address an aggregator's services that are, in turn, based on services beyond the aggregator's control? In the role of web-service provider, your initial instinct may be to reject outright the idea that you can guarantee any level of service when it's affected by elements outside of your control. Indeed, crafting an SLA in such an environment can be quite a challenge. But the lack of support for *pass-through SLAs* merely reflects the immaturity of the web-services universe, since we certainly have such commitments in other areas of commerce.

If you buy an automobile, for instance, the warranty you receive from the manufacturer covers many parts supplied by third parties. If a fuel pump fails, it doesn't matter whether a third-party supplier made it; the car manufacturer will still cover the repairs. In fact, you'll probably never know that a third party was involved. It may surprise you to know that in a recent product year, Ford and Chrysler outsourced 50 percent and 70 percent of their vehicle components respectively.[24]

Like pass-through warranties, aggregated or composite web services are covered by pass-through SLAs. Aggregators must learn to manage the quality of the services they purchase, just as automobile manufacturers manage their suppliers. This requires that aggregators and their providers enter into high-quality SLAs so that the aggregators can, in turn, enter into SLAs of comparable quality with their own customers.

Even though an aggregator can't directly influence the services it receives from others, it does have some control over its business and technology relationships with upstream providers. Some aggregators do a better job of managing these relationships than others, and it's the *results* of such good relationship management as indicated by measurable service levels that an aggregator and its customers should look for in an SLA.

Penalties and Incentives

The final purpose of an SLA is to create an ongoing financial motivation for the provider to achieve the service levels under all circumstances. An SLA typically defines financial penalties to be paid by the provider to the customer in case the agreed-to service levels aren't achieved. In most cases, the penalties are capped at or below the total amount paid by the customer to the provider, which rarely compensates the customer for its actual loss. This points, again, to the need for insurance and other mitigations in order to protect a business from losses greater than those addressed by SLA penalties. Beyond simple penalties, an SLA should also provide continuous motivation for the provider to restore the level of service to that which was agreed to, even if the level of service drops below the initial threshold defined in the SLA.

How can SLA penalties be structured to motivate a provider to maintain its service levels, once a service-level target has been missed? It's human—and business—nature to cease trying to maintain or improve services once a penalty threshold has been exceeded.

Consider a typical SLA component, such as an availability guarantee, when measured on a monthly basis. What happens when something goes wrong, and the service level dips below the penalty threshold early in the month, as illustrated in Figure 19-1?

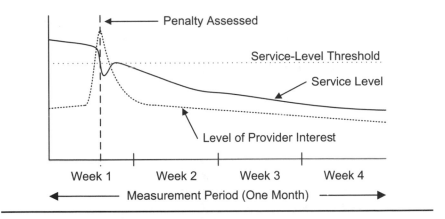

Figure 19-1: Loss of Provider Interest After Assessment of Penalty

As you can see, the provider's interest (based at least in part on the fear of reduced profits) peaks as the service level begins to degrade to the point that the penalty will be incurred, as indicated by the dashed vertical line. However, once that point has been passed, the provider loses interest, for nothing the provider can do will have any further impact on its revenues. No matter how hard it tries, the provider can't recover its loss from missing the monthly goal. Even if the service continues to perform poorly, the provider knows it won't incur any additional penalty. The provider loses the motivation to deliver high availability for the remainder of the month. In fact, the provider's attention may be diverted to solving another problem for a different customer, where such efforts can make a difference to the provider's bottom line. This one's already a lost cause for the current month; the provider has no further motivation, so the service level continues to decline.

As Chris Overton pointed out in his paper, "On the Theory and Practice of Internet SLAs," "An SLA penalty has motivational force only near its boundary." [25] Overton illustrated this effect as shown in Figure 19-2.

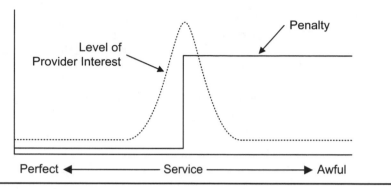

Figure 19-2: A Single-Penalty Threshold ©2001 Keynote Systems, Inc., www.keynote.com. Reproduced by permission.

Note that the x-axis in Figure 19-2 isn't *time* as it is in Figure 19-1, but rather the quality of service. So long as the quality of the service remains high, the level of the provider's interest remains fairly low, because the provider has nothing to lose if the service level drops slightly. So long as the service doesn't degrade to the point at which the penalty kicks in, there will be no effect, and hence there's no incentive to maintain the service at the highest possible level.

As the quality of service approaches the threshold at which the penalty will be assessed, the provider's level of interest increases rapidly, peaking at the point at which the penalty is assessed. Once the service degrades further, however, the provider's interest drops quickly, for the provider realizes that no matter what it does, the effect of the penalty cannot be reversed, and no further penalties will be assessed, at least for the current evaluation period.

The challenge, therefore, is to design a system of penalties and incentives that will create a *continuous* motivation for the provider to maintain as high a level of service as possible. In other words, if the service is already acceptable, the SLA should motivate the provider to improve it; and if the service isn't acceptable, the SLA should motivate the provider to fix it, no matter how much the provider has already lost due to penalties.

Nagging Little Penalties

Overton refers to "the large cumulative effect of these nagging little penalties" as a way to create continuous motivation for providers. Rather than one large penalty that's imposed at a single service-level threshold, suppose an SLA is constructed with *multiple* penalty thresholds spread over a broader range of service levels. The results would then look more like Figure 19-3.

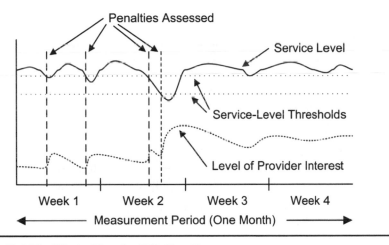

Figure 19-3: The Effect of Nagging Little Penalties

As compared to Figure 19-1, Figure 19-3 shows that by assessing penalties *each time* the service drops below the agreed-to level, the provider's interest—and hence the urgency of its response—actually increases over time. In the earlier example, this urgent response occurred only once.

More importantly, look at what happens during the drop in service level during the second week. An initial penalty is assessed as the service level crosses the first threshold. Although the provider's interest is increased, the service level continues to fall. But there's a second service-level threshold that's crossed a day later, and this event *really* gets the provider's attention.

In a well-designed SLA, there are increasingly severe penalties assessed at subsequently more significant service-level thresholds, for it's the threshold one hasn't quite reached and the threat of others

to follow that provide the motivation to respond promptly and sufficiently.

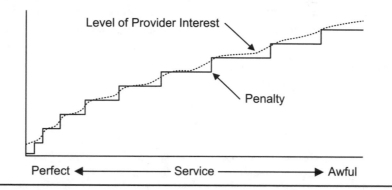

*Figure 19-4: The Cumulative Effect ©2001 Keynote Systems, Inc., www.keynote.com.
Reproduced by permission.*

Note in Figure 19-4 that the provider's level of interest increases
continuously as the level of service continues to deteriorate, as
compared to Figure 19-2. In other words, no matter how bad things
get—and how many penalties the provider has already incurred—an
additional penalty will be assessed if the level of service continues
to diminish. If the level of service is quite high, the provider is motivated to keep it there, since even a slight degradation will cause the
assessment of some penalty.

To accomplish this, the SLA *penalty budget*—the total amount available to be paid to the customer—should be allocated over many
relatively small time periods, preferably daily. Longer periods such
as monthly or quarterly cause the provider's initial motivation to be
diluted by the impression that it still has "plenty of time" to fix the
problem, and still not be penalized. If a penalty is assessed early in a
long period, the provider's motivation will be diluted by the idea that
it's too late to compensate for prior poor performance. It's also important to have not just one, but several service-level penalty thresholds, so that the sum penalty increases non-linearly as the service
level decreases.

Automated SLAs

Today, virtually all SLAs are human-readable documents that are prepared and negotiated manually. The only technologies associated with SLAs are for measurement, reporting, and the use of load balancing, routing, and capacity-on-demand to meet service levels. In the years to come, however, we can expect to see machine-readable SLAs expressed in XML that are negotiable and manageable by automated systems. This is feasible because unlike in other types of IT outsourcing, virtually all web-services SLA metrics are based on data that are easily measurable. Most other SLAs involve some degree of human interaction, and are therefore difficult to automate.

SLAs can be represented as *policies* much like security and privacy policies. Once the standards and tools are in place, web services may include multiple service-level offerings, possibly at different price points. A prospective customer will then be able to select the level of service that provides the best balance of performance, risk, and cost—perhaps even through an automated system. The two parties' systems could then establish communications on the basis of the service level offered and accepted. This assumes that not only will the syntax and semantics of XML-based SLAs be standardized, but that similar standards will exist for contractual terms and conditions and the mechanisms by which service levels are measured and reported.

While most of this chapter has been written with the interests of the customer in mind, progressive providers will recognize that it's also in their best long-term interest to create and execute service-level agreements that accurately reflect the needs of their customers. And lest you think this doesn't apply to you, consider that virtually all web-services providers will also be consumers—because if you're a provider, you're also likely to be an aggregator.

Chapter 20

Providing External Services

Eventually, we'll all be users of web services, even if only because the applications, appliances, and mobile devices of the future will contain web-services requestors. Many of us will also use web-services technologies for integration behind our corporate firewalls. But relatively few of us are going to take the next step and provide external web services to others. If you're in this group, you'll face a number of challenges that don't concern those with less ambitious web-services goals. The strategic issues associated with publishing web services and making them available to parties outside of your control are the focus of this final chapter of *Loosely Coupled*. Many of these issues are similar to those encountered when internal systems are exposed over the World Wide Web. They include the following:

- **A service mentality**. If your company currently produces software or other products, you'll find that web services change the way you deliver value to your customers.
- **Revenue models and payment mechanisms**. If your services will generate revenues, how will you measure and bill for usage? If you're developing an aggregated, revenue-based service, you'll need a plan for *settlements*—a way to share revenues with your upstream service providers.

- **Contracts**. Although web services streamline the technological aspects of linking with external organizations, the selection of strategic business partners will still require human intervention, negotiations, and formal contracts. The advent of web services will place even more pressure on those parts of your organization that are responsible for establishing business-partner relationships.
- **Application and infrastructure robustness**. If your services will be based on legacy applications, are the applications up to the task? Can they handle the increased load? Will the applications, your infrastructure, and your staff be able to meet the criteria specified in your service-level agreements (SLAs)?
- **Semantics**. Have you and your partners agreed on the semantics of your services? Are the semantics based on existing standards, or does your company have the clout to create and mandate de-facto adoption?

A Service Mentality

Is your company prepared to be in the services business? Do the various departments, executives, managers, and individuals understand the differences between products and services? If your company has previously delivered software or data in the form of products, it has some important changes to consider. The Internet has already altered the nature of software-product packaging and delivery, and web services will hasten that change. For example, many software products depend on an Internet connection for registration or real-time help facilities. Delivering a service requires a very different mindset than delivering a product. You might think you're delivering the same thing, but you're not.

Consider the difference between cordless phones and cellular phones. You can buy them at the same stores, but the business models and the economics behind them are quite different. Cordless phones are traditional products. You pay for them up front, take them home, and use them. If all goes well, that ends your relationship with the manufacturer, distributor, and retailer, at least as far as that phone is concerned. If the phone fails, you'll once again interact with the manufacturer or the retailer, but it's assumed by all parties that that's a rare occasion.

Cell phones are very different. The cell phone itself is almost incidental to the service; it's the service you're really buying, not the phone. You'll select a cellular phone according to its features and price, but first you'll choose a service according to its coverage, price, and other policies. You'll have an ongoing, long-term relationship with your service provider. If all goes well, your service relationship will outlast your phone, which you may well replace without switching providers.

Consider the warranty differences, too. For the cordless phone, the warranty covers just the hardware. For the cell phone, there's also a service-level agreement. It's not too sophisticated, and it certainly gives the cell-phone provider many outs—but it does give you certain remedies for dropped calls and the like.

If you're currently a software publisher, your primary commitment to the customer is that the software works as promised. The warranty you provide with your software probably only covers the media on which the software is delivered: You'll replace defective CD-ROMs. Most shrink-wrapped software is sold as-is, bugs and all.

But like cellular-phone providers, web-services providers promise to deliver value on an ongoing basis. The relationships (and the revenue streams) are continuous. If you don't continue to meet and anticipate the customer's needs as they change over time, you'll run the risk of losing that customer. Consider these differences carefully as you shift to a services-oriented distribution model. The implications are both subtle and significant.

Revenue Models and Payment Mechanisms

If you're planning a fee-based service, you'll need systems to measure usage and collect payment. If the equivalent of the service you plan to offer is currently available as packaged software, you'll also have the challenge of converting customers from flat-fee pricing (they buy a copy of software and are entitled to unlimited use) to usage-based pricing (where they pay little or nothing up front, and instead pay as they go).

Pricing is more art than science, and customer habits and perceptions have a great deal to do with how changes will be accepted. But all revenue models boil down to two options: flat-rate and usage-based, with a variety of combinations. The advantages of the flat-rate model are that it's unquestionably simpler, and provides predictability for the customer. On the other hand, flat-rate pricing discourages entry-level customers, whose usage may initially be low but could increase over time.

Usage-Based Pricing

Usage-based pricing is a fairly straightforward option to implement technologically and economically, so long as the total amount charged to each customer during each billing period is at least a few dollars. For smaller amounts, the costs of invoicing and credit-card processing become too great a percentage of the value of the transactions themselves. Using traditional invoicing and credit-card technologies, there's a minimum-billing threshold below which it's no longer economical to charge for the service. There are three ways to solve this problem: minimum charges, bundling, and micropayments.

Monthly Minimum

If customers won't utilize your service to the extent that you can afford to invoice them or charge their credit cards, one option is to set a minimum monthly fee to cover the cost of billing, and then charge for incremental use above a predetermined threshold. This is the model frequently used by cellular-phone providers in the U.S. For a flat monthly fee, the customer is entitled to some number of minutes. Usage beyond that level is billed on a per-minute basis. The same pricing structure can be applied to web services.

Bundled Charges

If you have a separate revenue-based relationship with your customers, you can combine the usage fees for web services with other charges. For example, you can collect a small amount for a service that modifies an order or shipment, since you can add that fee to the invoice you'll otherwise generate for the goods or shipment.

This is the model used by telephone companies that offer incremental services such as voicemail, Caller ID, and three-way conferencing. It wouldn't be economical to generate separate invoices for these services, but they can be billed as add-ons to larger monthly charges.

Depending on your business and your relationship with third parties, it may be possible in some cases to include your charges with those of other vendors such as a telephone company, cellular provider, cable-TV company, or utility company. In the U.S., for example, some companies use "900" telephone numbers as a way to collect fees for telephone-based services without having to issue their own invoices.

Micropayment

Finally, you might want to consider a *micropayment* technology, although at the time of this writing, none has achieved any significant level of acceptance. Many micropayment vendors have tried and failed to build sustainable businesses. All sorts of wallets and credit systems have been invented, patented, launched—and abandoned. But to many observers, micropayments seem like a valuable concept that should eventually catch on, and web services may be the catalyst.

To date, most micropayment systems have been used not for services, but for the delivery of *content* over the World Wide Web. They've been based on the assumption that consumers would pay small amounts ranging from fractions of a penny to perhaps a few dollars for the right to view and possibly download web-based entertainment, information, or software. The challenge, of course, is that it can cost more to collect such amounts than is worthwhile. Most solutions have been based on the aggregation of multiple small accounts, which in turn means that the micropayment vendor must have enough volume and sources of content that aggregation is economically feasible. No micropayment aggregator has come close to achieving this critical mass.

However, the economics change when micropayments are used for *services* rather than for content. It's one thing to charge a few pennies to download a document, particularly when consumers may only view one or two documents per month. But in the business-to-business world of web services where requestors are more likely to use those services more frequently, the aggregated revenues per requestor will be greater. Micropayments may finally succeed for web services where they failed for content. Time will tell.

Aggregation and Settlements

As web-services usage weaves its way into the fabric of business technology, an increasing number of web services will themselves be based on other web services. In some industries and applications, these aggregated web services will become the norm rather than the exception. Not only will they be architecturally more complex than those that are self-contained, but billing and accounting for such web services will also require sophisticated systems.

Luckily, there are precedents and technologies in other industries that can be applied to these problems. For instance, an international long-distance telephone call requires the cooperation of multiple telephone companies, but the customer receives only a single aggregated phone bill each month. Three or more carriers may be involved, yet their charges are integrated and presented together. (In the U.S., the deregulation of long distance means that we now receive separate bills for local and long-distance services, but this wasn't always the case.)

The method telephone companies use to compute and share revenues is referred to as *settlement*, and it's practiced in many other industries as well. Settlement-based systems are designed to handle huge numbers of transactions at very low per-transaction costs. As aggregation becomes increasingly common, expect a number of schemes to surface to manage settlements in the web-services environment.

Today, there is no generic solution to settlements that works across industries. Instead, each industry has its own system, such as those for telephone, cable TV, travel reservations, or inter-bank ATM usage. But in the future, we can expect to see the creation of more general-purpose settlement services that can be used by aggregators of virtually any type of web services.

Contracts and Human-Process Overhead

Given all we've discussed regarding the automation of business integration, you might think that web services will streamline every aspect of the processes two companies use to integrate their systems. While this may be true for their IT departments, web services will likely *increase* the pressure on legal departments and others who have responsibility for negotiating the non-technological aspects of external web-services projects.

For all but the most trivial web services, your company is going to need contracts and service-level agreements, just as they're needed for less-automated business relationships today. In addition, there are four issues that will actually increase the burden on those responsible for creating and managing these third-party relationships: capacity, granularity, location, and privacy.

Capacity

In the past, the IT department was often considered the bottleneck in any project that involved linking with external business partners. The rest of the company didn't care whether the obstacles were due to connectivity, security, syntax, or semantics—it always just seemed to take too long and cost too much.

That changes with web services. Once your IT department is ramped up with a few external web-services projects under its belt, other departments will take note of how much more quickly and less expensively these projects are completed. But the bottleneck will simply move to another department. Once technology is no longer the obstacle but the enabler, organizations will find that their legal departments and others that handle external business partners become bogged down with the details of establishing and maintaining new relationships.

Granularity

Although in some industries the trend towards aggregation will increase, in other industries the opposite will be true. Today you may obtain credit-card processing and credit-risk analysis from a single vendor. In turn, that vendor obtains processing and risk information from third parties, combines them, and presents the bundled or aggregated services to you as one.

As more companies become adept at both providing and subscribing to external web services, it will be increasingly possible and practical to *dis-aggregate* one-stop services, and obtain web services on an à la carte basis. This in turn will increase the number of unique business relationships that must be managed.

Instead of being packaged as large monolithic services, many applications will instead begin as simple frameworks to which you can add web-services components. What today you license from a single vendor, may in the future be built from discrete services obtained from dozens of providers. This increased granularity will further burden those who are responsible for vendor relationships.

This added administrative strain may seem to be at odds with the simplification and cost-reduction objectives of web services, and in some cases the savings may not outweigh the shift of responsibility to non-IT departments—especially in cases where the costs of shifted responsibilities are not considered in advance.

Location

In terms of commerce, the World Wide Web has blurred state, provincial, and national borders. Even now, we're still sorting out the implications of cross-border Internet-based transactions: What laws apply? Who has the right to tax transactions? If lawsuits are filed, which jurisdictions apply? And how can you reliably determine a requestor's location, anyway?

Those who manage web-services contracts will have to track the rapidly changing laws, regulations, and policies of Internet-based commerce. As the geographic scope of business relationships continues to expand and you consider obtaining web services from providers in foreign countries, the need for knowledge of laws in other locales will increase.

Privacy

If your web services deal with consumer data, you'll also face the challenge of privacy—already an issue today in credit-card processing. When you request authorization for a customer's credit-card transaction, you're implicitly divulging that customer's identity and something about his or her purchasing habits to the credit-card processor.

In practice, this is rarely an issue, but it illustrates the complexity of the privacy problem and highlights what it means to build web services that are, in turn, built upon other web services. When you pass your data or that of your customers through to a third party, what assurances do you have that it won't be passed to a fourth or a fifth? What obligations do you have to protect yourself and your customers, and how do you write those into your contracts with suppliers?

The privacy of healthcare records has also become a major concern with the passage in the U.S. of the Health Insurance Portability and Accountability Act of 1996 (HIPAA). You may not think you're in the healthcare business, but if you offer your employees an intranet portal to manage their benefits, you may well be transmitting those employees' confidential medical data through web services to third parties. In this case, you may be required to comply with the HIPAA regulations.

The European Union has adopted generally stricter privacy laws than exist in other regions. Even if your company is located outside of the EU, you may be obligated to comply with its regulations if you obtain web services from EU countries (or vice versa).

Application and Infrastructure Robustness

If your company already supports e-commerce on the World Wide Web, then you already have some idea of what it takes to develop, deploy, and operate Internet-based services. Unlike traditional applications that operate within the controlled environment of your organization, both e-commerce and web services must meet the needs of external business partners—and in some cases, the public. This increases the demand for robustness of your infrastructure and applications. The following are points to consider as you evaluate the suitability of your existing systems and applications to support external web services.

Availability

Perhaps the most basic consideration is the requirement for availability or *uptime*. If your web services are to be available to the public, you'll most likely need to aim for 100 percent uptime. That in turn implies requirements for redundancy, updated operating procedures, and perhaps additional staff, all of which increase costs.

Scheduled Downtime

An always-on web service obviously can't be shut down to perform
backup or maintenance operations, so you'll need to have the tools
and procedures in place to perform backups and upgrades on the
fly. Even if you don't have a 100-percent uptime target, you still may
need very different maintenance procedures than those you currently
have in place. This can be quite a challenge for legacy applications
that have been used—perhaps for decades—only in controlled, in-
house environments where it's been acceptable to schedule downtime.

The addition of a loosely coupled, reliable asynchronous messaging layer and its associated queuing mechanisms (as discussed in
Chapter 9) allow a system that must be taken offline on occasion to
accept requests on a 24/7 basis.

Globalization

Will your web services be used from other countries or perhaps
worldwide? Time-zone issues could certainly affect your uptime
requirements, but international support can also mean that your applications and infrastructure must be re-designed for multinational
character sets, foreign languages, documentation, and support. These
challenges aren't unique to web services; they've long been issues on
the World Wide Web. But they could be new requirements for your
legacy applications and existing support systems.

Global performance is yet another issue. You may want to deploy
your web services via a *web services delivery network,* as discussed in
Chapter 15, in order to provide them from points as close as possible
to the locations of your international requestors.

Version Control

Unlike web services, applications that use *thin clients* such as web
browsers can be updated at will. For example, if you change the content of your e-commerce web site, visitors aren't required to take any
actions in order to receive the changes. The next time they visit the
web site, they'll see the new content. It's just that simple—there's no

need for coordination or synchronization. This is an important benefit of any thin-client system.

However, web services require that both the provider and the requestor be synchronized with regard to the latest specifications for the interface. You can accomplish this in a loosely coupled manner using the *delayed binding* methodologies described in Chapter 10, but you'll still have to develop new procedures to modify your supporting applications. You can't make a change, and just assume your requestors will automatically pick it up. You've got to link your change-management process with process you use to update published definitions and schema.

Transaction Processing

Do the web services you plan to publish use applications that currently require the locking of database records? If so, consider what will happen if those records are locked for extended periods of time on behalf of external requestors, or if an application fails to receive the message to unlock a record. This is the problem discussed in detail in Chapters 11 and 12, and you should be aware that there may not be an off-the-shelf solution available or compatible with your legacy environment. Until the protocols and tools for managing loosely coupled transactions are available, you'll have to develop or purchase ad-hoc solutions to this problem.

Peak and Burst Loads

By exposing your applications as external web services, will you still be communicating with the same parties, or will the number of business partners increase? It's quite possible that the load on the applications and other systems will grow in either case. Not only might you need to increase the capacity of both applications and related components, but you may need to redesign or re-code because of the underlying architectural changes.

If your web services will operate in real time, you may need to expand the infrastructure to meet peak and burst loads that are substantially greater than the average loads your current less-demanding environment supports—particularly if your web services are based on the

RPC style of interaction. You might be able to get by using the same *load-balancing* techniques that are often used with e-commerce web servers. But you may instead be better off adopting a reliable asynchronous messaging model, and inserting a message queue between your front-end processors and your applications. These are the issues covered in Chapter 9.

Redundancy

If high uptime is required, you may need to re-deploy your web services on a high-availability platform using redundant components at every level. It's not just a matter of throwing additional hardware at the problem; your applications may have to be completely redesigned and re-written in order to operate properly in a modern *n*-tier configuration.

Third-Party Licenses

Do the licenses you currently have for third-party applications and utilities permit them to be used to support external users? If not, you may be faced with substantial costs for additional licenses.

This became a significant problem when databases were first deployed as the back ends to dynamic web sites. At that time, many of the database-software licenses were written for a maximum number of *simultaneous users*. This raised the question of what constitutes a *user* in the connectionless environments of the World Wide Web. If ten users are currently viewing a database-driven web site, for example, does that count as ten database users? It's a matter of interpretation. Technically speaking, there may be only a single user connected to the database, or only one instance of an application running on an application server. But another view taken by some database-software vendors is that every person currently viewing web pages constitutes a database user, even if no database transaction is currently pending on behalf of that user. Which interpretation is correct? The answer can make a huge difference in the cost of your software licenses.

The same problems exist for web services as for browser-based e-commerce, so you should review your license agreements and find out to what extent they permit the use of third-party software in such an environment, if at all.

Security

You've probably spent years trying to protect your internal applications and back-end databases from being reached from beyond your firewall. But once you start providing external web services, you're actually going to encourage others to access these applications and data remotely over a publicly accessible, unreliable network that's vulnerable to denial-of-service and other attacks and abuses. The good news is that these challenges and the solutions to them are similar to those you may have already faced when exposing your applications over the World Wide Web, and your experiences there may help you solve the same problems in the web-services environment.

In Chapters 13 and 14 we covered the security problems you'll face, as well as the solutions available to solve them. The implications could be substantial for your existing applications and infrastructure, which were probably not designed to accommodate such demands.

Outsourcing Strategies

You may be committed to solving your application problems in house, but when it comes to infrastructure challenges, you should consider third-party help. We discussed web-services networks (WSNs), web-services providers (WSPs), and other deployment options in Chapter 15, and you may well find that outsourcing your infrastructure to such a third party is the best solution.

Semantics

If you intend to be a provider of or a requestor to external web services—or even if you only plan to use this new technology for internal application-integration chores—your greatest challenges will probably come from the lack of semantic standards and from having to resolve semantic inconsistencies.

We've discussed the problem of semantics throughout this book, but admittedly never suggested a specific solution. That's because there's no one-size-fits-all answer. It's different for every case. In Chapter 5, we illustrated the problem of business semantics using the web-services pyramid, and you'll recall from that discussion that semantics occupied the entire top third of the pyramid. Although there are other missing pieces in the technology stack, ultimately they'll be found through horizontally adopted standards. Once these mid-level technologies become commonplace, they'll merge with the other long-since-accepted protocols such as TCP/IP and HTTP.

As you plan for the deployment of external web services, don't begin with the protocols. Instead, focus on the issues surrounding semantics. Are you lucky enough that standards for your application already exist? If not, who will define them? Is your company the 800-pound gorilla with the political clout (and obligation) to set the standards for all parties? If not, is it part of a consortium that should take on this responsibility? Or is there a hardware or software manufacturer or a major systems integrator in your industry that's capable of drafting the initial standards and building consensus?

In any case, you also must ask: Is the party who will establish the business-semantics standards qualified to do so? Just having read a few books on XML doesn't adequately prepare someone to create an XML schema that will probably affect your company and others in your industry for decades to come. This requires careful planning by someone who has done it before.

Once you're past the business semantics, and assuming you've done your homework regarding critical components (see Chapter 5) and the timing of your launch (Chapter 18), you should be able to reap the rewards of providing external web services—particularly those *unintended consequences* that can deliver a long-term return on your investment.

Web services are already changing the way things work. But their simplicity and eventual ubiquity make it tempting to use them only tactically, to solve small problems more efficiently than you have in the past. As you plan for more complex web services within your own organization and beyond, keep in mind that understanding and investing in loose coupling—in all of its many manifestations explored in this book—are the keys that will bring you the greatest returns.

Appendix

A Strategic Checklist

Whenever I'm asked to help a client develop a strategy for web services or plan a specific web-services project, I begin with a checklist. Not only does it remind me what to ask about and review, but it's also a great tool to get a feel quickly for how various individuals and departments perceive web services, and how they're likely to interact during and after the planning and execution of web-services projects.

Inventory

Well before you start planning specific web-services projects, take some time to survey the assets, processes, procedures, and policies in your company that will ultimately affect the successful outcome of your web-services efforts.

☐ **Strategy**. Is there a formal strategy for the use of web services within the company? Has senior management signed off on it? Has it been communicated to the IT staff? Is it adhered to?

☐ **Grass-roots projects**. Are any grass-roots web-services projects already underway? (It may be hard to find them in a large organization.) Are programmers and teams sharing their experiences, or is each project an island? (See Chapter 16.)

☐ **E-commerce**. What e-commerce systems and web sites are in place? When might it be mandatory or helpful for them to be web-services enabled?

☐ **ERP and CRM**. Does the organization have enterprise-resource planning (ERP) or customer-resource management (CRM) systems? To what extent are they web-services enabled, or capable of being so? (See Chapter 6.)

☐ **Other silos**. Aside from ERP and CRM, are there other monolithic applications or suites that already have or should have web-services interfaces? (See Chapter 6.)

☐ **Mergers and acquisitions**. Are there any planned or anticipated M&A activities that could benefit from web services as an integration tool?

☐ **EAI**. Are any enterprise-application integration (EIA) tools in use? Have they been updated to use web-services interfaces? Are efforts underway to convert to those interfaces? (See Chapter 6.)

☐ **EDI and VANs**. Is the company involved with electronic-data interchange and/or work with a value-added network? What are the future EDI/VAN plans? Is there a plan in place to migrate these applications to web services? (See Chapter 6.)

☐ **Manual integration**. Look for sneakernets and swivel-chair integration. Sometimes they're hard to find, because people have become so used to such procedures that they don't realize things could be improved. Indeed, some people's jobs may depend on these manual processes. (See Chapter 6.)

☐ **Kludgy integration**. Likewise, look for technologies such as screen scraping that could be replaced by web services. (See Chapter 6.)

☐ **Integration costs**. Determine what percentage of the organization's IT budget is spent on integration-project development, maintenance, and operations. This will allow you to set a target for savings using web-services technology for integration. (See Chapter 6.)

☐ **Object technologies**. What object-oriented (OO) technologies and platforms are in use? Have any components been wrapped with web-services interfaces yet? (See Chapter 7.)

☐ **Business-process tools**. Does the company use business-process modeling (BPM) or similar tools? To what extent have the vendors of those tools embraced and supported web services? (See Chapter 12.)

☐ **Transaction management**. Are any of the organization's applications based on a transaction-processing management system (TPMS)? Does that system or its vendor support external transactions, managed by another TPMS, perhaps even those of other vendors? (See Chapter 11.)

☐ **Messaging**. Does the company use a messaging system that could support asynchronous web services? (See Chapter 9.)

☐ **Security policies**. Is a formal security policy in place? Has it been updated to address the security requirements of web services? (See Chapter 13.)

☐ **Network firewalls**. Evaluate the firewall architecture. How well will it contain and protect internal web services? How difficult will it be to enable external web services while protecting back-end databases and other assets? (See Chapter 14.)

☐ **VPNs**. Are any virtual private networks being used to link departments, divisions, remote offices, or external business partners? To what extent could these VPNs also be used to support web services with those same parties? (See Chapter 14.)

☐ **Authentication systems**. Does the organization use application-independent authentication for single sign-on? Can these systems support authentication for web services? (See Chapter 14.)

☐ **Digital credentials**. Are any digital-identity systems already in use, such as encrypted email or digital signatures for documents? To what extent could the same certificates and key infrastructure be utilized for web-services? (See Chapter 14.)

☐ **Business semantics**. Does the company currently utilize any XML-based document or messaging schemes, either industry-specific or horizontal? The issue here is whether your company already has in-house experience with XML and the specific standards appropriate for web services. (See Chapter 5.)

☐ **Industry standards**. What are the politics of the company's industry? Who controls (or would control) inter-company XML standards? What standards are already in place? How firm are they? What controversies surround them? (See Chapter 20.)

☐ **Launch date**. When do various managers and executives believe the company should launch its first external web service? Why do they believe those dates are the right ones? (See Chapter 18.)

☐ **Insurance**. How well—if at all—does the existing insurance coverage address the risks associated with web services? Consider lost revenues and profits, loss of data and trade secrets, and breaches of confidentiality and privacy. (See Chapter 20.)

☐ **Risk management**. Is formal risk management practiced within the IT department? If so, evaluate how the processes might affect simple and complex web-services projects. (See Chapter 20.)

☐ **Legacy application robustness**. If existing applications will be exposed as web services (internally or externally), will they be able to handle the increased demands placed upon them? (See Chapter 20.)

☐ **Infrastructure**. Likewise, how well will the existing IT infrastructure and staff cope with the demands of 24/7 operation and potentially greater utilization? (See Chapter 20.)

☐ **Outsourcing agreements**. Does the company have any existing outsourcing relationships? What's the overall prejudice for or against outsourcing, and in what specific disciplines?

☐ **Software licenses.** Do the existing licenses for individual applications, suites (such as ERP and CRM), and back-end database systems permit their use over the Internet? Do the licenses distinguish between interactive and machine-to-machine use? Are web services or APIs explicitly addressed within the licenses? (See Chapter 19.)

☐ **Service level agreements.** What's the level of SLA experience within the organization? Does the company either use the SLAs of other parties, or perhaps have SLAs of its own? How well do the IT and legal teams collaborate on SLAs? Which department typically takes the lead role in SLA negotiations? (See Chapter 20.)

Project Requirements

After you've surveyed the organization's readiness for web services, you can gather the requirements for specific web-services projects.

☐ **Roles.** Will the company be a provider, requestor, and/or aggregator?

☐ **Contexts.** Will the web service be external (linking with systems controlled by more than one team), internal (behind a single firewall), or intra-system? (See Chapter 2.)

☐ **Interaction.** Does the service require real-time synchronous interaction, or can it be asynchronous? (See Chapter 8.)

☐ **Messaging style.** Must the messaging model be RPC-style, or can self-contained documents be used? (See Chapter 10.)

☐ **Legacy systems.** Can the team support, maintain, and enhance the necessary legacy applications? Are the original developers still available? Do you even have the source code? Will you need a third-party consultant or systems integrator to add functionality or increase the scale of the applications? (See Chapter 20.)

☐ **Transaction processing**. Will the project require distributed-transaction processing? In particular, will web services on one system be allowed to lock records on another? If so, the complexity of the project will be substantially greater than it would otherwise. Can non-ACID compensating transactions be used instead? (See Chapter 11.)

☐ **Transformations**. In addition to the basic web services, will any transformation services be required? Are there requirements that suggest the transformations should be provided either by third parties or internally? Do such services already exist? (See Chapter 8.)

☐ **Intermediaries**. Are other third-party services needed, such as non-repudiation, logging, and auditing? (See Chapter 8.)

☐ **Vertical hubs**. Will the project involve the use of an industry-specific intermediary? Does the intermediary already exist, or is it being created simultaneously? (See Chapter 15.)

☐ **Service switching**. Are there requirements for interchangeable web services, possibly front-ended by a software switch that can either fail-over from one service to another, or perform service-selection optimization? (See Chapter 15.)

☐ **In-transit confidentiality**. What are the security (confidentiality) requirements for data while in transit between endpoints? (See Chapter 13.)

☐ **SSL**. Are the confidentiality requirements limited to in-transit and single-hop? If so, it may be possible to use SSL, and take advantage of its low cost and ubiquity. If SSL isn't sufficient, taking the next step may well push the project across the boundary separating simple from complex web services. (See Chapter 14.)

☐ **In-storage confidentiality**. What are the encryption requirements for data when stored either at the endpoints or by intermediaries? (See Chapter 13.)

☐ **Authentication.** Does the service require authentication? Are usernames and passwords sufficient, or are digital certificates necessary? What certificate infrastructure is appropriate? Will it be necessary to link the authentication systems of providers and requestors? In other words, must there be a shared-identity context? (See Chapter 13.)

☐ **Durable authentication.** Must authentication information be retained with the documents so that credentials can be verified after transactions have been completed? For how long thereafter? (See Chapter 13.)

☐ **Credential consolidation.** If the web service will perform actions on behalf of others, is it necessary to pass through credentials to third parties, or is it more appropriate to present a single identity on behalf of all requestors? (See Chapter 13.)

☐ **Outbound authorization.** What rules must be enforced restricting the rights of users or systems to issue web-services requests, possibly on behalf of the organization? (See Chapter 13.)

☐ **Availability.** Can the web service be shut down for maintenance, backups, and upgrades? Or must it operate 24/7? (See Chapter 20.)

☐ **Throughput and latency.** How many transactions per second must be processed? What are the peak and burst requirements, in addition to the averages? At specified traffic levels, what maximum latencies (turnaround times) are allowed? (See Chapter 20.)

☐ **Revenue model.** Will fees be charged for the use of the web service? If so, on what basis will those charges be calculated? (See Chapter 20.)

☐ **Payment mechanisms.** Are any systems required to support accounting and the collection of fees? For example, will a micropayment system be needed, or a system that handles settlements between multiple providers? (See Chapter 20.)

☐ **Laws and regulations**. Are the web services subject to any legal or policy constraints, such as preservation of documentation, privacy (e.g., HIPAA), or use of encryption technologies across international borders? (See Chapter 20.)

☐ **Globalization**. If requestors in other countries or regions will use your web services, must additional languages, character sets, or currencies be supported? (See Chapter 20.)

☐ **Support**. What support obligations are associated with the service? Who will be responsible for problem determination and resolution? On what timeframes, and at what locations?

☐ **Licensing**. What components must be licensed from third parties? Licensed components could include not only software, but lists and databases as well. (See Chapter 20.)

☐ **Update**. How frequently are updates to the service expected? What tools and systems are required to manage the revision process? (See Chapter 20.)

Planning

Once you complete your inventory and understand the existing situation and the requirements for the new web service, you're ready to create a plan for its development, deployment, support, and operation.

☐ **Segregate by complexity**. A web service is generally complex if the interaction is asynchronous, if high availability is required, or if your side is the provider and the requestors are outside of your control. (See Chapter 16.)

☐ **Stepping stones**. A simple project doesn't require strategic planning, but you would still do well to map out a development process that increases complexity incrementally. (See Chapter 17.)

☐ **Web-services pyramid**. Expand the web-services pyramid to reflect the current state of technologies, protocols, and standards. (See Chapter 5. You'll also find the most up-to-date version of the pyramid at www.rds.com/webservices/pyramid.)

- [ ] **Critical components**. Identify your project's critical component(s), which will account for the 20 percent of technologies that will require 80 percent of your time and other resources. They're also likely to be found among the least-mature technologies towards the top of the pyramid. (See Chapter 5.)

- [ ] **Milestones**. Determine where each critical component falls on the Software Implementation Cost Curve. (See Chapter 18.)

- [ ] **Industry adoption lifecycle**. Based on whatever information and opinions you can gather, create an *adoption life cycle* curve for web services in the company's industry. (See Chapter 18.)

- [ ] **Launch date**. According to the company's intended role in the adoption life cycle (early adopter, early majority, etc.), determine the optimal date on which to launch the project. (See Chapter 18.)

- [ ] **Start date**. Using traditional project-management methods, work backwards from the launch date to determine the start date—which may already be past. (See Chapter 18.)

- [ ] **Early development**. Look again at the *software implementation cost curve* for the critical components, and determine how mature each component will be as of the start date. This will help answer the following six checklist items. (See Chapter 18.)

- [ ] **Standardization**. Will the project begin before some of the associated standards are approved and implemented? Will the standards be firm, or still in a state of flux? (See Chapter 18.)

- [ ] **Standards bodies**. If the web-services project will be started prior to the adoption of final standards for any critical component, join the associated standards body, or at least subscribe to the appropriate mailing lists. (See Chapter 18.)

- [ ] **Development tools**. Will tools exist at the time the project begins? Will they be mature or first-generation? (See Chapter 18.)

- [ ] **Interoperability**. Will implementations from different vendors be compatible, or will they have to be tweaked to achieve interoperability, or even modified post-launch as the standards and implementations continue to evolve? (See Chapter 18.)

☐ **Third-party documentation**. Will third-party books and training be available, or will software vendors be the only sources for these materials and services? (See Chapter 18.)

☐ **Consultants vs. staff**. Will the project be starting so early that no experienced consultants are available? Or (at the other extreme) will the company probably be able to hire developers who have previous experience with the critical-component technologies? (See Chapter 18.)

☐ **The Solution-Evolution Timeline**. Determine where the critical-component technologies are in their own life cycles. For those that aren't available yet as inexpensive shrink-wrapped products or as services themselves, keep your options open so that one implementation can be swapped out for another, more mature one in the future. (See Chapter 15.)

☐ **Outsourcing plan**. Defer decisions on what to outsource and what to do in house, both during development and as part of the operational infrastructure.. Not only does this allow you to obtain competitive proposals, it also makes it easier to change your mind *after* the service is implemented and deployed and the technology and requirements have changed. (See Chapter 15.)

☐ **RFPs**. Whenever a Request for Proposal is issued to a software vendor, ask that they provide documentation of current web-services interfaces, as well as a non-binding statement of future web-services intentions.

☐ **Point-to-point services**. Assume that any point-to-point web service will, in fact, become a one-to-many service.

☐ **The network effect**. The number of one-way links between n parties is $n*(n-1)$. Assume that n will become at least 4x and possibly 10x what you've been told to expect. Do the math and consider the implications.

☐ **Contracts**. Discuss the contractual issues with your legal, purchasing, sales, and business-development departments as early in the process as possible. (See Chapter 20.)

☐ **Update cycles**. Application service providers (ASPs) often use 6-12 week update cycles. ISVs use 18-24 months. Delayed binding used in conjunction with web-services means new specifications and descriptions can be published at any time—so plan for near-continuous update and improvement cycles.

☐ **Usage measurement**. Determine how usage will be measured and reported. Within the applications? Using an XML firewall? Or perhaps via a third-party service? (See Chapter 20.)

☐ **Service level agreements**. Write SLAs early, preferably during the requirements-gathering phase of your projects. If a web service will depend on others as in an aggregated service, determine the pass-through impact of the upstream vendors' SLAs. (See Chapter 19.)

Evangelizing

As one of those who now understand web services and loose coupling (as opposed to those who just think they do), you now have the additional responsibility to explain and clarify web services to the rest of the world, or at least to the rest of your team.

☐ **Elevator pitch**. Develop your own versions of the 30-second introduction—one each for technical and non-technical audiences. (See Chapter 2.)

☐ **Training**. Consider leading a series of one-hour informal classes for your team. Cover the highlights of one chapter in this book during each session. At the same time, also seek outside training for your organization.

☐ **Expectations**. Do what you can to eliminate the hype surrounding web services. Dispel the notions that web services will offer your company any long-term competitive advantage, or that you're likely to achieve such a high state of automation that you can identify and link with new business partners without human intervention. Set realistic expectations. (See Chapter 3.)

☐ **Loose coupling quiz**. As an evangelist of web services, you should be able to explain how each of the following relates to loose coupling. (See Chapter 10 for the answers.)
- synchronous versus asynchronous interaction
- RPC- versus document-style messaging
- the use of routing and dynamic message routes
- coarse-grained interfaces
- data-type, language, and OS independence
- agreement by convention versus published schema
- delayed binding
- transformations versus enhanced applications
- reuse versus broad applicability
- unanticipated consequences

———————

This checklist isn't cast in concrete; it's a constantly evolving document. I'm continuously revising my personal copy based on my real-world experience, and so should you. You'll find an updated version at www.rds.com/webservices/checklist.

Notes

[1] John Hagel, *Out of the Box* (Harvard Business School Press, 2002, ISBN 1578516803).

[2] Phil Wainewright, *Web Services Infrastructure* (2002). www.philwainewright.com/pubs/wp/WSIpaper.pdf

[3] OSF, *OSF DCE Application Development Guide Revision 1.0* (1993, ISBN 0136438261).

[4] Charles Phillips, "Stemming the Software Spending Spree." *Optimize* (2002). http://www.optimizemag.com/issue/006/roi.htm

[5] Inspired by an article by Alan Kotok, "Tell Me About Web Services, and Make It Quick." WebServices.org (2002). http://www.mywebservices.org/index.php/article/view/429/

[6] The Stencil Group, "The Emerging Web Services Market" (2002). ©2002 The Stencil Group, Inc. Reprinted by permission. http://www.stencilgroup.com/ideas_scope_200203atkws.html

[7] Remarks made by John Hagel during a panel discussion entitled "BIG Brains: Forecasts for 2002 and Beyond," May 29, 2002, sponsored by the San Francisco Business Interest Group.

8   Clay Shirky, "Web Services: It's So Crazy, It Just Might Not Work." XML.com (2000). http://www.xml.com/lpt/2001/10/03/webservices.html

9   Ibid.

10   Jon Bosak and Tim Bray, "XML and the Second-Generation Web." ScientificAmerican.com (1999). http://www.sciam.com/1999/0599issue/0599bosak.html

11   Tom Yager, "The Future of Application Integration." InfoWorld.com (2002). http://www.infoworld.com/articles/fe/xml/02/02/25/020225feintro.xml

12   Christopher Kock, "The ABCs of ERP." CIO.com (2002). http://www.cio.com/research/erp/edit/erpbasics.html

13   The Stencil Group, "How Web Services Will Beat the 'New New Thing'." *Rap* (2001). http://www.stencilgroup.com/ideas_scope_200106newnew.html

14   Tim O'Reilly, "Amazon Web Services API." *O'Reilly Networks Weblog* (2002). http://www.oreillynet.com/cs/weblog/view/wlg/1707

15   Philip A. Bernstein and Eric Newcomer, *Principals of Transaction Processing* (Morgan Kaufman, 1997, ISBN 1558604154).

16   Theo Härder and Andreas Reuter, "Principles of Transaction-Oriented Database Recovery." *ACM Computing Surveys*, vol. 15, no. 4, pp 287-317 (1983,ISSN 0360-300). http://doi.acm.org/10.1145/289.291

17   Bernstein and Newcomer, *Principals of Transaction Processing.*

18   Jon Udell, "Connecting with Web Services." InfoWorld.com (2002). http://www.infoworld.com/articles/fe/xml/02/06/10/020610feappdevtci.xml

19   Jack McCarthy, "A Fundamental Shift." InfoWorld.com (2002). http://www.infoworld.com/articles/ct/xml/02/04/08/020408ctsw.xml

[20] Evans Data, from a survey of over 400 development managers at companies with more than 2000 employees, as cited in a press release from Vordel Limited, 2002. http://www.vordel.com/news/press/02_03_19.html

[21] http://www.projectliberty.org/

[22] Geoffrey A. Moore, *Crossing the Chasm* (HarperCollins, 1991, ISBN 0887305199).

[23] The publication of an O'Reilly book is an easy-to-spot milestone, so at the suggestion of my clients, I've nicknamed this *The O'Reilly Curve*.

[24] S. Brunnemeier and S. Martin, *Interoperability Cost Analysis of the U.S. Automotive Supply Chain* (Research Triangle Institute, 1999). http://www.mel.nist.gov/msid/sima/interop_costs.pdf

[25] Chris Overton, *On the Theory and Practice of Internet SLAs* (Keynote Systems, 2001). http://www.keynote.com/downloads/SLA_Theory-and-Practice-060802.pdf

Index

.NET 35, 40, 110
80/20 rule 53

A

abort (in transactions) 148, 152–155
acceleration, XML 208
accounting 51
ACID (properties of transactions)
      149–162
acts of God 286
adapter 74. *See also* connector
adoption strategies 38, 240–241,
      256–258, 262
advantage, competitive 42
aggregation 102–104, 248
   service-level agreements for 287
   settlements for 300
ANSI 19
API. *See* application-program interface
      (API)
appliance 218
application-based security 201–205
application-program interface (API) 29
application firewall. *See* proxy, XML
application server 21, 218
application service-provider (ASP) 41

architecture
   application 40, 93–94
   distributed-object 85–86
   three-tier 21
ASP. *See* application-service provider
asynchronous interaction 113–129
   loosely coupled 133–136
   reliable messaging in 165
   security for 176–177
   service-oriented architectures for 99,
      107–109
   simple projects using 248
atomic (property of transactions) 148,
      149
attacks
   denial-of-service (DoS) 193
   downgrade 194
   replay 193
auditing, security-policy 210
authentication 48, 177, 179–185, 247,
      248
   bi-directional 180–182
   durable 184–185
   host-based 203
   loosely-coupled model of 180
   multi-party 183
   network-layer 200
   peripheral-service 206

web-services network 212
XML firewall 208
authorization 48, 177, 185–186, 247
   durable 186
   host-based 203
   loosely coupled model of 185
   network layer 200
   peripheral-service 206
   service-level for 186
   web-services network 213
   XML firewall 209
availability 303–307
   high 242–243
   service level for 277

B

backup 52
bandwidth 171
basic-grade web services 243
benefits of web services 29
Bernstein, Philip
   Principles of Transaction Processing 147,
      155, 322
billing 51
binding, delayed 85, 94, 133, 140–141
binge/purge 38
body, message 190–191
Bosak, Jon 322
BPR. *See* business-process reengineering
Bray, Tim 322
brittleness 31
broadcast 101
broad applicability 133, 143
brokers. *See* objects, brokers
Brunnemeier, S. 323
burst loads 124–128, 305–306
business logic 136–137, 159
business model 41–42, 51
business process
   application integration and 67–68
   enterprise-application integration and
      12–17, 80
   orchestration of 163–170
   reengineering 14, 15

service-oriented architectures and
   109–112
web services and 26

C

cancellation risk 157–159
CDN. *See* content-delivery network
chasm, adoption-curve 257–258
choreography 49
claims 285. *See also* remedies
client/server 38
commercial-grade web services 243,
   248
commit 148
   one-phase protocol 151–152
   two-phase protocol 152–155
Common Object Request Broker
      Architecture (CORBA) 14, 20,
      40, 86–89
compensation. *See also* transactions,
      compensating
   in orchestration 165
competitive advantage 42
complexity, web-services 58, 241–244
components 28–29
   critical. *See* critical components
confidentiality 178, 186–192
   host-based 202
   in network-layer security 200
   peripheral-service 206
   web-services network 212
   XML firewall 208
connectivity, service levels for 277
connector 77. *See also* adaptor
consistency (property of transactions)
      149–150
content-delivery network (CDN) 232
context, security 172–173
contracts 50, 296, 300–303
cookies 176
CORBA. *See* Common Object Request
      Broker Architecture
correlation, message 99
costs 30, 230–231, 265–271

credentials
  consolidation of 182–183, 186
credit-card processing 302–303
critical components 55, 244, 251–254,
      259–260, 271–272
CRM. *See* customer-resource manage-
      ment
Crossing the Chasm (Moore) 256
customer-resource management (CRM)
      14, 69–77
CyberCash 14, 22

D

database 148
data silos. *See* silos
data types 133
DCE 20
DCOM. *See* Distributed Common Ob-
      ject Model
denial-of-service 193
deployment 217–236
DISA 19
discovery 141
discovery agency 96
Distributed Common Object Model
      (DCOM) 14, 20, 30, 35, 87–89
distributed web-services network
      (DWSN) 226–227. *See also* web-
      services network
documents
  integrity of 179
  interaction, style of 109–112, 133,
      136–138, 164
  self-contained 119–120, 159
downgrade attacks 194
downtime 304
due diligence 276–277
durability (property of transactions)
      150
DWSN. *See* distributed web-services
      network

E

e-commerce 14, 21, 64, 69, 79–80

EAI. *See* enterprise application integra-
      tion
early adopters 257
early majority 257
EDI. *See* electronic data interchange
EDIFACT 19
EJB. *See* Enterprise Java Beans
electronic data interchange (EDI) 14,
      41, 44
elements, message 190–191
email 12, 39, 108, 115, 119–122
encoding 111
encryption 48
  element-level 189–193
  end-to-end 188
  storage 189
enterprise application integration (EAI)
      14–16, 64, 75–81
Enterprise Java Beans (EJB) 30, 71, 85
enterprise resource planning (ERP)
      14–15, 64, 67–70, 76–80
envelope, message 190–191
ERP. *See* enterprise resource planning
      (ERP)
European Union (EU) 303
Evans Data 323
event-driven design 113, 117–118
eXtensible Markup Language. *See* XML
external web services. *See* web services,
      external

F

fast-track strategy 240–241, 254–255
FAX 11–13, 42
File Transfer Protocol (FTP) 221
fire-and-forget 99
firewall
  network layer 197–201
  XML. *See* proxy, XML
force majeure 286
Forrester Research 63–64
FTP. *See* File Transfer Protocol
future-proofing 15, 95, 204

G

Gartner Research 38–39, 63–64, 78
gateway. *See* proxy, XML
globalization 304
guarantees 276–277

H

Häerder, Theo 149, 322
Hagel, John 38, 39
  Out of the Box 16, 17, 321
header, message 190–191
Health Insurance Portability and
      Accountability Act of 1996
      (HIPAA) 303
heterogeneity 133, 139
high availability 242–243
hops 224, 229–231
host-based security 201–205
hub 77. *See also* broker; *See also* vertical
      hubs
hype, web-services 37–45
HyperText Transfer Protocol (HTTP)
  RPC-style interaction and 110
  security issues related to 176, 198

I

IBM 40, 228, 232, 233, 239
identity. *See also* authentication; *See
      also* credentials
identity passthrough 183
incentives 288–290
independent software vendor (ISV)
      217–219, 228
infrastructure 52, 296, 303–307
innovators 257
insurance 286
integration 63–81
  swivel-chair 66–67
integrity 177–179, 187
  component 178–180
  document 179
  end-to-end 178
  host-based 202

network-layer 199
peripheral-service 205
web-services network 212
XML firewall 208
interaction
  asynchronous. *See* asynchronous
        interaction
  synchronous. *See* synchronous interac-
        tion
  web-service model 96
interfaces 28, 97–98
intermediaries 51, 101–102, 174
internal web servies. *See* web services,
      internal
interoperability 171
isolation (property of transactions)
      150, 160–161
ISV. *See* independent software vendor

J

Java 14, 23–24, 40

K

Kerberos 180
Keynote Systems 290, 292
Kick, Christopher 322
Kotok, Alan 321

L

laggards 257, 262
latency, service level for 278–279
late majority 257
launch date 255–256, 262–263
LDAP. *See* Lightweight Directory-Ac-
      cess Protocol
lead time 263–265, 268–271
Liberty Alliance 206
licenses, software 217, 306–307
life cycle, adoption 256–258
Lightweight Directory-Access Protocol
      (LDAP) 206
lingua franca 40
loads, system 124–128, 305–306
load balancing 306

locking, resource 150–151, 160–161
logging 246
long-lived transactions. *See* transactions, long-lived
loose coupling 31, 131–144
  business processes and 164
  security and 204
  transactions and 158–160

M

maintenance 52, 277, 286, 304
managed-service provider (MSP) 234, 235
mapping, data 77
Martin, S. 323
maturity 38
McCarthy, Jack 322
measurements, service-level agreement 284–285
mediation 221–222. *See also* transformation
message-exchange patterns (MEPs) 98–101
message and messaging 98, 133
  asynchronous. *See* asynchronous interaction
  encryption 190–191
  one-way 112
  queuing. *See* queuing, message
  reliable 156, 165. *See also* asynchronous interaction
  routing. *See* routing
  security 201
Meta Group 68
methods 111
micropayments 51, 299–301
Microsoft
  .NET internals 35
  Java and 23–24
  Passport 206
  SOAP, invention of 45
  TCP/IP, implementation of 232
milestones 57
mobile devices 23
Moore, Geoffrey 267, 323

Crossing the Chasm 256
MSP. *See* managed-service provider
multicast 101

N

negotiation, contract 50
network-layer security 197–201
Newcomer, Eric
  Principles of Transaction Processing 147, 155, 322
NNTP 39
non-repudiation 48, 178, 192–193
  host-based 203
  network layer 200
  peripheral-service 206
  web-services network 213
  XML firewall 209

O

O'Reilly, Tim 143, 322
O'Reilly Curve 268, 323
object-oriented programming 29, 83–89
objects
  brokers 85
  distributed 85–86
  web services and 83 89
Object Management Group (OMG) 86
one-phase commit protocol 151–152
Open Software Foundation (OSF) 20, 321
ORB. *See* objects, brokers
orchestration 49, 163–170
OSF. *See* Open Software Foundation
outsourcing 224–225, 235–236, 307–308
Out of the Box (Hagel) 16, 321
Overton, Chris 289–292, 323

P

pass-through service-level agreements 287–288
Passport, Microsoft 206
payment mechanisms 295, 297–298

peak loads 124–128, 305–306
penalties 288–292
performance 138. *See also* scalability
peripheral-service security 205–206
persistence (of authentication) 184–185
Phillips, Charles 321
PKI. *See* public-key infrastructure
platforms, security 195–216
platforms, web-services deployment 40
portal 247
pricing 298–299
Principles of Transaction Processing (Bernstein and Newcomer) 147, 322
privacy 302–303
procedural design 116–117
project management
  complex projects and 251–272
  simple projects and 245–250
  strategies for 239–244
provider 96
proxy, XML 217, 218, 226–231
  security 207–211
  service-managed 210–216
psychographics 257
public-key infrastructure 180
publish/subscribe 100–101
publisher, software. *See* software publisher
pyramid, web-services 55–57

Q

quality of service (QoS) 50, 242–243, 277–279
queuing, message 113, 121–129, 306

R

Ray Tomlinson 12
redundancy 306
reliability 123–124
  messaging. *See* messaging, reliable
  transaction 156
remedies, service-level agreement 279–282. *See also* penalties

Remote Method Invocation (RMI) 14, 20, 40, 87–89
Remote Procedure Call (RPC) 20, 22, 119, 133
  interaction 109–112
replay attacks 193
request-to-prepare message 153, 155
request/response 99–101, 105, 110–111
requestor 96
reservations, in orchestration 168
resilience. *See* reliability
resource locking. *See* locking, resource
resource manager 152, 156
reusability 30, 143
Reuter, Andreas 149, 322
revenue models 295, 297–298
risks 231
  cancellation 157–159
  security, internal 204–209
RMI. *See* Remote Method Invocation
RosettaNet 14, 19–20, 41
routing 101–102, 133, 138–139, 165
RPC. *See* Remote Procedure Call

S

SalCentral 246
scalability 31, 124–128
scheduled maintenance. *See* maintenance
schema 41, 140–141
Scott, Tony 171
screen scraping 67
Secure Sockets Layer (SSL) 173, 196–216, 221, 248
security 48, 247, 248, 307
  challenges of 171–194
  host-based 201–205
  in-storage 175–178
  in-transit 173–174
  management 209
  multi-hop 174–175
  network-layer 197–201
  peripheral-service 205–206
  policy, auditing of 210
  solutions for 195–216

security context 172–173
semantics
  complex projects and 252
  EDI, history of 19
  external services and 296, 307–308
  loose coupling and 133
  missing piece from web-services pro-
    tocols 41, 48
  web-services pyramid and 57
server
  application. *See* application server
  messaging 121, 122
service-level agreement (SLA) 273–294
service-oriented architecture (SOA) 29,
    91–112
  aggregated 103–104
services, transformation 51
service switching 223
settlements 51, 295, 300
SGML 44
Shirky, Clay 40, 43, 322
silos
  application integration and 65, 76
  ERP backlash and 15, 69
Simple Mail Transfer Protocol (SMTP)
    39, 122
single signon 49, 206
SLA. *See* service-level agreement
SMTP. *See* Simple Mail Transfer Pro-
    tocol
SneakerNets 66–67
SOA. *See* service-oriented architecture
SOAP
  integrity of messages 179
  security of 198
software-as-service 236
software publishing 236
solution-evolution timeline 244, 266
SSL. *See* Secure Sockets Layer
staffing 52
standards 44
Standard General Markup Language
    (SGML) 44
start date, project 263–265

state
  distributed 166, 169
  maintenance of 106
Stencil Group 28–29, 321, 322
stepping-stone strategy 240–241,
    246–249, 254–255
storage, encrypted 189
store-and-forward 121
stovepipes. *See* silos
strategy 239–244
  adoption 240–241
Sun Microsystems 23–24, 25, 44, 87,
    232
switching. *See* service switching
swivel-chair integration 66–67
synchronization 99
synchronous interaction
  asynchronous, compared to 113–114
  defined 104–106
  deployment options for 229–231
  message-exchange pattern (MEP) 99
  RPC-style 110
  tight coupling of 133
syntax 17, 19, 41, 48, 133

T

TCP/IP 47
  security of 198
Telex 11
termination, consistent 148
three-tier architecture. *See* architecture,
    three-tier
thresholds, in service-level agreements
    291–292
timeline
  integration-history 64
  software-technology 84
  software-evolution 266
  solution-evolution 219
timeouts 105
timing, project 258–259
tipping points 258
Tomlinson, Ray 12
topology 224

TP monitor. *See* transaction-processing
        monitor
transaction-processing monitor 148
transactions 48, 147–162, 305
    compensating 160–162
    long-lived 156, 160
transaction coordinator 152, 156
transaction manager 152
transformations 51, 133, 142–143, 208,
        222–223. *See also* mediation
trust 32–36, 43, 48, 157
two-phase commit protocol 152–155
types, data. *See* data types

U

Udell, Jon 156, 322
unintended consequences 308
United Nations (U.N.) 19
unit of work 148
UserLand Software 45

V

value-added network (VAN) 18
value-added reseller (VAR) 253
VAN. *See* value-added network
vendors, independence from 229–231
version control 304–305
vertical hubs 226
virtual private network (VPN) 196–
        216, 221, 248
virus protection 209–210
visibility 38
vote (in transactions) 154
VPN. *See* virtual private network

W

Wainewright, Phil 18, 321
warranties 297
waste 271
web-services delivery network (WSDN)
        231–232, 304
web-services network (WSN). *See
        also* distributed web-services
        network

deployment option of 219–226
measurement of service levels 285
outsourcing strategy for 307–308
security solution of 211–213
web-services provider (WSP) 234–236,
        307
web services
    benefits of 29
    external 31, 33–35, 248, 295–308
    interaction model of 96
    internal 31, 33
    intra-system 31, 35–36
    pyramid 55–57, 220, 244
workflow 16, 163–170
WSDN. *See* web-services delivery
        network
WSN. *See* web-services network
WSP. *See* web-services provider

X

X/Open 20
X12 19
Xerox 45
XMethods 246
XML 14, 17, 41
    acceleration of 208
    gateway. *See* gateway
    integrity of elements in 179
    proxy. *See* proxy, XML
    schema 41, 253

Y

Y2K 14, 21–22
Yager, Tom 322

About the Author

Doug Kaye is a technology-management consultant, author, and lecturer based in northern California. Drawing upon nearly three decades of experience in the roles of CEO and CTO, he spends much of his time communicating technology concepts to business executives and business issues to technologists.

Kaye literally wrote the book on web hosting: *Strategies for Web Hosting and Managed Services* (John Wiley and Sons, 2002), considered by many customers and vendors alike to be the definitive resource of the high-end web-hosting industry. He also publishes the the *IT Strategy Letter* (an electronic newsletter), and has been a frequent contributor to *Internet World* and *The Web Host Industry Review*.

In recent years, Kaye's stints have included executive positions with Organic Online, goodcompany.com, and NextMonet.com. Previously, he was founder and CEO of Rational Data Systems.

In his spare time, he and his wife enjoy flying their airplane to remote locales and on charitable missions for Angel Flight, transporting patients to and from treatments for serious diseases.

For more information, contact Doug at doug@rds.com and visit www.rds.com.

Also by Doug Kaye:

Strategies for Web Hosting and Managed Services
John Wiley and Sons, 2002, ISBN 0471085782

"This is the most complete collection of information about hosting I've ever seen."
>—Phil Windley, Former CIO, State of Utah

"The ultimate resource for selecting a complex Web hosting vendor."
>—Rawlson King, The Web Host Industry Review

"WOW! Get this book…If you are looking to learn what it takes to get a company to host your web site(s), this is the book for you. If you don't truly understand what it takes to set up a large web site, this book is a MUST read!… I give this book an A+ as it is one of the top two technical books I've read."
>—reberrya, Denver, Colorado (on Amazon.com)

"The content in this book is amazing."
>—Matt Alland, HostCompare.com

"If you're looking for a 'how to think' approach to the problem of outsourcing your hosting, this book is the place to start!"
>—Scott Loftesness, Glenbrook Partners

"…very impressed…A great job in making it interesting enough for experienced business consumers while keeping within the grasp of the first timer."
>—Chris Ridabock, CEO, CanXCentral Inc.

"You have written the single best source of information on this new industry that I know of—both technically and from a business perspective."
>—Benn Stratton, The Stellar Corporation

"This is a well-written, no-nonsense book that gets right to the point. An excellent guidebook to building a web-hosting strategy. Lots of information with available updates. Gets to the point—ideal for executives and other IT decision-makers."
>—davissyor (on Amazon.com)

Quick Order Form

• FAX orders: 415.459.0103. Complete and send this form.
• email orders: sales@rdspress.com
• World Wide Web: www.rdspress.com/sales

Please send

___ copies of *Loosely Copupled—The Missing Pieces of Web Services* @US$39.99

I understand that I may return any of them for a full refund—for any reason, no questions asked.

Name: _____

Address: _____

_____

City:_____ State: _____

ZIP:_____ Country:_____

Telephone: _____

FAX: _____

email address:_____

Please add my email address to the following lists:
❏ The *IT Strategy Letter* newsletter (a free email subscription)
❏ Announcements of new books, essays, seminars, etc.

Please send more information on:
❏ Books   ❏ Speaking/seminars   ❏ Mailing Lists   ❏ Consulting

Shipping: US: $4.00 for first book. $2.00 each additional book.
International (estimated): $10.00 for first book. $5.00 each additional book.
Sales tax will be added for books shipped to California addresses.

Payment: ❏ VISA   ❏ Master Card   ❏ Amex

Card number: _____

Name on card:_____ Exp. date: _____

Signature: _____